Pope Fiction

Pope Fiction

Patrick Madrid

Basilica Press
SAN DIEGO

Contents

5

Dedicated with love to my son, Jonathon,
and with filial affection to
Pope John Paul the Great

Acknowledgments

I would like to give special thanks and recognition to Brian Paul, my colleague and friend, for his vital assistance in preparing this book.

My thanks also go to David Palm, Steve Ray, Marcus Grodi, Fr. Ray Ryland, Jeff Cavins, David Hess, and Jim Moore, each of whom took time from their busy schedules to read and critique the manuscript and then offer many insightful comments and helpful suggestions, all of which improved upon my initial efforts. I also thank Kinsey Caruth, who designed the cover, and John O'Rourke from Loyola Graphics, for his technical advice and page-layout prowess. Thank you all, and may God reward you.

Each of the pope fictions answered in this book could have been discussed in far greater detail, but space considerations wouldn't permit it. Some, such as the section on Pope Alexander VI's "line of demarcation" (page 196) and the arguments raised by the sedevacantists (page 272), merit a much lengthier analysis than you will find here. Indeed most of them deserve entire volumes devoted to refuting them. This book, though, is more an appetizer than a main course. Its aim is to provide food for the mind at a popular, not scholarly, level; enough to feed and satisfy our common hunger for the truth, but also, hopefully, to whet

the reader's appetite for further study and deeper understanding of this marvelous gift of Christ to His Church:
the papacy.

Foreword

My wife sat at the opposite end of the couch from me, not to mention at the opposite end of the theological spectrum. We were both Evangelical Protestants then. She was firmly convinced that the Reformation was right, and I was feeling a growing suspicion that maybe it wasn't.

With books on the early church fathers, Mary and the sacraments strewn around our living room, we began to watch the video of Pope John Paul II's visit to Denver in 1993. As he made his entrance into Mile High Stadium with the crowd waving enthusiastically, my eyes followed the Holy Father as he circled the stadium in the Popemobile. I was mesmerized as I observed the dynamic relationship between this man from Rome and the diverse crowd assembled there to greet him.

My heart began to beat faster and faster, until suddenly and quite unexpectedly I started to cry. With tears running down my face and this new burst of emotion flowing from my heart, I wanted to stand up and proclaim to those in the stadium, "I know what you know — he's the Vicar of Christ!"

Confused by my tears, my wife asked, "What's the matter with *you*?"

I looked at her and said, "You don't understand! You weren't raised Catholic." Pointing to the image of the pope on the television, I exclaimed, "That's not Billy Graham, or Pat Robertson, or Oral Roberts! He is the Vicar of Christ

— my Father in the faith, and those people in the stadium
are my family."

As a Protestant pastor, I had been engaged in an intense study of the Catholic Church for nearly a year. My
reading focused on the sacraments, Church authority, the
relationship between faith and works, the Eucharist, and
Tradition. I was convinced that the Church that embodied
the facts was indeed the Catholic Church. The interaction
between the Pope and visible, united family of Christian
believers assembled in Mile High Stadium made all my intellectual conclusions become real with the impact of that
united family as a continuation of salvation history. Surprisingly, seeing the visible head of the church brought my
quest for truth into focus.

And, not very long after that, I became Catholic.

Several years later, in 1998, while covering for EWTN
the papal visit of Pope John Paul II to St. Louis, I was again
captivated by the extraordinary response of the young people anticipating his arrival into the Kiel Center. Earlier in
the day I had spoken to a cameraman who worked for another major television network. He had commented that
though he was not practicing any particular faith at the
time, he found the papal visit interesting, never having
witnessed this much "fuss" over one man. Moments before the Holy Father's entrance, baseball's home-run slug-
ger Mark McGwire leaned down to kiss the ring of Pope
John Paul. This encounter displayed on the giant indoor
screen caused an eruption of applause from the crowd.
Then the Holy Father made his entrance into the arena to
a throng of awe-inspired youth. A brilliant sea of camera
flashes accompanied Pope John Paul II's arrival as eager-
faced youths struggled to get a glimpse of him, some with

tears streaming down their cheeks. The applause was so deafening that though the young people around him were screaming, "John Paul II, we love you!" it appeared as if they were only mouthing the words. I glanced over at my cameraman friend. He had left his camera post and was standing next to me with his mouth wide open. Then without any shame he began to cry. Somehow the presence of the Vicar of Christ in the same room melted his heart and touched him deep within. Like that cameraman, I with millions of others have realized deep within our hearts that we yearn to be fathered. We call the Pope "The Holy Father" because he extends heaven's paternal presence.

Since our entrance into the Catholic Church, my wife and I have experienced a profound sense of certitude concerning Christ and His kingdom. This is due to the awareness that Jesus did not leave the care of his flock to whoever felt like preaching or teaching or to an individual who experienced a private inner nudging to start a church. No, after much study about the papacy, I knew that when I saw Pope John Paul II at Mile High Stadium, I was witnessing the manifestation of Christ's decision to lead and guide me in truth.

Today, in bible studies and prayer groups around the world, important topics such as baptism, faith, salvation, heaven, and healing are discussed. While there are many questions, there are also many answers to each of these topics. But how does the average individual with little or no theological training come to conclusions about such important topics? Do they take the word of a man or woman leading a local Sunday school class? Do they randomly choose a book off the shelf of their local Christian bookstore? With over 25,000 Christian denominations to choose from, how does the believer know for certain that his or her denomination is correct? As a Protestant pastor for over twelve years, I too faced many difficult decisions in areas of doctrine, church discipline and church government. During my years as a pastor, I studied under many of the popular bible teachers of our day. While fascinated by the various teachings I received, there was always the question in the back of my mind, "Who says you are right?" In other words, by what authority did they speak? Or what's more, by what authority did I speak?

Throughout the Old Testament, God exercised His authority through earthly leaders such as Noah, Moses and David. While they were mighty men, they occasionally lapsed into times of personal weakness. We today do not disregard or discount their authority on account of their frailties, rather, we take courage in the fact that they were like us. Those who either doubt or dismiss the papacy due to the past failures of men or choose to believe a skewed version of church history due to an anti-Catholic bias, fail to see God's authority hidden in fragile flesh. Like the Creator of heaven and earth coming to us veiled in human flesh, like Jesus continually offering his body and blood under the appearance of bread and wine, He continues to govern and lead his flock by bestowing his authority upon mere mortals. This divine accommodation not only confounds the devil but continues the celebration of the mystery of the incarnation.

Interestingly, it was in the midst of a multiplicity of opinions about the very identity of Christ that Jesus established Peter as the first pope. Jesus asks a simple question in Matthew 16:

"Who do men say that the Son of man is?" And they said, "Some say John the Baptist, others say Elijah, and others Jeremiah or one of the prophets." He said to them, "But who do you say that I am?" Simon Peter replied, "You are the Christ, the Son of the living God." And Jesus answered him, "Blessed are you, Simon Bar-Jona! For flesh and blood has not revealed this to you, but my Father who is in heaven. And I tell you, you are Peter, and on this rock I will build my church, and the powers of death shall not prevail against it. I will give you the keys of the kingdom of heaven, and whatever you bind on earth shall be bound in heaven, and whatever you loose on earth shall be loosed in heaven."

Similar to the cacophony of voices today, Jesus received four answers to one question, "who do men say that the Son of man is?" What should grab our attention is the fact that all four answers were wrong. But what is more arresting is the realization that today the question would not receive four wrong answers, but thousands of wrong answers.

To assure that his flock would continually hear his voice, Jesus appointed Peter as the head of his church. Through the assistance of the Holy Spirit, the Church has for two thousand years clearly heard the voice of the Great Shepherd. The deposit of faith, that truth which has been protected and taught from generation to generation, has not always been an easy word, nor a popular word, but a sure and needed word.

The very fact that you are reading this foreword says that you are interested in spiritual things. I encourage you not to approach this book simply as fodder for your predetermined theological position, but approach the book with a hungry heart, eager to embrace all that Jesus has for you. Jesus said that if you want to be his disciple you must continue in his word, for it is when you continue in his word that you will be truly free.

If you are like me, you want the sure foundation on which to build your life. If you are tired of spending your life trying to determine the voice of Christ rather than spending your life obeying him, then *Pope Fiction* is for you. In this book you will receive answers to many questions concerning the papacy. Patrick Madrid does a masterful job of answering common objections to the papacy as well as accurately teaching the Church's position on the subject. Though the mystery of God's gift to the Church of the papacy can never be fully understood this side of heaven, this book will help you better understand this great treasure.

— Jeff Cavins

Introduction

As my friend Rita pulled to the side of the road to check her map, she noticed that the car that had been behind her for the last mile or so also stopped, and pulled alongside.

Thinking the middle-aged woman in the other car had stopped to offer assistance, Rita rolled down her window and smiled. "Could you help me with some directions, please?" she asked through the rolled up window of the other car. The woman couldn't hear her through the glass, but she understood the question. Staring hard at Rita, she shook her head and scowled.

Perplexed, Rita pantomimed the motion of turning the window handle, saying, "Could you roll down your window, please?" The woman shook her head again and her scowl deepened. Then, leaning across the front seat of her car, her face inches from the window, she mouthed slowly and clearly: "I HATE THE POPE." Then she made an obscene gesture with her finger, pulled back onto the road, and drove off.

Dazed, Rita wondered what could have provoked such a bizarre expression of hostility. Then it dawned on her: The bumper sticker on her minivan read "Follow me, I'm behind the pope!" and included a picture of a smiling Pope John Paul II. Apparently, it so offended the woman that she had to go out of her way to let Rita know.

Was she an anti-Catholic Evangelical Protestant? A Jehovah's Witness on her way home from a meeting at the

Kingdom Hall? A secularist of no particular religion? Perhaps she was a "pro-choice Catholic" who hates the pope because his efforts to defend the sanctity of unborn life clash with her agenda to "Keep Abortion Legal." Maybe she's mad that he won't compromise Catholic teaching that the sacrament of holy orders is reserved to men. Who knows?

There is one thing we do know. A lot of people dislike, even hate, Pope John Paul II, not because of his personality or ethnicity or whatever, but because they don't like the Catholic Church. The pope is the flesh-and-blood reminder of that Church and its teachings — he *personifies* Catholicism — and for some this is particularly offensive. Some make their dislike for the papacy felt in articles, tracts and videos, calculated not merely to refute Catholic teaching, but to undermine the trust Catholics have in the Church and the pope.

Millions believe myths and legends and historical inaccuracies about the papacy, almost all of which were concocted centuries ago by critics of the Church. Many labor under the twin burden of ignorance and an unwillingness to be shown the truth, heirs of a generations-old anti-Catholicism handed down from family, friends, social circles, and over 200 years of subtle American Protestant propaganda.

But there's hope. John Henry Newman, a Protestant scholar who converted to Catholicism in 1845 and became a leading apologist and later a cardinal, said in his book *Apologia Pro Vita Sua*, "When I was young . . . I thought the pope to be the antichrist. At Christmas 1824–5 I preached a sermon to that effect." If Newman could be brought to see the truth, so can that angry driver who HATES THE POPE.

In this book we'll meet some of the bad popes, men who

lived ruthless, immoral lives while in the office of Bishop of Rome. We'll see why their wicked behavior, while deplorable, does not injure the Catholic Church's teachings regarding papal infallibility, Petrine primacy, or apostolic succession. We will examine situations in which popes have made poor administrative and political decisions, were cowards, connived with secular powers for base objectives, and even came perilously close — but never all the way — to the edge of leading the Church astray in their teaching. We'll also see the papacy for what it is: a human office that was divinely established. A special function of unity and stability within the Church, yet one that is occupied by men who are as vulnerable to sin and human weakness as any of us.

As the old saying goes, man proposes and God disposes. There is no truer example of this than the papacy. In spite of the countless human schemes and intrigues that have swirled around the Chair of Peter for two thousand years, the Lord God has had His hand on it since the moment Christ spoke the words to Simon the fisherman: "You are Rock and upon this rock I will build My Church." Often, His hand was there to steady that chair and prevent it from toppling when bad or incompetent popes sat upon it. Other times it was there to shield it during the many cyclones of controversy and heresy which battered the Church over the ages. The Lord has kept His promise to be with the Church always, and this promise has been kept, *par excellence*, in the office of the papacy.

The following thirty myths and misconceptions about the papacy are ones you are likely to run across, some of them regularly, in the media, among non-Catholics and misguided Catholics, and in popular culture. As apostles for Christ, we have work to do when we encounter them. We are called by Christ to speak the truth with charity and try to dispel misunderstandings about the Church whenever we can. The myths and misconceptions that form the vast body of "Pope Fiction" are widespread and pernicious — but like other ills, they can be counteracted and cured with a healthy dose of the facts.

1

Peter was not the first "pope." He didn't have any special primacy or jurisdiction over the other apostles or other early Christians. In fact, he denies this by referring to himself as merely a "fellow presbyter" (1 Peter 5:1) — an office lower than an overseer (bishop). If anything, Paul had a greater authority than Peter.

Although St. Peter never called himself "pope" in Scripture, he did indeed have a special apostolic primacy and jurisdiction. The Scriptural evidence for this is substantial and explicit. Let's take a tour of the major scriptural monuments that testify to his primacy. As we trace the outlines of Simon Peter's presence in the New Testament, one thing soon becomes clear: Christ promised that Peter would have a special primacy and leadership among the Apostles, but that role wasn't fully assumed by him until after Christ's earthly ministry came to a close. But once the Lord had ascended into heaven, once the infant Church was on its feet and moving forward with the message of the Gospel, then we see Peter step fully into his ministry.

The Galilean fisherman

Who was this man Peter? His story is as dramatic as any in Scripture. It begins with an unusual conversation on the shore of Lake Galilee. It ends, painfully, a thousand miles away and thirty years later in a Roman arena. Scripture is filled with information about him and tells us much about what kind of a man he was: A Galilean fisherman, hotheaded, intense in his relationships. He was called away from his fishing boat by Jesus Christ to be one of the original Twelve Apostles. He walked the dusty hills of Palestine, shoulder-to-shoulder with the Lord for the next three years, sharing the hardships and triumphs of His ministry, witnessing the miracles, performing miracles himself at Christ's command. He heard the Gospel preached directly from Christ's mouth. He sat at the table of the Last Supper and watched Christ celebrate the first Eucharist. That very night, his fear overwhelmed him and he abandoned his Master just as the sorrowful mystery of His Passion began to unfold. Under oath he denied even knowing Christ, preferring to skulk in the shadows while his closest friend was being interrogated, tortured, and executed.

But after the Resurrection, Peter changed. He was imbued with God's grace in a special way and left cowardice behind. As the Book of Acts records, he very quickly became the Apostle Christ wanted him to be: courageous, humble, unswervingly dedicated to his apostolate. The leadership he showed only partially during the Gospel accounts of Christ's earthly ministry blossomed and was fully actuated, beginning with the day of Pentecost. He was a man transformed by God's grace, energized and consumed by his burning love for Christ and His Church. His cowardice gave way to courage. His hotheaded brashness was forged, gradually, into a steely determination and wisdom that didn't flinch or run in the face of opposition. Peter went from being a boisterous, roughneck fisherman, to an Apostle, a teacher, a leader, a father figure, a true *papa* to the Church.

A profile in courage

In Acts 1, Simon Peter rallies the other Apostles and leads them in taking the first step along the path of apostolic succession. They choose Matthias to replace the suicide traitor, Judas. In Acts 2, he explodes onto the scene in a dazzle of zeal and miracles, beginning with a penetrating sermon to the crowds in Jerusalem on the day of Pentecost — a sermon that resulted in over *three thousand* conversions and baptisms that very day. In Acts 15, at the Council of Jerusalem, we see the last glimpse of St. Peter in Scripture. He delivers apostolic teaching at the assembly of Apostles and disciples that stilled the debates raging back and forth and caused the whole assembly to fall silent. The Lord delivered special revelation regarding the status of the gentiles to Simon Peter (cf. Acts 10), and it was through Peter that this revelation was given to the Church at the council. In essence, Peter was saying to the Church: "Here is what we have to do, brothers. The Lord delivered the answer to me."

At this point in the biblical narrative, Peter fades from our view, at least in the pages of Scripture, and Paul carries the story to its abrupt conclusion in Chapter 28 of Acts.

Peter strides through the first fifteen chapters of Acts performing miracles, rebuking the high and mighty who oppose Christ, personally welcoming the converted Saul into the Church, planting churches that flourish even to this day, receiving revelation from heaven, teaching, admonishing, encouraging and leading. Decades later, when his supreme hour finally arrived, he fulfilled Christ's prophecy about him: "When you are old, you will stretch out your hands, and someone will lead you where you do not want to go" (John 21:18).

In A.D. 65, Simon Peter was arrested in Rome by the pagan authorities for the crime of being a Christian. He was bound and led by soldiers to Nero's circus. There, he was nailed upside-down to a cross and left to die. Afterward, his body was hauled a few hundred feet away and thrown into a shallow grave. No one at that moment could have known that on that site, over that forlorn and abandoned corpse, would be raised the universal focal point of the Christian religion: St. Peter's Basilica and the Vatican.

In that final act of following his Lord, Simon Peter made good on a promise he once made, spoken in haste: Lord, "even though I should have to die with you, I will not deny you!" (Mark 14:31). His martyrdom, the supreme act of his courage and fidelity to Christ, was his final act of strengthening his brethren.

Peter was a man of many impulses, good and bad. One moment he could argue vociferously that he would *never* betray Christ, that he would stay with Him loyally always. The next moment he could succumb to his fears and sink into cowardice and betrayal — the way he once sank beneath the water he was walking on, when he took his eyes off Christ.

Diamond in the rough

The Gospel accounts show Simon Peter as a rustic, unsophisticated, good man with a huge heart that brimmed with love for his Lord. He was truly a "sign of contradiction." Christ had chosen a fisherman to be the prince of His Apostles. Peter wasn't the smartest of the group, nor was he well prepared for his global mission with polished rhetorical skills or honed leadership and management experience. Rather, Christ chose in Peter a man who would be shaped and formed into the Rock on which He would build his Church.

This very first argument — "Peter was no pope, he had no special authority, he was just one of the group" — is pure fiction, and an odd one at that. It's odd because the biblical and historical evidence that disproves it is so overwhelming, so obvious, that it is strange to see people actually trying to use it against the Catholic Church. But we can and should assume only the best motives in someone who levels this charge. The person making this claim may simply be unaware of the vast amount of evidence to the contrary. It's our job as apostles of Christ, as sons and daughters of the Church He established on the Rock of Peter, to present the evidence clearly and charitably. Let's examine that evidence in detail.

Always first

Perhaps the most telling New Testament clue about the importance of Simon Peter is how often he is mentioned. The answer is staggering. Of the Twelve Apostles, he is by far the one mentioned most often in Scripture. He appears

195 times under his various names (Simon, Peter, Cephas, Kephas). The next most often mentioned Apostle is St. John, who comes in at a whopping *twenty-nine times.* St. James the Greater is mentioned nineteen times, St. Philip fifteen, and the numbers dwindle rapidly for the others. Does this in itself prove St. Peter's primacy? No, but it does shed considerable light on his importance among the Twelve. What does that light reveal?

Among other things, we see that when the Twelve Apostles are listed by name (Matt. 10:2-5; Mark 3:16-19; Luke 6:14-17; and Acts 1:13). St. Peter's name is always first — and Judas Iscariot is always listed dead last. Far more commonly, through, the New Testament refers to simply "Peter and the others," as if to say that the tempestuous fisherman signified in himself the unity of the whole apostolic college.

There are many other biblical signs of St. Peter's pre-eminence among the Apostles. He is the only one who receives a name change from Christ. Name changes given by God that we read about in Scripture have huge significance and imply an elevation in importance and a special mission given to that person by God (e.g., Abraham, Jacob). Peter was Simon, but Christ calls him "Rock" (Matt. 16:18). He was also singled out in a unique way by Christ to receive a special authority, symbolized by the "keys of the kingdom of heaven." Christ promised, "Whatever you (singular) bind on earth will be bound in heaven, and whatever you (singular) loose on earth will be loosed in heaven" (Matt. 16:19). Later, in Matthew 18:18, the same promise of authority to bind and loose was extended to the other Apostles, but there is no mention of the keys. That role was entrusted to Simon Peter alone.

Christ's promise to give the keys to Simon has been seen

by many Scripture scholars as a parallel to the episode of Shebna and Eliakim in Isaiah 22:15–25. In that passage, God announces through Isaiah that the wicked prime minister of Israel, Shebna, will be deposed. And in his place, Eliakim, a good man, will be installed. Here we see a striking parallel in the language with the Lord's words to Simon Peter in Matthew 16:18–19.[1]

He put his hand in the hand of the Man Who stilled the water

St. Peter was the lone Apostle Christ called out of the fishing boat to walk on water. This episode tells us a lot about the man Simon Peter:

During the fourth watch of the night, he came toward them, walking on the sea. When the Disciples saw him walking on the sea they were terrified. "It is a ghost!" They said, and they cried out in fear. At once Jesus spoke to them, "Do not be afraid." Peter said to him in reply, "Lord, if it is you, command me to come to you on the water." He said, "Come." Peter got out of the boat and began to walk on the water toward Jesus. But when he saw how [strong] the wind was he became frightened and, beginning to sink, he cried out, "Lord! Save me!" Immediately, Jesus stretched out his hand and caught him and said to him, "Oh you of little faith. Why did you doubt?" After they got into the boat, the wind died down. Those who were in the boat worshipped him, saying, "Truly, you are the son of God."[2]

---

[1] More will be said about this parallel passage in chapter 5.
[2] Matt. 14:25–33.

Several subtle but important details about Simon Peter emerge here. First, we see he rises above the confusion and consternation of the other Apostles and settles the issue (granted, this frightening moment of action wasn't an example of settling a *dogmatic* issue or anything that involved teaching, but it's still an example of Simon Peter taking the lead in settling a question, once and for all).

Second, Peter's faith in Christ was so strong that he did something that seemed impossible: he jumped over the side of the boat — in the middle of a storm! — and walked to Christ on the surface of the water.

Third, his faith was weak enough that when he realized what he was doing, he faltered and began to sink. And in the moment when his faith failed him, he raised his eyes to the Lord and called out for help. The Lord drew him up and saved him from the waves that would have swallowed him.

Christ's mild, exasperated rebuke, "Oh you of little faith," rings in our ears down to this day. Like Simon, the popes are mere men, prone to the doubts and fears and weaknesses that afflict all of us. They aren't supermen. But they do have Christ's promise to guide and protect them as they carry out their mission of leading the Church. "Oh you of little faith," we can almost hear Christ chiding us today. "I know the storm is raging around you. But I am there with you, keeping Peter from sinking beneath the waves."

Simon Peter as leader

At the tomb of Christ, St. John waited, apparently out of deference, to allow St. Peter to enter ahead of him (John

20:6). It was to Simon Peter first among the Apostles that God first revealed the Resurrection (Mark 16:7). The risen Christ appeared to him first, before he appeared to the other Apostles (Luke 24:34).

A particularly significant biblical fact is that on at least one occasion, Christ preached the gospel of forgiveness and salvation to the crowds from St. Peter's fishing boat (Luke 5:3). Luke makes a point of mentioning that the boat Christ chose belonged to Simon. Is this an irrelevant detail, thrown into the narrative by Luke, almost as an afterthought? Not at all. The significance of Christ preaching to the crowds from Simon Peter's boat was not lost on Luke, nor was it lost on the early Christian readers of his Gospel. This passage, by the way, is where the often-heard Catholic term for the Church — *the barque of Peter* — comes from. ("Barque" is an archaic word for boat.)

Shielded from the devil

St. Peter was told by Christ, "Simon, Simon, behold Satan has demanded to sift all of you (Greek: *humas* [plural]) like wheat, but I have prayed for you (*sou* [singular]) that your (*sou* [singular]) faith may not fail. And once you (*su* [singular]) have turned back, strengthen your brethren (Luke 22:31–32). We can't underestimate the force of these words and the impact they had on the theology of the early Christians. Let's break this startling warning down into its component parts.

First, as we saw above, Christ was speaking to Peter alone. This was another of the many examples where the Lord identified Simon Peter, alone among the Apostles, for some special task or to grant him a unique authority. In this case, it was a revelation of the pivotal role he would play in the terrifying drama of the Passion that was about to unfold.

Second, the matter Christ was speaking about here was not trivial or peripheral; it was the most extreme form of danger that could threaten the Church. Peter was being told to brace himself for an imminent attack by the single most formidable and ferocious enemy the Church would face: Satan. This clear and present danger was so ominous that Peter, like any of us, if we were in his sandals at that moment, would have been paralyzed with fear if Christ hadn't added His personal promise of protection. "Simon, Satan has demanded to sift all of you like wheat, *but I have prayed that your faith may not fail.*"

Christ's words here imply that this attack would be beaten back, ultimately, by the faith of one man: Simon Peter. According to Christ, it all boiled down to him. The devil wanted to destroy all the Apostles (and succeeded, it seems, in destroying Judas Iscariot), but Christ prevented that spiritual slaughter by protecting Peter. In the same way, down through the ages, Christ has continued to protect His flock by strengthening and protecting the shepherds, those who hold the office of the papacy. Even popes who lived wicked lives were protected from the full force of Satan's aggression. None of them ever succumbed to the ultimate diabolical attack which has as its aim the subversion of the gospel and the evisceration of the Church; exactly what would result from a pope formally teaching error.

Third, this promise of special protection carried with it the chilling revelation that, even so, Peter would stumble and nearly fall during the ordeal that was about to engulf the Apostles (cf. Luke 22:32–34). "And *once you have turned back*, you must strengthen your brethren." Even though he was hand-picked by Christ, filled with the Holy Spirit, and especially protected for his combat with Satan, Simon Peter was still quite vulnerable to sin, even the sins of abandoning Christ and swearing three times, under oath, "I do not know Him."

"Feed My sheep"

We see in Luke 22:31–32 a unique role being given by Christ to Simon Peter. His faith would be protected by the Lord so that he could carry out a special apostolic mission. After the storm of doubt and fear had passed, he would have to strengthen his brethren. Peter's position among the Apostles was not one of tyrant or overlord. He was the leader, yes, but he was also the servant of the others (cf. Luke 22:24–30). It's no coincidence that immediately before Christ entrusted Peter with his special role, he told the Twelve: "Let the greatest among you be as the youngest, and the leader as the servant." (This passage is the primary biblical basis for one of the pope's official titles: *Servus Servorum Dei* [Latin: Servant of the Servants of God]).

There are other biblical examples of St. Peter's primacy. One of the most striking is the episode where Christ makes him the shepherd of His Church, telling him, again in the singular form, "feed My lambs . . . tend My sheep . . . feed My sheep" (John 21:15–17).[3] In Acts 1:13–26, St. Peter leads

---

[3] An important detail about Peter's authority in the Church emerges when we look at the original Greek text here. *Poímaine*, the Greek word

the other Apostles in choosing Matthias as successor to Judas. He leads them in preaching to the crowds in Jerusalem on the day of Pentecost (Acts 2:14). He performs the first Pentecost miracle (Acts 3). He speaks in the name of all the Apostles and for the whole Church when the Twelve are brought before the Sanhedrin for a trial (Acts 4).

It is to St. Peter that God sent the revelation that gentiles are to be allowed into the Church (Acts 10), and he is the Apostle who first welcomes them into the Church (Acts 11). St. Peter's dogmatic pronouncement was accepted and caused all disputes to cease at the Council of Jerusalem (Acts 15). After his conversion and healing from blindness, St. Paul went to visit St. Peter to have his teachings confirmed by him (Gal. 1:18). Notice that in Galatians 2:1–2 Paul repeats this link to Peter's authority, if indirectly, when he says he received "by revelation" the call to go and present himself to "those of repute." Clearly, Peter was the foremost of "those of repute" in Jerusalem. He was seen by Paul as the very touchstone of orthodoxy. How do we know this? Because Paul went out of his way to establish his credentials as a bona fide apostle — not one of the original Twelve (an issue he sometimes seemed rather touchy about), but an apostle nonetheless. The lesson here is that Paul knew that his great learning was in itself irrelevant to the issue of authority (modern Catholic theologians, take note!).

The biblical evidence that Simon Peter had a primacy

---

translated here as *tend*, has a strong meaning that is lost in English. Among the meanings of the command *poímaine* are "rule," "govern," and "shepherd" (cf. Joseph H. Thayer, *Thayer's Greek-English Lexicon of the New Testament* [Grand Rapids: Baker Book House, 1977], 527).

among the Apostles is wide and deep. The corroborating testimony from the early Church Fathers (presented in a later chapter) makes this fact undeniable (though, unfortunately, some still deny it). There is no doubt that — in spite of his weaknesses, his mercurial personality, and his fears and insecurities — under the grace of the Holy Spirit, Simon Peter became a rock of unity, a shepherd to his Master's flock.

Was he just a "fellow presbyter"?

Having said all that, what should we make of St. Peter's reference to himself in 1 Peter 5:1 as a "fellow presbyter"? After all, the biblical evidence speaks overwhelmingly of his special role among the Apostles. It shows us that Simon Peter was the leader, specially chosen by Christ to "strengthen his brethren." Does his humility in 1 Peter 5 signal that he was unaware of his special role as chief of the Apostles? Is it possible that he had no idea that Christ had conferred on him a unique authority?

The answer is found in this same passage. *"Clothe yourselves in humility in your dealings with one another,"* he says, "for God opposes the proud but bestows favor on the humble. So humble yourselves under the mighty hand of God, that He may exalt you in due time" (1 Peter 5:5). Since he was cautioning his Christian audience to be humble, it makes perfect sense that he would take his own advice and, setting an example for them, speak of himself in humble terms. And in doing so, he was following Christ's command, "Whoever wishes to be great among you shall be your servant, whoever wishes to be first among you shall be your slave" (Matt. 20:26–27).

St. Peter's humility shouldn't blind us to the substantial body of biblical evidence showing that he did receive a special apostolic preeminence and authority from the Lord Jesus Christ — evidence that critics of the papacy often ignore or strain to explain away.[4] And they forget that popes down through the ages have followed suit, referring to themselves as "a fellow bishop" when writing to other bishops.

St. Paul, like St. Peter, was also humble when referring to himself. He was by far the most prominent and prolific New Testament writer, responsible for about half of the New Testament, but he said, "I am the *least* of the apostles, not fit to be called an apostle, because I persecuted the Church of God" (1 Cor. 15:10). Elsewhere he said, "To me the very least of all the holy ones, this grace was given" (Eph. 3:8). On numerous occasions he called himself a mere *deacon*, the very lowest level of ordained ministry in the Church (cf. 1 Cor. 3:5, 4:1; 2 Cor. 3:6, 6:4, 11:23; Eph. 3:7; Col. 1:23, 25). But clearly, St. Paul had an authority far greater than that of a deacon. After all, he had the authority to ordain presbyters and bishops (cf. 1 Tim. 1:6).

As with St. Peter, these examples of St. Paul's humility are balanced by statements of his authority: "Although I have the full right to *order* you to do what is proper, I rather urge you out of love" (Philemon 8–9), and 1 Thessalonians 2:7: "[A]lthough we were able to impose our weight

---

[4] It's interesting to note that the Gospels of Matthew, Luke, and John, offer an abundance of passages showing Simon Peter's special leadership role among the Apostles. Mark's, however, avoids most of them. Since Mark was Peter's personal scribe and disciple, the silence in his Gospel about Peter is very possibly due to Peter's humility and reticence about his own status.

as apostles of Christ. Rather, we were gentle among you, as a nursing mother cares for her children."

Robbing Peter to pay Paul

Those who claim Peter had no special authority because he spoke of himself as a "fellow presbyter" must reckon with these instances of St. Paul calling himself a mere deacon (even lower than a presbyter). To be consistent, they would have to argue that St. Paul had even less authority than St. Peter. Of course, they won't be willing to do that.

St. Peter's calling himself a "fellow presbyter" doesn't disprove his primacy any more than St. Paul's habit of calling himself a "deacon" proves he had no authority greater than that of a deacon's. The practice of self-effacement among the Apostles was a testament to their humility, not some sort of evidence that they saw themselves as having no authority.

Non-Catholics recognize that the issue of the primacy of Peter and his successors, the bishops of Rome, is absolutely fundamental to the entire doctrinal structure of the Catholic Church. Over the centuries, countless books and articles have been written by critics of the Catholic Church, each aimed at proving that St. Peter had no special primacy and that the papacy is not what it claims to be: the ongoing presence of Petrine primacy for the Church in the person of the bishop of Rome.

The house that Christ built

If it could be shown that Peter himself was oblivious of having the special primacy the Catholic Church claims he had, it would be fair to say that the Catholic Church's claims for the papacy are seriously jeopardized. Worse yet, if the rest of the early Church was equally oblivious to that claim and to the notion that Peter's successors, the bishops of Rome, enjoyed a primacy of authority among bishops, the Catholic Church would be a house of cards waiting to fall.

Happily, Christ chose far more durable materials to build His house, the Church:

> Every one then who hears these words of mine and does them will be like a wise man who built his house upon the rock; and the rain fell, and the floods came, and the winds blew and beat upon that house, but it did not fall, because it had been founded on the rock.[5]

---

[5] Matt. 7:24–25.

2

Catholics claim that in Matthew 16:18, Christ built His Church on Peter, the rock. However, in the original Greek, Jesus said He would build His Church on the *petra* (large rock). Peter, on the other hand, is called *petros* (small rock). Clearly, Jesus was contrasting Peter with the Rock of the Church, not claiming that Peter was the rock. In fact, in 1 Corinthians 10:4, Paul specifically says that "the Rock was Christ," not Peter.

~

A lot of Catholics get tripped up on this one. There are some pope fictions that sound very convincing, right out of the box, and this is one of them. Who, after all, can resist being impressed by a technical sounding objection that appeals to the "original Greek" of the biblical text? Such an argument seems impressive and very difficult to argue against, especially if you aren't equipped with a knowledge of the vocabulary and grammar rules of biblical Greek. And that pretty much describes the vast majority of people walking the planet. So, when someone comes along with an argument against the papacy that hinges on the precise meaning of a perfect passive indicative participle or the gender of a declension ending, most people's eyes will glaze over quickly and they find themselves at the mercy of the "Experts."

Don't let this happen to you. The *petros/petra* argument — seems convincing at first, but falls apart upon closer inspection. Before we get into the gory details surrounding the Greek terms at issue here, let's take a few moments and meditate prayerfully on Scripture's message where it describes that pivotal moment in Christ's earthly ministry:

> Now when Jesus came into the district of Caesarea Philippi, he asked his disciples, "Who do men say that the Son of man is?" And they said, "Some say John the Baptist, others say Elijah, and others Jeremiah or one of the prophets." He said to them, "But who do you say that I am?" Simon Peter replied, "You are the Christ, the Son of the living God." And Jesus answered him, "Blessed are you, Simon Bar-Jona! For flesh and blood has not revealed this to you, but my Father who is in heaven. And I tell you, you are Peter, and on this rock I will build my church, and the powers of death[1] shall not prevail against it. I will give you the keys of the kingdom of heaven, and whatever you bind on earth shall be bound in heaven, and whatever you loose on earth shall be loosed in heaven.[2]

Christ rocks our world

This is the classic, though certainly not only, Scripture passage that Catholics down throughout the centuries

---

[1] Various Bible translations render the Greek *"pulai hadou"* as "the gates of hell," "the gates of sheol," "the gates of hades," the "jaws of death," etc. The literal meaning is the "gates of Hades."

[2] Matt. 16:13–19.

have turned to for demonstrating that Christ conferred on Simon Peter a unique office and primacy among the Apostles. It shows us several things.

First, we see that there was confusion as to Christ's identity. The confusion was checked when Simon spoke up, providing the correct answer to that christological question.

Second, as the Lord explained, this correct answer wasn't the result of mere human ingenuity or intellectual effort. Simon had received a revelation from God the Father that enabled him to deliver the correct answer. Illuminated by God's grace, he cut through the clutter of erroneous theological speculations the others were offering and answered correctly.

And third, neither Christ nor the Father gave the answer directly. Rather, the teaching about Christ's identity and mission was given *through* St. Peter. He who was to be entrusted by Christ with the keys of the kingdom was even then, without realizing it, fulfilling his new role in the Apostolic college. In Matthew 16:18, Christ taught *through* Simon Peter. The Lord's post-Ascension practice of teaching the Gospel and delivering revelation through his chosen followers, the Apostles and disciples, actually begins here in the backwater Galilean town of Caesarea Philippi.

And that brings us to the next point: the importance of the *setting* of Matthew 16:18. If you want to open a successful business, real estate experts will tell you the three most important things to remember are: Location, location, and location! You can't be too careful when it comes to deciding where you open your doors to the public. This axiom is especially true when we consider what happened in Matthew 16.

Jesus knew the power of symbolism and used it frequently when teaching. The location of His exchange with

Simon Peter in Matthew 16:18 took place at a small town
called Caesarea Philippi. The ancients knew it as Panias,
since it had been dedicated to the god Pan. When Philip
Herod became the tetrarch for that region, he saw a chance
to curry favor with Imperial Rome by changing the name
from Panias to the Latin "Caesarea Philippi," which essentially means "Caesar's (city) from Philip." It's located in
northeast Israel, high in the foothills of the Mount Her-
mon range, where the borders of Lebanon, Syria, and Israel meet. The ruins of that ancient site lie clustered at the
base of a huge rock promontory that rises dramatically to a
height of some 200 feet. The side of the rock facing south is
a sheer cliff, dotted with niches that are still visible today,
where pagan idols once stood. Writing around the year
A.D. 79, the Jewish historian Flavius Josephus describes
the scene:

> At this spot a mountain rears its summit to an immense
> height aloft. At the base of the cliff is an opening into an
> overgrown cavern. Within this (cavern), plunging down
> to an immeasurable depth, is a yawning chasm, enclosing
> a column of still water, the bottom of which no sounding
> line has been found long enough to reach. Outside and
> from beneath the cavern well up the springs from which,
> as some think, the (River) Jordan takes its rise.[3]

Fr. Stanley Jaki, whose book, *And On This Rock*, provides a fascinating explanation of the history and significance of Caesarea Philippi, describes the place as it would
have looked when Christ and the Apostles were there:

> A splendid pagan city lying in clear sight of a huge wall of
> rock. At the top of that wall there glitters the white marble

---

[3] *The Jewish War*, 1:21:3.

of a temple dedicated to Caesar. At the bottom, there is an outwardly idyllic sanctuary of Pan. Immediately to the left of that sanctuary there is a fathomless cavity full of water, one of the three sources of the Jordan.[4]

From ancient times, that cave was known to the local inhabitants as "The Gates of Sheol," the gates of the underworld.

Forget about the competition

Try to imagine the scene: Christ is speaking to the Apostles, using that huge rock as the backdrop. On top of the rock stands a temple, inside of which stands a pagan idol, a false god. Two key parallels here are striking:

a) Christ is the true God, not Caesar, not Pan, nor any other pagan divinity.

b) The false god's church (temple) sits atop a rock, but Christ will build His Church on *the* rock, Simon, son of Jonah.

The importance of this passage leaps into view when we see how Christ used the symbols of a gigantic rock and a pagan temple atop it to contrast with His Church and the rock on which it would be built. Simon, the brash and impulsive fisherman, would be the new rock.

But many non-Catholics will have none of this, believing that the alleged difference in meaning between the Greek words *petros* and *petra* nullifies all this talk about symbolism and parallels. "Christ wasn't referring to Simon Peter

---

[4] Stanley L. Jaki, *And On This Rock* (Manassas: Trinity Communications, 1987), 20–21.

when he said 'On this rock I will build My Church,' " they say. "He was referring to Himself, or to Simon's confession of faith, or to something else altogether, but not Simon himself."

A rock by any other name is still a rock

There are two basic problems with this argument. First, any linguistic distinction between the Greek nouns *petros* and *petra*, the masculine and feminine forms, was confined to examples found here and there in ancient Greek poetry, but there was no longer any difference in meaning at the time of Christ. This fact is acknowledged even by prominent Protestant scholars (the late Oscar Cullmann and D. A. Carson, to name two). For this reason, when Jesus called Simon *Petros*, He was not *contrasting* him with the rock (*petra*) on which He would build His Church, He was identifying Simon as that very rock. Indeed, if the Lord had wanted to designate Simon a small rock or pebble, His words would most certainly have been rendered using the Greek term *lithos*, which means pebble or small rock.

This fact is important to keep in mind when we consider the *petros/petra* argument raised by non-Catholics. We can't forget that *Petros*, the Greek name for rock, is a translation of the actual Aramaic name that Christ conferred on Simon. That name was *Kepha*, as John 1:42 proves conclusively. This is why the reminder that there was an underlying Aramaic original of St. Matthew's Gospel, from which the Greek version was translated, is so important. Once we get back to the original language, the apparent *petros/petra* conundrum evaporates. This is why there's no substance to the charge raised by some non-Catholics, that *petros* means a stone or a pebble.

The second problem with the *petros/petra* argument is that it ignores the fact that in their daily lives, Jesus and the Apostles didn't speak to each other in Greek, but in Aramaic, the common language of the Jews in Palestine at that time.[5] What we read in Matthew 16:18 is the Greek rendering of the Aramaic conversation between the Lord and Simon Peter.

How can we know for sure this is true? Scripture tells us that the word Christ chose for Simon's new name was *Kephas*, the Aramaic word for rock. When Jesus and Simon met for the first time, the new name was foretold. Here's how St. John described the scene:

> Andrew, the brother of Simon Peter, was one of the two who heard John and followed Jesus. He first found his own brother Simon and told him, "We have found the Messiah" (which is translated Anointed). Then he brought him to Jesus. Jesus looked at him and said, "You are Simon, the son of John; you will be called Kephas" (which is translated Peter).[6]

This passage makes it clear that the name Christ intended to confer on Simon was Kephas, rock. St. John was careful to help the Greek-speaking Christians who knew no Aramaic or Hebrew by translating into Greek two key

---

[5] A vivid example of this common use of Aramaic is found in Mark 15:35, which recounts Christ's anguished cry in Aramaic as he hung on the cross: *"Eloi, Eloi, lema sabachthani?"* (My God, my God, why have you forsaken me?). Cf. Matthew 27:46.

[6] John 1:41–42.

terms he had preserved in Hebrew and Greek: "Messiah" (Hebrew) and Kephas (Aramaic). This is a clear indication that although the Greek-speaking Christians came to know Simon the Fisherman-Apostle as "Petros," that was actually a translation of his actual new name, Kephas. This is clear from other passages of Scripture that refer to Peter as "Cephas," such as John 1:42 and Galatians 2:9, 11.

Those early Church Fathers who comment on the subject, affirm that the Gospel of Matthew was originally written in Aramaic, or possibly Hebrew, and only later translated into Greek for the benefit of Greek-speaking Christians. Bishop Papias is recorded in Eusebius's *Ecclesiastical History* as saying that St. Matthew wrote his Gospel in the "Hebrew (*Hebraidi*) language."

> St. Irenaeus and Eusebius maintain that he wrote his Gospel for the Hebrews in their national language, and the same assertion is found in several writers. Matthew would, therefore, seem to have written in modernized Hebrew, the language then used by the scribes for teaching. But, in the time of Christ, the national language of the Jews was Aramaic, and when, in the New Testament, there is mention of the Hebrew language (*Hebrais dialektos*), it is Aramaic that is implied. Hence, the aforesaid writers may allude to the Aramaic and not to the Hebrew. Besides, as they assert, the Apostle Matthew wrote his Gospel to help popular teaching. To be understood by his readers who spoke Aramaic, he would have had to reproduce the original catechesis in this language, and it cannot be imagined why, or for whom, he should have taken the trouble to write it in Hebrew, when it would have had to be translated thence into Aramaic for use in religious services.[7]

---

[7] A reference to the Targums, Aramaic translations of the Hebrew

Eusebius (*Ecclesiastical History*, 3:24:6) tells us that the Gospel of Matthew was a reproduction of his preaching, and this we know, was in Aramaic. An investigation of the Semitic idioms observed in the Gospel does not permit us to conclude as to whether the original was in Hebrew or Aramaic, as the two languages are so closely related. Besides, it must be borne in mind that the greater part of these Semitisms simply reproduce colloquial Greek and are not of Hebrew or Aramaic origin. However, we believe the second hypothesis to be the more probable, viz., that Matthew wrote his Gospel in Aramaic.[8]

Early evidence

The patristic testimony that Matthew wrote first in Aramaic is substantial:

Scriptures. "*Targum* is the distinctive designation of the Aramaic translations or paraphrases of the Old Testament. After the return from exile Aramaic gradually won the ascendancy as the colloquial language over the slowly decaying Hebrew until, from probably the last century before the Christian era, Hebrew was hardly more than the language of the schools and of worship. As the majority of the population ceased to be conversant with the sacred language it became necessary to provide translations for the better understanding of the passages of the Bible read in Hebrew at the liturgical services. Thus to meet this need it became customary to add to the portions of the Scriptures read on the Sabbath an explanatory oral translation — a Targum. At first this was probably done only for the more difficult passages, but as time went on, for the entire text" (Dr. Franz X. Schühlein, "Targum," *The Catholic Encyclopedia* [New York: Robert Appleton Co., 1912], vol. XIV, 454). E. Jacquier, article "Gospel of Matthew" in the *Catholic Encyclopedia*, 1913; electronic version available at www.knight.org/advent/cathen/10057a.htm.

[8] Jacquier, "Gospel of Matthew."

Let us now recall the testimony of the other ecclesiastical writers on the Gospel of St. Matthew. St. Irenaeus (*Against Heresies*, 3:1:2) affirms that Matthew published among the Hebrews a Gospel which he wrote in their own language. Eusebius (*Ecclesiastical History*, 5:10:3) says that in India, Pantaenus found [a copy of] the Gospel according to St. Matthew written in the Hebrew language, the Apostle Bartholomew having left it there. Again, in his *Ecclesiastical History* (6:25:3:4), Eusebius tells us that Origen, in his first book on the Gospel of St. Matthew, states that he has learned from tradition that the First Gospel was written by Matthew, who, having composed it in Hebrew, published it for the converts from Judaism.

According to Eusebius (*Ecclesiastical History*, 3:24:6), Matthew preached first to the Hebrews and, when obliged to go to other countries, gave them his Gospel written in his native tongue. St. Jerome has repeatedly declared that Matthew wrote his Gospel in Hebrew (*Epistle to Damasus* 20; *Epistle to Hedib.* 4), but says that it is not known with certainty who translated it into Greek. St. Cyril of Jerusalem, St. Gregory of Nazianzus, St. Epiphanius, St. John Chrysostom, St. Augustine, etc., and all the commentators of the Middle Ages repeat that Matthew wrote his Gospel in Hebrew. . . . St. Jerome uses Matthew's Hebrew text several times to solve difficulties of interpretation, which proves that he had it at hand. Pantaenus also had it, as, according to St. Jerome (*On Illustrious Men*, 36), he brought it back to Alexandria. . . . [A]ll ecclesiastical writers [until Erasmus in the sixteenth century] assert that Matthew wrote his Gospel in Hebrew, and, by quoting the Greek Gospel and ascribing it to Matthew, thereby affirm it to be a translation of the Hebrew Gospel.[9]

---

[9] Jacquier, "Gospel of Matthew": While patristic testimony on this

So far, so good. When the Lord renamed Simon, he named him *Kepha*, not *Petros*. In Aramaic, there is no masculine or feminine distinction for the noun *Kepha*, and it has only one meaning: a rock. Christ said to Simon, "You are *Kepha*, and upon this *kepha* I will build My Church." At this point you might wonder why the Greek text has Jesus using different words for Peter and the rock on which He would build His Church, if there was no difference. In short, it doesn't. Jesus utilizes two forms of the same word. In Greek, unlike English, nouns have gender (the same is the case with German). In Greek, *petra* is a feminine noun — unsuitable to be used as the name of a man. To remedy this, Matthew changes it to the masculine form of the word: *petros*. That's all there is to it.

The rock that will not roll

It's clear from the context of Matthew 16:18 that the primary meaning of the rock referred to is Peter.[10] To see this, you actually have to start in Matthew 7:24–27:

---

point is valuable and authoritative, the modern school of biblical studies rejects this thesis out of hand. There are a number of modern-day biblical scholars who are sifting through the textual and patristic evidence and find themselves departing from the current view and championing the patristic testimony. Good examples of recent scholarly work in this area are found in Jean Carmignac, *The Birth of the Synoptics* (Chicago: Franciscan Herald Press, 1987); Claude Trésmontant, *The Hebrew Christ* (Paris: O.E.I.L., 1983); and, briefly, in William G. Most, *Free From All Error* (Libertyville: Prow Books, 1985).

[10] There are, of course, completely valid secondary meanings for the word "rock" in Matthew 16:18. The *Catechism of the Catholic Church*, for example, points to an alternate meaning, Peter's *profession of faith*,

> Everyone who hears these words of mine and does them
> will be like a wise man who built his house upon the rock;
> and the rain fell, and the floods came, and the winds blew
> and beat upon that house, but it did not fall, because it
> had been founded on the rock. And every one who hears
> these words of mine and does not do them will be like a
> foolish man who built his house upon the sand; and the
> rain fell, and floods came, and the winds blew and beat
> against that house, and it fell; and great was the fall of it.

Was Jesus Christ foolish? Of course not. And he wouldn't
give advice that He Himself didn't follow. So, since He was
indeed a wise man, when it came time to build God's own
house, the Church (cf. 1 Timothy 3:15), he did exactly what
he told his disciples to do: He built it firmly on the rock of
Simon. What other possible reason could Jesus have had
for renaming Simon "Rock" at that moment? If He were
intending to contrast Simon with the rock, he picked a
strange time to change his name to rock. It would have
been as if Jesus had changed Simon's name to "Faith," in
order to make the point that Simon had no faith. That
notion is every bit as silly as it sounds. And that leaves
those who deny that Peter is the rock of Matthew 16:18

---

as being the rock on which the Church would be built by Christ (cf.
CCC 424, 442), an interpretation echoed by some early Church Fathers.
But the *literal* meaning of the rock is Peter himself, as the *Catechism*
affirms (cf. CCC 552, 586). Secondary or figurative meanings are al-
ways built upon the literal meanings, not the other way around. The
literal meaning — in this case, that Simon Peter is the rock spoken of in
Matthew 16:18 — establishes the possibilities for secondary meanings.
Ultimately, we must search for the primary intent of the inspired author.
Only then can we build upward and locate the figurative meanings that
can be inferred from a given passage.

between a rock and a hard place. They haven't been able to come up with a viable alternative reason for why Christ would change Simon's name to Rock at that moment.

A Protestant opinion

The preeminent Protestant New Testament scholar of his day, the late Dr. Oscar Cullmann, wrote:

> The Gospel tradition has simply preserved the fact that Jesus marked off Simon among the Twelve by giving him the name 'rock.' According to OT [i.e., Old Testament] models (Gen. 17:5, 15; 32:29; Isaiah 62:2, 65:15) and Rabbinic usage nicknames either refer to a particular situation as a promise or else they lay upon those who bear them a specific task . . . This name cannot be explained exclusively in terms of Peter's character. To be sure, Jesus knows his zeal, exuberance and energy as well as his lack of courage. When he gives Simon the name Peter, he knows the many sided strength of his temperament. On the other hand, these qualities unfold only in the discharge of the task laid upon him.[11]

The fact that St. Paul refers to Jesus Himself as a Rock in 1 Corinthians 10:4 has no bearing on who the Rock is in Matthew 16:18. God calls Abraham the "rock" from which the Israelites were hewn (Isaiah), but that doesn't mean He Himself isn't the "eternal Rock" (Isaiah 26:4–5). Similarly, Christ changes Simon's name to rock, but that doesn't conflict with the fact that Christ was the "rock"

---

[11] Cullmann, "Petros," Gerhard Kittel, Gerhard Friedrich, eds., *Theological Dictionary of the New Testament* (Grand Rapids: Eerdmans, 1968), vol. 6, 103.

that followed Israelites in the desert. Scripture says Christ is the "light of the world" in John 1, and it says that God's people are the "light of the world" (Isaiah 49:6). You get the point.

Biblical authors use a wide range of terms and symbols, and they aren't always interchangeable (just take a look at the way St. Paul and St. James use the term "faith" in Romans 3:28 and James 2:24). To determine the identity of the Rock, we must look at the immediate context — not a letter written by a different author, to a different audience, in a different place, discussing a different topic. Sometimes, that's what happens when people are looking for something, anything, to use as an argument against the papacy. It's sloppy exegesis and, unfortunately, it lurks at the heart of the *petros/petra* fiction.

3

In Matthew 16:23, Jesus calls Peter "Satan," and tells him that he's on the side of men, not God. If, as the Catholic Church claims, Jesus had just made Peter the pope in the preceding verses (18–19), there's no way He would have turned around and reprimanded him in this way, calling him Satan. This is proof that Peter was not being made pope in Matthew 16:18–19.

This argument is like the dog that's all bark and no bite. It's not nearly as formidable as it seems, once we dig deeper into the facts surrounding the episode. True, Christ used a harsh word to rebuke the impetuous Peter, but this doesn't negate His earlier promises about Peter's primacy.

Before we prove that point, let's first clarify a minor but important point. In Matthew 16:18–19, Christ was not making Simon Peter the first pope — he was promising that he *would* do that at a later time. That time came after the Resurrection, when Christ turned to Simon Peter and told him to "feed My sheep and tend My lambs" (John 21:15–17). As we look at the many Scriptural evidences for Peter's primacy, it's important to see all of them against

the backdrop of Christ's promise in Matthew 16:18. Peter
didn't assume the fullness of his office as pope all at once.
He entered into it gradually, and only fully so, from the
Day of Pentecost forward.

As for Christ's rebuke, we must keep in mind what He
meant when He called Peter "Satan." Was he literally identifying Peter as being the Fallen One? Obviously not, since
a few verses earlier, Christ had just promised to entrust him
with the keys of the kingdom of heaven. Rather, the Lord
was speaking figuratively. He had just finished telling the
Apostles that He would have to suffer and be killed. Peter
resisted this horrifying prediction; a perfectly natural human reaction. As it happened so often in the past, Peter
and the other Apostles didn't fully recognize Christ's divine mission, a mission which included his suffering and
death on the cross. Now, as before, the deeper meaning of
his words was lost on them.

When Peter responded to Christ's grim prediction with
a hearty, "God forbid, Lord! No such thing shall ever happen to you!" he was being protective of his friend. Christ
knew this, of course, and his response — "Get behind me,
Satan! You are an obstacle to me" — pointed out that, in
spite of Peter's natural desire to shield his Lord from suffering, he wasn't thinking with Christ. "You are thinking
not as God does, but as human beings do" (Matt. 16:23).

What did Jesus really mean?

The word "satan" literally means adversary or opponent.
By his effort to stop Christ from going up to Jerusalem,
suffer at the hands of the Jewish leaders, and be executed,

Peter was unwittingly opposing God's plan of salvation. Christ used the word "satan" to emphasize just how contrary Peter's thinking was to His mission as Redeemer. This wasn't an identification of Peter as "satanic" in the strict sense of the word. Rather it showed the gravity of the situation facing Christ and how important it was that He fulfill His mission. Any effort, however inadvertent, to prevent Christ from keeping his appointment with death on Calvary, was worthy of such a rebuke.

Does this event somehow contradict the doctrine of papal infallibility? Not at all. Notice, first of all, that Peter hadn't yet been made the head of the Church. In verse 18 of this passage, Jesus said, "You are Peter (Rock), and upon this rock I *will* build my church." This refers to a future event. So too in verse 19, when Jesus said "I *will* give you the keys of the kingdom of heaven," this authority had not yet been conferred on Peter. Both of these promises were fulfilled later. For this reason alone, the issue of papal infallibility is completely irrelevant.

A double-edged sword

And let's not forget that the logic of this pope fiction ("Jesus had just made Peter the pope in the preceding verses, there's no way He would have turned around and reprimanded him in this way, calling him Satan") can be turned against itself. Christ's promise, in Matthew 16:18, to make Simon the rock on which his Church would be built holds.

In Matthew 16:18–19 Christ said: "Blessed are you, Simon, son of Jonah. You are rock, and on this rock I will build My Church. . . . I will give to you the keys of the kingdom of heaven. Whatever you bind on earth will be bound in heaven, etc. . . ." The construction of this address to Simon leaves no room for the possibility (as many non-Catholics argue) that Christ renamed Simon *Petros* as a way to show how insignificant and useless he was, rather than in comparison with identifying the *petra* on which He would build His Church. Why?

The context won't allow it. Why? Because, if Jesus had intended the meaning inherent in this pope fiction, He would have engaged in a bizarre and inexplicable wordplay: a) Jesus calls Simon "blessed." b) He tells Simon he received revelation from God the Father. c) He gives him the new name of Petros. d) He turns right around and *mocks* Simon by telling him that he's really just a pebble, and that He intends to build His Church on a *real* rock, a big rock, not Peter. And, finally, e) after his moment of mocking Simon and his ironic new name, Christ shifts back to praising him, saying, "I give you the keys of the kingdom of heaven. Whatever you bind on earth is bound in heaven, and whatever you loose on earth is loosed in heaven."

You're not the boss of me!

The problem with this picture is clear. It just doesn't make sense for Christ to praise, honor, and elevate Simon and, in the next breath, mock him, and then go back to entrusting him with authority and honor. But that stilted interpretation is exactly what many non-Catholics want to force onto this passage. Why? Because they can't bring themselves to acknowledge that Christ was entrusting Simon Peter with special duties and primacy. For to do that would amount to an admission that the pope has *authority*, and that is something very unpleasant for many non-Catholics to contemplate. Rather than submit to the primary teaching authority Christ established to guide his Church, the papacy, many non-Catholics grasp at the Reformation principle of *sola scriptura* (Latin: the Bible alone). They can avoid obedience to the Church by claiming to go by the Bible alone. And that is simply the "every man for himself" path that leads only to divisions, fragmentations, and disunity.[1]

But there's another, more fundamental reason why Catholic teaching about the papacy isn't jeopardized by an appeal to Christ's stinging rebuke of Peter. The Catholic Church claims that the popes, starting with Peter himself, are guarded from formally teaching error. There's no claim made that popes, including Peter, cannot be wrong in their private opinions. Clearly, Peter was incorrect in his thinking, as the Lord showed him, but his was simply an error in judgment. He wasn't proclaiming a dogma to be held by all. He simply misunderstood what was about to happen in Jesus's future. Nothing more, nothing less.

---

[1] For a full-scale critique of the Protestant doctrine of *sola scriptura*, see Robert Sungenis, Patrick Madrid, et al., *Not By Scripture Alone* (Santa Barbara: Queenship, 1997).

4

In Galatians 2:11–14, Paul recounts a time when he publicly rebuked Peter for false teaching, saying "When Kephas came to Antioch, I withstood him to his face because he was clearly wrong." This fact single-handedly shatters the Catholic claim that popes are infallible and that they are the ultimate authority. If Peter were the first pope, he was clearly in error, so he wasn't infallible. Furthermore, he couldn't have been the ultimate authority in the Church, or Paul would never have dared to rebuke him as he did.

The two objections stuffed into this pope fiction — Peter was in error (therefore he was not infallible) and Paul rebuked him (therefore Peter had no special authority over Paul) — seem convincing. In fact, many opponents of the papacy have appealed to this classic "proof text" to disprove Catholic claims about papal authority and infallibility. But they too ultimately fail to prove what papal critics think they do. Let's stop and ponder the Scripture passage in question before moving on to our answer.

But when Cephas came to Antioch I opposed him to his face, because he stood condemned. For before certain men came from James, he ate with the Gentiles; but when they came he drew back and separated himself, fearing the circumcision party. And with him the rest of the Jews acted insincerely, so that even Barnabas was carried away by their insincerity. But when I saw they were not straightforward about the truth of the gospel, I said to Cephas before them all, "If you, though a Jew, live like a Gentile and not like a Jew, how can you compel the Gentiles to live like Jews?"[1]

The irony here is that it was specifically to Peter that the Lord had given the revelation regarding the gentiles being allowed into the Church without needing to observe the Mosaic ceremonial laws, such as Kosher food restrictions. That's what exasperated Paul when he saw what Peter did. It's easy to imagine him pounding his fist on the table in frustration, saying, "You of all people, Peter! God gave *you* the revelation that cleared up this Gentile issue once and for all, and look at you! You're not abiding by the policy which you *yourself* laid down at the Council of Jerusalem" (cf. Acts 15).

But St. Paul's exasperation notwithstanding, when you get right down to it, this passage has nothing to do with *teaching*, but with personal actions. Paul rebuked Peter for what he saw as hypocritical *behavior*, not for heretical teaching. And this is a crucial point. For as far as papal infallibility is concerned, personal behavior has nothing to do with it. What Peter did in this situation may or may not have been correct, but regardless, this passage can't help the critics of papal infallibility. Why? Because the Catholic teaching on papal infallibility rests on the issue of what the

---

[1] Gal. 2:11–14.

pope formally teaches to the Church as a whole, not the personal decisions he makes about how to act in a given situation.

Vatican I, the council which defined the dogma of papal infallibility, explained the parameters of the doctrine of infallibility. It defined formally what the Church had always held and believed: That the pope is infallible precisely when he teaches officially. This charism does not extend to personal attitudes or actions. The fact that papal infallibility is grounded firmly and only in the teaching office of the papacy was echoed at Vatican II:

> The Roman Pontiff, head of the college of bishops, enjoys this infallibility in virtue of his office, when, as supreme pastor and teacher of all the faithful — who confirms his brethren in the faith — he proclaims by a definitive act a doctrine pertaining to faith or morals.[2]

The source of the controversy

So, let's get back to Galatians 2. According to St. Paul, St. Peter had been eating with Gentile Christians when he heard that a group of Jewish Christians were on their way to visit him. Now that may not sound like a big deal, but in those very early days of the Church, it was. This was the era when the young Church was still struggling to perceive and explain to the world its identity as something distinct from the Judaism that had given it birth. The earliest Christians grappled with the question of how much of a role, if any, Jewish precepts such as circumcision, Kosher

---

[2] *Lumen Gentium* 25.

food laws, and various dietary restrictions imposed by the Law of Moses, should play in Christianity.

Eating and drinking with Gentiles was a a serious matter for devout Jews of the first century. It violated a whole raft of Kosher laws handed down by Moses and, as amazing as this may seem to us today, this aversion to eating with Gentiles threatened to tear apart the unity of the early Church. One faction of Christians, known as the "Judaizers," believed that all the Jewish precepts and ceremonial aspects of the Mosaic Law — including circumcision — must be kept completely intact within Christianity. They were the minority. It wasn't until the Apostles met in the first plenary council of the Church (cf. Acts 15), that this question was finally resolved. The decision of the Church, under the direction of the Holy Spirit (Acts 15:28–29), was to completely abandon all the restrictions and ceremonial practices of the Mosaic Law, leaving Gentile converts free to enter the Church without undergoing circumcision or following Kosher food laws.

With this in mind, let's think about St. Peter's actions. He knew very well that the Jewish Christians who were coming from Jerusalem to visit him would be rattled by finding him dining with Gentile Christians. So he thought it best to stop the practice, at least temporarily. He did this, it seems, to avoid scandalizing his visitors and to avoid a controversy.

When St. Paul discovered this he was unhappy, and when the opportunity presented itself, he confronted Peter and upbraided him for this. As he explains in Galatians 2, he felt Peter and the others who followed his example "were not on the right road in line with the truth of the gospel." If, as Christians, Jews and Gentiles are absolutely equal in the eyes of God, St. Paul reasoned correctly, and if the various ceremonial obligations of the Law of Moses, such as circumcision and kosher laws, had been abolished by Christ's redemptive sacrifice on the Cross, why did Peter do what he did?

It cuts both ways

Even though St. Paul tagged St. Peter with the charge of "hypocrisy," the case was not as clear-cut as that. Nor can non-Catholics use Galatians 2 with impunity to attack the Catholic Church's teaching on papal infallibility and the primacy of Peter. This passage becomes a double-edged sword.

First, Peter may not have been committing nearly as big a *faux pas* as St. Paul's complaint in Galatians 2, taken at face value, makes it appear. (I can just imagine the Protestant reader reaching this statement and rolling his eyes. "See? These Catholics ignore what Scripture says and try to explain it away." But I ask for patience and an open mind here. Read on, and see, in light of some things Paul himself did, if Peter's hypocrisy was really as damning as it might appear.) Remember that, in addition to being the shepherd of the whole Church, he had the special charism of being sent as an "apostle to the circumcised" — the Jews (cf. Gal. 2:7). So he naturally would be expected to have had a special sensitivity to the attitudes and concerns of Jewish Christians.

His action was an attempt to keep from making waves with the Jewish Christians — something the Apostles at the Council of Jerusalem itself sought to do with their decrees (cf. Acts 15:22–29). In these decrees, the council bound

Gentile Christians to observe certain regulations in order to keep them from offending the sensitivities of Jewish Christians (cf. verses 19–21). St. Peter did essentially the same thing when he avoided a situation that would have caused controversy and scandal.

St. Paul did what?

The exquisite irony here is that St. Paul himself heartily endorsed the very practice he rebuked St. Peter for following — the practice of avoiding scandal and controversy over eating habits. In his Epistle to the Romans, he admonished:

> Then let us no longer judge one another, but rather resolve never to put a stumbling block or hindrance in the way of a brother. I know and am convinced in the Lord Jesus that nothing is unclean in itself; *still it is unclean for someone who thinks it is unclean.* If your brother is being hurt by what you eat, your conduct is no longer in accord with love. Do not because of your food destroy him for whom Christ died. So do not let your good be reviled. For the kingdom of God is not a matter of food and drink, but of righteousness, peace, and joy in the Holy Spirit; whoever serves Christ in this way is pleasing to God and approved by others.
>
> Let us then, pursue what leads to peace and to building up one another. For the sake of food, do not destroy the work of God. Everything is indeed clean, but it is wrong for anyone to become a stumbling block by eating; it is good not to eat meat or drink wine or do anything that causes your brother to stumble.[3]

---

[3] Rom. 14:15–21; cf. 1 Cor. 8:7–13.

It could be that St. Paul himself was the real hypocrite for condemning St. Peter for something he himself admitted to doing and encouraged others to do.[4]

Another twist of irony makes it even more futile for non-Catholics to cite Galatians 2 as a proof text against papal infallibility. If St. Paul's rebuke of St. Peter over the issue of his hypocrisy somehow undermines the Catholic claim of Peter's primacy, watch what it does to St. Paul's authority.

The Epistle to the Galatians captures St. Paul at his most stern; condemning the Judaizers and their efforts to force circumcision and other Jewish ceremonies into the Christian faith. He begins his critique by asking, "Am I now currying favor with human beings or God? Or am I seeking to please people?[5] If I were still trying to please people,

---

[4] In fact, this very question was a source of disagreement between St. Augustine and St. Jerome, both of whom sought to interpret Galatians 2 in a way that made sense out of this curious episode. St. Augustine maintained that Peter sinned venially in his behavior. St. Jerome argued that Peter acted out of charitable concern for the Jews, and therefore can't be charged with any sin at all. St. Jerome suggested that the whole incident may have been something of a virtuous ruse, an apparent run-in, pre-planned by Peter and Paul as a way to show the Christian community (remember that at that time, many Christians still harbored a deep suspicion of Paul because of his earlier career of persecuting the Church [cf. Acts 8:1–3, 9:1–2; Gal. 1:13–14]), that Paul had apostolic authority. It would also have served, Jerome theorized, as a good object lesson in humility for the community. If Peter himself would receive a rebuke from Paul, the former Christian-killer, how much more should the rank and file Christian be docile and humble (cf. St. Augustine, *Letters: Volume I* (New York: Fathers of the Church, Inc., 1951), *Letter* 40, 75, 81, 82).

[5] It's no coincidence that St. Paul begins his Epistle to the Galatians

I wouldn't be a slave of Christ" (Gal. 1:10). Clearly, his goal is to please God, regardless of what others may think. But notice what happens. He warns in Galatians 5:2: "It is I, Paul, who am telling you that *if you have yourselves circumcised, Christ will be of no benefit to you.*" Yet he himself, when faced with the problem of unruly Judaizing Christians in Lycaonia, had his disciple Timothy circumcised:

> He reached Derbe and Lystra where there was a disciple named Timothy, the son of a Jewish woman who was a believer, but his father was a Greek. The brothers in Lystra and Iconium spoke highly of him, and Paul wanted him to come along with him. *On account of the Jews in that region, Paul had him circumcised*, for they all knew that his father was a Greek.[6]

This is where the dilemma arises for those who see in Galatians 2 a disproof of Catholic teaching on papal infallibility and Petrine primacy. If Peter can be discredited and disqualified as pope because he was hypocritical for "withdrawing from table fellowship" with Gentile believers, then Paul's credibility and authority is ruined all the more because he had Timothy circumcised "on account of the Jews" who would have balked if Timothy had remained uncircumcised.

Obviously, in spite of his warnings in Galatians 5:2, St. Paul's authority wasn't squandered because he made a pru-

---

with a pointed reminder of his apostolic authority: "Paul, an apostle, not through a human being but through Jesus Christ and God the Father who raised him from the dead, and all the brothers who are with me, to the churches of Galatia, grace to you and peace from God our Father and the Lord Jesus Christ" (Gal. 1:1–2).

[6] Acts 16:1–3.

dential decision to have Timothy circumcised. He didn't see circumcision as something that had to be performed in order to be a "true" Christian and thus appropriate Christ's saving grace (*that* would have been a clear violation of his own teaching). No, it seems he chose that course of action so as to avoid needless tension and scandal with the Jews whom he sought to evangelize.

In the same way, St. Peter's "hypocrisy" can be explained quite reasonably as a decision to avoid similar tensions with Jewish Christians. Just as St. Paul's actions surrounding his decision to have Timothy circumcised "on account of the Jews" can be seen, on one hand, as "hypocritical" (given his pointed statements in Romans, 1 Corinthians, and Galatians), in the full light of the facts, St. Peter's actions regarding the Judaizers can also be seen, from a practical and pastoral standpoint, as being legitimate and understandable.

But in any case, we find ourselves being drawn back to the same conclusion: St. Peter's actions in this case have nothing to do with his office as Chief of the Apostles, nor do they undermine or disprove the Catholic teaching on papal infallibility. They were simply his personal deeds, done at a moment of vexing uncertainty for all concerned.

Can the pope be rebuked?

We're still left with that nagging question about St. Peter's authority. Did he have some sort of preeminent authority among the Apostles? And if he did, how could it be that St. Paul would have dared to oppose him in so brash a way? The answer to this question is ultimately uncertain, but St. Jerome's theory that it was an object lesson in humility is a solid one. It may be that St. Peter indeed made a mistake and St. Paul was right to rebuke him for it. And such a rebuke wouldn't conflict with the special primacy that Christ had given to St. Peter.

Popes have been rebuked, privately and publicly, by other Catholics since the time of St. Peter. True, such cases are infrequent, but they have happened. For example, the great Dominican, St. Catherine of Siena, traveled to Avignon, France in 1376 to confront Pope Gregory XI about his (and several of his predecessors') seemingly permanent intention to remain absent from the diocese of Rome. She admonished the pope publicly, pleading with him to withdraw from his strange exile in France and come back to Rome, where he belonged. Her rebuke worked. It was so well-placed, so appropriate and necessary, that the pontiff was cut to the heart and accepted the wise counsel of that heroic nun. Ignoring all pressure exerted by the King of France and others to keep him there, he left France forthwith and returned to Rome.

In the case of Peter and Paul, such a rebuke must have been similarly well-placed and efficacious. After all, it was to St. Peter alone among the Apostles that the Lord revealed that Gentiles should be admitted to the Church without having to submit to Jewish ceremonies and that the Church was free to abandon the dietary restrictions imposed by the Law of Moses (cf. Acts 10:9-43). So whom better to remind about this freedom in Christ than the very man to whom Christ gave this revelation?

Notice, too, St. Paul's language in Galatians 2. As you read the text, it seems evident that he was eager to explain the circumstances surrounding his public correction of St. Peter. Perhaps he felt he *needed* to give an account for his actions. After all, to rebuke Peter himself, the Apostle to whom Christ had entrusted the keys of the kingdom, was an action that no Christian before Paul had ever presumed to take.

To use a contemporary example, let's imagine that a President of the United States were engaged in a televised "Town Hall" meeting with American citizens in a large U.S. city. Now, imagine that in front of the whole audience, one of the citizens whose turn it was to ask the president a question took the opportunity to rebuke him for some bad decision he had made in his foreign affairs policy. A dramatic scene? Yes. Out of the ordinary? By all means. Shocking? Of course. But when you get right down to it, such a rebuke, as dramatic as it may be, wouldn't imply that the president doesn't possess the jurisdiction or authority proper to his office. It wouldn't mean that he wasn't the president. And it certainly wouldn't mean that the citizen who issued the rebuke had an authority equal to that of the president. No. The most it would mean is that the president may have deserved such a correction, even if delivered from a private, "rank and file" citizen.

Similarly, although the legitimate need for publicly rebuking or correcting a pope has been, happily, relatively rare in the life of the Church, it isn't at all inconsistent with the claim that Peter (and the popes after him) was the head of the Church.

And finally, there's an important point that should be made to Protestants who still insist that popes can't be infallible, because they are sinful, weak men. Protestants believe in the teaching infallibility of three "sinful and weak" men. Two were murderers (Moses and Saul of Tarsus), the third was a murderer *and* an adulterer (King David). In spite of their sins, God still was able to use them to teach infallibly. The same is true of Peter and the popes.

5

Even if Jesus Christ had given Peter a special primacy, there is nothing in Scripture that suggests his authority was passed on to his alleged "successors."

~

This is one of those subtle, "I'll meet you half way" arguments that are sometimes thrown at Catholics by those who recognize and admit the strength of the biblical evidence for Peter's primacy, but who are unwilling to concede that this primacy exists today in the office of the papacy. At the very least, we can be thankful that the person using this line of reasoning is willing to admit that Peter did have a primacy. The task now is to show that this primacy was transmitted from Peter to each of his successors, the bishops of Rome.

The continuation of Peter's ministry is tied closely to the continuation of the apostolic ministry in general. Before we can tackle the specific issue of the succession of Peter's office as bishop of Rome, we must first outline the biblical evidence for the overarching doctrine of apostolic succession itself. If it can be established that apostolic authority was intended by Christ to continue in the Church, even after the deaths of the original Apostles, we can also make the case that Peter's unique role as pope was to continue as well.

The *Catechism of the Catholic Church* explains the doctrine of apostolic succession as a perpetual mission intended by Christ to be carried out in a special way, for as long as the Church sojourns on earth:

> In order that the mission entrusted to them might be continued after their death, [the apostles] consigned, by will and testament, as it were, to their immediate collaborators the duty of completing and consolidating the work they had begun, urging them to tend to the whole flock, in which the Holy Spirit had appointed them to shepherd the Church of God. They accordingly designated such men and then made the ruling that likewise on their death other proven men should take over their ministry.[1]

An unbroken chain

Jesus Himself implied that there would be an unbroken continuation of the apostolic office until the end of the world. When He chose the men who would be His Apostles, the men he would send to the four corners of the world with the saving message of the gospel, he knew that they could not accomplish their mission personally, in its totality. This mission would be initiated by the original Apostles, but it would eventually need to be handed on to appointed men who would succeed them. In their turn, as the Catechism explains, they would hand on their apostolic mission to others.

---

[1] CCC 861.

This mission is to wage a war of love. Its prime objective: to conquer the whole world in the name of and for the glory of Christ the King. It is carried out by all baptized Christian men and women, but in a particular way by those men — bishops, priests, and deacons — who have been entrusted with the unique charism of the apostolic office. Each of them shares in the ministry of Christ's apostles, bishops most fully. This mandate from Christ is to conquer the world with love, a campaign that will last until the end of the world, the only weapons brought to bear being faith, hope, and a burning charity.

This is precisely the mission of redemption that the Father gave Christ His Son in the Incarnation. And Christ, when his earthly ministry was complete, entrusted that mission to His Apostles: "As the Father has sent Me, so I send you" (John 20:21). The Apostles clearly understood that their "being sent" included their own eventual selection and commissioning of men who would carry on the mission after they had died.

At the Last Supper, in reference to the Holy Sacrifice of the Eucharist, Christ commanded the Apostles to "do this in memory of Me" (Luke 22:19). If this practice was to continue after the Twelve were dead and gone (and we know it did), then other men would have to be able to succeed to their ministry, being invested with the power to perform the same priestly action.[2] Since Christ promised

---

[2] Christ's Last Supper command to "do this in memory of Me" is part of the accomplishment of the prophecy of the Eucharist in Malachi 1:10–12. From the earliest times, the Fathers and doctors of the Church linked this prophetic passage of Scripture with the doctrine of the Sacrifice of the Mass (cf. the *Didache* 14:3; St. Irenaeus, *Against Heresies*

that he would be with His Church "until the end of the world" (Matt. 28:20), we can be sure that the Church's need for apostolic authority would continue, too, until the end of the world when Christ will return to take His Bride, the Church, to heaven with Him.

There is a parallel here with the power Christ gave His Apostles to forgive and retain sins (John 20:21–23). Was this power to forgive sins designed to end when the apostolic age came to a close? Obviously not. The powers and duties of the Apostles, including the authority to forgive sins in the sacrament of confession, were to be passed on to successors. This is the Catholic doctrine of apostolic succession.

Adios, Judas. Hello, Matthias

There is ample biblical evidence to show that the Apostles understood that their ministry would be handed down in the Church. We see it immediately in those uncertain days after the Crucifixion and Resurrection, as soon as a vacancy arose in the Apostolic college.

> In those days Peter stood up among the brethren (the company of persons was in all about a hundred and twenty), and said, "Brethren, the scripture had to be fulfilled, which the Holy Spirit spoke beforehand by the mouth of David, concerning Judas who was guide to those who arrested Jesus. For he was numbered among us, and was allotted his share in this ministry. . . . For it is written in the book of Psalms, 'Let his habitation become desolate, and let

---

4:17:5; St. Justin Martyr, *Dialogue with Trypho the Jew* 41; St. Augustine, *Tractate Against the Jews* 9:13).

there be no one to live in it'; and 'His office let another take.' "[3]

After this, the Apostles voted to have Matthias take Judas's place among the Twelve. If the apostolic office was to end with the death of the Apostles, there would have been no need to replace Judas. This passage indicates that this ministry was to continue beyond the apostolic age.

Other actions of the Apostles give firm foundation to the Catholic teaching on apostolic succession. They traveled throughout the Middle East, ordaining successors, and leaving them in various cities to head up the churches there. While engaged in just such a journey, St. Paul wrote to a bishop named Titus: "This is why I left you in Crete, that you might amend what was defective, and appoint elders in every town as I directed you" (Titus 1:5).

Paul tells Timothy to keep on keepin' on

Similarly, St. Paul wrote to Timothy, another young bishop he had ordained: "Do not lay hands too readily on anyone" (1 Tim. 5:22). Why would he give Timothy this advice? Because the office of bishop has a unique and very important authority, and each bishop should be very careful to choose worthy men to carry on this special mission in the Church. He emphasizes this point again when he says, "So you, my child, be strong in the grace that is in Christ Jesus. And what you heard from me through many witnesses entrust to faithful men who will have the ability to teach others as well" (2 Tim. 2:1–2). We can see

---

[3] Acts 1:15–17, 20.

quite clearly in this section of Paul's Epistle to Timothy the first few links in the two-thousand-year chain of apostolic succession:

1. I Paul have received an apostolic mission from Christ (cf. 2 Tim. 1:1).
2. I have given you, Timothy, this apostolic ministry and authority through the laying on of my hands when I ordained you a bishop (cf. 2 Tim. 1:6).
3. Be careful, Timothy, in handing on this apostolic ministry you possess to others, so that they in turn will be wise enough to hand it on to the next generation of bishops (cf. 2 Tim. 2:2).

The early Church provides us with a rich testimony to the doctrine of apostolic succession. Among the many authoritative voices that speak of apostolic succession as an undisputed fact, as early as the year A.D. 80, St. Clement, bishop of Rome, gave a simple, eloquent explanation of how this happened. This passage from his *Epistle to the Corinthians* is one of the classic examples of extra-scriptural corroboration of apostolic succession in the early Church:

> The Apostles preached to us the gospel received from Jesus Christ, and Jesus Christ was God's ambassador. Christ, in other words, comes with a message from God and the Apostles with a message from Christ. Both of these orderly arrangements, therefore, originate from the will of God. And so, after receiving their instructions and being fully assured through the Resurrection of our Lord Jesus Christ, as well as confirmed in faith by the word of God, they went forth proclaiming that the kingdom of God was at hand. From land to land, accordingly, and from city to city they preached, and from their earliest converts

appointed men whom they had tested by the Spirit to act as bishops and deacons for the future believers. . . . Our Apostles, too, were given to understand by our Lord Jesus Christ that the office of bishop would give rise to intrigues. For this reason, equipped as they were with perfect foreknowledge, they appointed the men mentioned before, and afterwards laid down a rule once for all to this effect: When these men die, other approved men shall succeed to their sacred ministry.[4]

You can't get more conclusive evidence than that. Notice that Pope Clement was writing before the end of the first century, while St. John the Apostle was still alive. As bishop of Rome, he was invoking the authority of apostolic succession in this very early letter as a way to demonstrate the continuity both of the Church's doctrine, and the authority it possessed, from the Apostles, to teach that doctrine. It's even more significant to note that Clement, bishop of Rome and successor to St. Peter in that office, was "strengthening his brethren" in Corinth through this pastoral letter. He was acting in the same capacity of leadership as Peter was told to by Christ.

No complaints from Corinth (or anywhere else)

And never is there an outcry from the Church at Corinth complaining that Clement was out of line for presuming to instruct and admonish another preeminent church. No. The clergy and faithful of Corinth revered Clement's letter, and had it read in church on Sunday along with Scrip-

---

[4] *Epistle to the Corinthians* 42, 44; translation by Johannes Quasten, *Patrology* (Westminster: Christian Classics, 1993), 1:45–46.

ture. The Corinthians complied as best they could with Clement's directives, never once showing shock or resistance to his authority. This is extremely important. If the doctrine of apostolic succession and the primacy of the Roman church was not already understood by Christians of the first century, there would have been an incredible backlash against Clement.

The Isaiah 22 connection

Now let's go back to Isaiah 22 and examine its special significance in light of Christ's words to Simon in Matthew 16:18. The Lord said, "You are Peter (rock), and on this rock I will build my Church, and the powers of death shall not prevail against it. I will give to you the keys of the Kingdom of heaven. Whatever you bind on earth shall be bound in heaven, and whatever you loose on earth, shall be loosed in heaven." Here Christ is promising to make Simon Peter, not just the rock on which he would build His Church, but also *the keeper of the keys* of the Kingdom and the one, authorized by Christ Himself, who would hold a personal authority to bind and loose. This authority was not Simon's own authority, but one given to him by Christ. That means he acts with Christ's own authority in a particular way in the life of the Church.

This duty is the equivalent of a "prime minister" in a kingdom, the King's trusted second in command. And that position is precisely the one occupied by Shebna, spoken of in Isaiah 22:15–25. Notice the strong parallel to Matthew 16:18:

Thus says the Lord God of hosts, "Come, go to this stew-
ard, to Shebna, *who is over the household*, and say to him:
'What have you to do here and whom have you here, that
you have hewn here a tomb for yourself, you who hew a
tomb on the height, and carve a habitation for yourself in
the rock? Behold, the LORD will hurl you away violently,
O you strong man. He will seize firm hold on you, and
whirl you round and round, and throw you like a ball
into a wide land; there you shall die, and there shall be
your splendid chariots, you shame of your master's house.
I will thrust you from your office, and you will be cast
down from your station. In that day I will call my servant
Eliakim the son of Hilkiah, and *I will clothe him with your
robe, and will bind your girdle on him, and will commit your
authority to his hand*; and *he shall be a father to the inhabitants of Jerusalem and to the house of Judah.* And *I will place
on his shoulder the key of the house of David; he shall open,
and none shall shut; and he shall shut, and none shall open.*
And I will fasten him like a peg in a sure place, *and he
will become a throne of honor to his father's house.* And they
will hang on him the whole weight of his father's house,
the offspring and issue, every small vessel, from the cups
to all the flagons. In that day, says the LORD of hosts, the
peg that was fastened in a sure place will give way; and it
will be cut down and fall, and the burden that was upon
it will be cut off, for the LORD has spoken."[5]

Several important points need to be made here. First, this
office of prime minister[6] in the House of Judah (i.e., the
Davidic Kingdom) was, second only to the King himself,

---

[5] Emphasis added.
[6] Cf. Stephen K. Ray's excellent discussion of the nature and history
of this office and how it relates to Matthew 16:18–19 in *Upon This Rock*
(San Francisco: Ignatius Press, 1999), 266–297.

the highest office in the land. The prime minister "is over the household," meaning that he exercises a unique, final authority in the name of the King. Similarly, in Matthew 16:18–19, Christ was commissioning Simon Peter to be His vice-regent or prime minister. Simon was to be given the same type of second-in-command authority in Christ's name.

Second, the holder of this office was identifiable for wearing certain vestments that pertained to the office. Although this is a minor point, it's worth noting in passing that the pope, too, has certain insignias and vestments (e.g., the pallium, the crozier, the Fisherman's episcopal ring) that identify him as the successor to Simon Peter.

Third, one of the functions of the prime minister, at least as it was to be fulfilled by Eliakim and his descendants, was to be "a father to the inhabitants of Jerusalem and to the house of Judah." This role of father figure didn't detract from or compete with the King's role as the ultimate "father figure" to the inhabitants of his kingdom. Rather, the prime minister shared in that role in a subordinate way, and reflected the "fatherhood" of the King to his people. In the same way, the bishop of Rome, successor of Peter, is the father figure to the whole Church. He is the *papa*, the visible center of unity for all Christians.

Fourth, the Prime minister receives the master key to the household, the key that overrides and supersedes all lesser keys held by other officials in the kingdom. What "he shall open, none shall shut; and what he shall shut, none shall open." The direct parallel with these prophetic words to those directed to Peter by Christ are unmistakable. As Christ's new prime minister, Simon Peter is promised the keys of the kingdom of heaven. What he binds, no one can loose, and what he looses, no one can bind. This authority is extended at a more general level to all the Apostles in Matthew 18:18.

Fifth, this office constituted a "throne of honor to his father's house." This means that Eliakim would bring glory and honor to his family because of the special role he would play in the Kingdom. Similarly, the Catholic Church recognizes the honor and glory that is proper to the office of the papacy, the successors of Simon Peter. This fact is echoed by St. Paul in 1 Corinthians 12, where he speaks about the Church as the Body of Christ: "if one member [of the Body] is honored, all rejoice together" (12:26). Also, the mention of the office being a "throne," a ceremonial chair, is quite interesting. The obvious parallel to the papacy is that the pope occupies the venerated "chair of St. Peter."[7] This is not a specific, particular throne or chair, of course, but the word "chair" symbolizes the seat of magisterial authority occupied by Peter and his successors.[8]

And finally, the entire context of Isaiah 22 is one of *succession*. It is this context more than any particular element in the passage that bolsters the Catholic claim that Peter would also have successors in his ministry. Shebna gave way to Eliakim, and Eliakim in due time would die and hand on that dynastic office of prime minister to his successor.[9]

---

[7] In Latin, the word for chair or throne is *sedes*, from which we derive in English the word *see*, as in the Holy See or Apostolic See.

[8] Cf. Matthew 23:2–4: "The scribes and the Pharisees *sit on Moses's seat*; *so practice and observe whatever they tell you*, but not what they do; for they preach, but do not practice. They bind heavy burdens, hard to bear, and lay them on men's shoulders."

[9] The historical and Scriptural evidence surrounding this fact is presented in Ray, *Upon This Rock*, 280–297.

The many elements that can be gleaned from Isaiah 22 leap out at us when we juxtapose them with the statements made by Christ to Simon Peter in Matthew 16:18–19. They are too many and too pointed to be mere coincidence. Christ was intentionally applying the same kind of language in Isaiah 22 — a passage that Simon Peter and the other Apostles, all Jews, would have known by heart — to his commissioning of Simon. As Stephen Ray explains in his book *Upon This Rock*,

> The Catholic Church has consistently taught from the first centuries that the office of Peter is an office that continues to exist and exercise the authority of the keys. What can we learn about succession from the ancient kingdoms and their office of vizier and steward "over the house?"
>
> The vizier was an office of supreme importance to the kingdom of Egypt.[10] It should be remembered that it was not a person, but an office. When the vizier died, the office did not. The office continued to exist, and in the event of death or displacement, another man would be appointed to fill the vacant office.[11]

If death itself could not overcome the Church, then the Church would last until the end of time. But for this to be true, the *foundation* on which that Church was built by Christ — the "Rock" — would itself have to endure as well. This fact is glimpsed earlier in Christ's words about the wise man who builds his house on the "rock" in Matthew 7:24–27. Regardless of how furiously the rain, winds, and floods might batter against that house, it would not fall because the rock on which it is built could not be dislodged

---

[10] Cf. the story of Joseph being installed by Pharaoh as his royal vizier (prime minister) in Genesis 41.

[11] Ray, 289–290.

or eroded. This is the rock on which Christ promised to build His Church. This "rock" is the blessed Apostle Peter and his successors in the papacy.

Since Peter himself would eventually die, there had to be some way for his position as the "rock," the prime minister of the Kingdom, to continue. Obviously, for that to take place, this office had to be able to be passed on to successors somehow. (Interestingly, Christ foretold Peter's death in the very passage where he gave him a special primacy, telling him to "feed my sheep and tend my lambs" [John 21:15–19]. Just as the office of Apostle is handed on to each generation through apostolic succession in the episcopacy, this perpetuation of Peter's special role takes place through his successors in the office of bishop of Rome — the popes.

Clearly, Christ's Kingdom would be established more firmly, more permanently than David's was. The Lord Jesus Christ's decision to install Simon Peter as His prime minister, his vicar, could not have been carried out in a way inferior to the Davidic model. As the Davidic Kingdom's office of prime minister would be perpetuated, even more so would the office of Christ's vicar on earth.[12]

A permanent position

The fact that Christ promised that He would be with His Church until the end of the world points to the continuation of the papacy. If the Church continued, as Our Lord said it would, it would need to retain (and even strengthen) its structure, and the papacy is central to this structure. As

---

[12] Cf. ibid., 289–293.

the Church grew and developed over the centuries, so did the papacy. Much like the tiny acorn that grows into a towering oak tree, the papacy we see in the New Testament is identical to the papacy of today, even though it didn't bear all the external features we have come to associate with the office. But this shouldn't surprise us. This development of the office of the papacy runs parallel to the development of the Church — growing from a mustard seed to a huge tree in which "the birds of the air come and make their nests" (cf. Matt. 13:31–32).

The earliest Christians were the students and disciples of the Apostles themselves. They are invaluable witnesses of the genuine apostolic teaching on such a crucial point. It's striking that the Fathers of the ancient Church were always and everywhere clear in their assertions that the Catholic bishops of their day were the sole, legitimate successors to the Apostles.

An early appeal to Roman authority

Around the year 180, less than a century after the Apostles lived, St. Irenaeus, the bishop of Lyons, wrote:

It is within the power of all, therefore, in every church, who may wish to see the truth, to contemplate clearly the tradition of the apostles manifested throughout the whole world; and we are in a position to reckon up those who were by the apostles instituted bishops in the Churches, and [to demonstrate] the succession of these men to our own times; those who neither taught nor knew of anything like what these [heretics] rave about. For if the apostles had known hidden mysteries, which they were in the habit of imparting to 'the perfect' apart and privily from the rest, they would have delivered them especially to those to whom they were also committing the churches themselves. For they were desirous that these men should be very perfect and blameless in all things, whom also they were leaving behind as their successors, delivering up their own place of government to these men; which men, if they discharged their functions honestly, would be a great boon [to the Church], but if they should fall away, the direst calamity.[13]

St. Irenaeus, like the other early Fathers, understood that the sacred ministry of Peter was also to continue through the bishops of Rome:

Since, however, it would be very tedious, in such a volume as this, to reckon up the successions of all the churches, we do put to confusion all those who, in whatever manner, whether by an evil self-pleasing, by vainglory, or by blindness and perverse opinion, assemble in unauthorized meetings; We do this, by indicating that tradition derived from the Apostles, of the very great, the very ancient, and universally known Church founded and organized at Rome by the two most glorious apostles, Peter and Paul; as also the faith preached to men, which comes down to our time by means of the successions of the bishops. For it is a matter of necessity that every church should agree with *this* Church [i.e., Rome], on account of its preeminent authority, that is, the faithful everywhere, inasmuch as the apostolic tradition has been preserved continuously by those [faithful men] who exist everywhere. The blessed Apostles, then, having founded and built up the Church,

---

[13] *Against Heresies*, 3:3.

committed into the hands of Linus the office of the epis-
copate. Of this Linus, Paul makes mention in the Epistles
to Timothy. To him succeeded Anacletus; and after him,
in the third place from the apostles, Clement was allotted
the bishopric.[14]

Notice what St. Irenaeus appeals to as the indisputable
authority that will verify his statement as true and authentic Christian doctrine. He appeals to apostolic tradition in
his effort to refute the various Gnostic attacks on the Catholic Church, and he locates and establishes the authority of
this tradition fundamentally in the person of the bishop of
Rome. He announces that it is "a matter of necessity that
every Church should agree with *this* Church, on account
of its preeminent authority." In doing so he is anchoring
his defense of orthodox Christianity squarely on the rock
of Peter. This is *the* place, according to St. Irenaeus, where
all Christians can be absolutely certain that "the apostolic
tradition has been preserved continuously."

And for those who still dispute this issue, saying that
the apostolic office was purely a temporary arrangement,
intended for the first generation of Christians only and to
cease with the death of the last Apostle, perhaps this question will give them pause: What other significant arrangement (aside from a period of providing a general revelation)
did Christ ever make for his Church that was intended to
be merely *temporary*?

---

[14] Ibid., 3:3.

Even the popes' critics knew the truth

We could enumerate many examples of early Fathers pointing confidently to the bishop of Rome as the successor of St. Peter,[15] but let's also introduce evidence that isn't complimentary to the pope. It's evidence which, nevertheless, makes the point that even critics of particular popes recognized that, as the bishop of Rome, the pope possessed a unique authority among bishops.

For example, in the middle of the third century, Firmilian wrote a diatribe against Pope Stephen in a letter to the venerable Bishop Cyprian of Carthage:

> In this respect, I am justly indignant at this so open and evident stupidity of [pope] Stephen: that although he glories so much in the place of his bishopric, and contends that he holds the succession of Peter, on whom the foundations of the Church have been laid, he should introduce many other rocks and establish the new building of numerous Churches, since he defends with his authority that baptism is found in them![16]

Note that Firmilian isn't denying Petrine succession or authority, but is actually using it to underline Stephen's alleged hypocrisy in the controversy regarding the rebaptism of heretics. Pope Stephen held firm to the orthodox teaching that baptism is a "once for all" sacrament, never

---

[15] Catholic writer Antoine Valentim has compiled an excellent series of quotes from the ancient Eastern Church Fathers who affirm the primacy and jurisdiction of the Bishop of Rome as well as the fact that he was the authentic successor of St. Peter. This collection is available on the Internet at web.globalserve.net/~bumblebee/ecclesia/patriarchs.htm.

[16] Firmilian of Caesarea, *Letter to Cyprian*, 75.

to be repeated. When the controversy in the early Church arose about whether heretics who had been reconciled to the Church should be rebaptized, Pope Stephen said no. Others, such as Firmilian and St. Cyprian, opposed him.

The buck stops here

When it came to the question of the succession of Peter's office in the papacy, there was no real argument among early Christians. This is what Catholic theologians sometimes call the "unanimous consent of the Fathers." The Catholic teaching that the bishops of Rome are truly successors of St. Peter and share in his unique ministry of leadership in the Church is something all the Fathers agreed upon, down through the centuries. The late Cardinal Yves Congar, O.P., a widely respected Catholic theologian, explained what the Catholic Church means by unanimous consent:

> In every age the consensus of the faithful, still more the agreement of those who are commissioned to teach them, has been regarded as a guarantee of truth; not because of some mystique of universal suffrage, but because of the gospel principle that unanimity and fellowship in Christian matters requires, and also indicates, the intervention of the Holy Spirit. From the time when the patristic argument first began to be used in dogmatic controversies — it first appeared in the second century and gained general currency in the fourth — theologians have tried to establish agreement among qualified witnesses of the faith, and have tried to prove from this agreement that such was in fact the Church's belief. As a matter of fact, a few testimonies sufficed, even that of one single man if his particular sit-

uation or the consideration accorded him by the Church
were such as to gibe to what he said the value of coming
from a quasi-personification of the whole Church at that
time. The decisive factor was not mere quantity but the
representative quality of the testimony. . . . Unanimous
patristic consent as a reliable *locus theologicus* is classical
in Catholic theology; it has often been declared such by
the Magisterium and its value in scriptural interpretation
has been especially stressed.

Application of the principle is difficult, at least at a certain level. In regard to individual texts of Scripture total
patristic consensus is rare. In fact, a complete consensus
is unnecessary: quite often, that which is appealed to as
sufficient for dogmatic points does not go beyond what
is encountered in the interpretation of many texts. But it
does sometimes happen that some Fathers understood a
passage in a way that does not agree with later Church
teaching. One example: the interpretation of Peter's confession in Matthew 16:16–19. Except at Rome, this passage
was not applied by the Fathers to the papal primacy; they
worked out an exegesis at the level of their own ecclesio-
logical thought, more anthropological and spiritual than
juridical. This instance, selected from a number of similar
ones, shows first that the Fathers cannot be isolated from
the Church and its life. They are great, but the Church
surpasses them in age, as also by the breadth and riches
of its experience. It is the Church, not the Fathers, the
consensus of the Church in submission to its Savior which
is the sufficient rule of our Christianity.[17]

The good Cardinal is quite right. It is the Tradition of
the Church (both the written Tradition of Scripture, and

---

[17] Yves M. J. Congar, O.P., *Tradition and Traditions* (San Diego: Basilica Press, 1998), 397–399.

the unwritten Tradition that is lived out and handed on in the Church's liturgies, prayers, councils, etc. Cf. 2 Thess. 2:15) that preserves the authentic deposit of faith.

His comment regarding the patristic interpretation of Matthew 16:18 — "Except at Rome, this passage was not applied by the Fathers to the papal primacy" — is inaccurate, as we'll see in a moment, but it is understandable. He was seeking to show an example of the authority of the Church when it comes to authentic interpretation of the deposit of faith. Even though some Fathers didn't interpret Matthew 16:18–19 according to the way the Church understands it, this doesn't deprive the Church of being able to show the antiquity and consistency of its position.

From the source's mouth

As we go back to the patristic sources and examine what the earliest Christians believed and taught about the primacy of St. Peter and his successors, the bishops of Rome, we see clearly that this belief was universal and continuous. Happily, in the first few centuries, Christ blessed His Church with an incredible succession of holy and wise popes. The history of the Church brims with popes who were fearless and effective in teaching the gospel and extending the borders of the Kingdom of Christ. Some of them were martyrs. Many of them are canonized saints. All of them received and shared in and labored under the protection of the special graces and charisms Christ promised to Peter: "I have prayed for you that your faith may not fail. . . . And when you have turned back, strengthen your brethren."

Good and bad, wheat and chaff

But we must also recognize that the history of the papacy isn't all good. There were disagreements and controversies between the popes and other bishops, yes. There were episodes of popes not acting decisively or wisely on behalf of the Church at those moments when the Church most needed their leadership. There were terrible instances of public scandal and hidden wickedness perpetrated by a handful of medieval popes. But these dark chapters are simply the proof that the Catholic Church is Christ's Church, not the pope's Church.

The examples of papal weakness and sin that some point to as evidence against the papacy are, in fact, merely echoes of the Gospel accounts of the conduct of the first pope, Peter, and the other original Apostles. Christ Himself chose these twelve men and, even so, all but one of them ran away from Him. One, Peter, denied even knowing Him. Another betrayed Him to his enemies. Not a good track record. But, again, it is proof positive that Christ is in charge here and is living in His Church. If the papacy and the succession of the Apostles through the episcopacy were of merely human origin and not divinely established and preserved by the Triune God, they would have collapsed centuries ago, under the weight of human weakness.

But that has never happened, nor will it. In spite of dungeon, fire and sword, these links in the chain of apostolic succession have never been broken. Neither, by God's grace, have the links been broken in the chain of Peter's successors, the bishops of Rome.

6

The pope is the beast spoken of in Revelation 13. Verse 1 says that he wears crowns and has "blasphemous names" written on his head. Verse 18 says that the numerical value of his name adds up to 666. The pope's official title in Latin is *Vicarius Filii Dei* (Vicar of the Son of God). If you add that up using Roman numerals, you get 666. The pope's tiara is emblazoned with this title, formed by diamonds and other jewels.

~

I wasn't very good at math in school, but even I can follow this argument and run the numbers well enough to show it's bogus. (Besides, answering this question is apologetics at its most fun!) The charge that the pope is the beast of Revelation 13, because his title adds up to 666, is especially popular with Seventh-Day Adventists, but it's also widely repeated in some Protestant circles.

Vicarius Filii Dei can be shown to have a numerical value of 666 in Latin. Here's how it works. Like many ancient languages, such as Greek and Hebrew, some Latin letters are also used for numbers: I = 1, V = 5, X = 10, L = 50, C = 100, D = 500 and M = 1000. The letter "u" is rendered as V and the letter "w," which doesn't exist in the Latin alphabet, would be rendered as VV. So this title would read in Latin as VICARIVS FILII DEI.

When calculating the value of a name or word, letters that don't have a numerical value are ignored. For example, drop out the no-value letters in my name, PATRICK MADRID, and you come up with 2102 — 1 (i) + 100 (c) + 1000 (m) + 500 (d) + 1 (i) + 500 (d) = 2102.

(By the way, this is one reason why, as far as I know, no one has yet accused me of being in league with the antichrist. The numbers just don't add up.)

But in the case of VICARIVS FILII DEI, they *do* add up to 666. Isolate the numbers and this is what you get: 5 (v) + 1 (i) + 100 (c) + 1 (i) + 5 (v) + 1 (i) + 50 (l) + 1 (i) + 1 (i) + 500 (d) + 1 (i) = 666.

But there are problems with this. The first is that *Vicarius Filii Dei*, or "vicar of the Son of God," is not now, nor has it ever been, an official title used by the bishop of Rome. The second problem is that virtually no one, including many unsuspecting lay Catholics, knows that this papal "title" is a fabrication. To an untrained ear, it sounds enough like one of the pope's real titles, *Vicarius Christi* (Vicar of Christ), to pass the test. Unfortunately for those who traffic in this particular piece of pope fiction, the real title, *Vicarius Christi*, adds up only to a measly 214, not the infernal 666. In fact, none of the pope's official titles, such as *Servus Servorum Dei* (Servant of the Servants of God), *Pontifex Maximus* (Supreme Pontiff), or *Successor Petri* (Successor of Peter), will add up to 666. That's why you never see any of them used by anti-Catholics.

Wrong name, wrong number

If the person making this claim disputes these facts, ask him to furnish an example of the alleged title, *Vicarius Filii Dei*, being used officially by a pope. You won't encounter papal decrees, conciliar statements, or other authentic, official Catholic documents in which the pope calls himself the "vicar of the Son of God." Why? Because no such examples exist. *Vicarius Filii Dei* has never been an official title of the pope.

But, as they say, old habits die hard. One Seventh-Day Adventist apologist was so incensed with me for having written an article in which I said that *Vicarius Filii Dei* has never been an official title of the pope that he wrote me the following rebuttal:

> I am a Seventh-Day Adventist and wish to dispel the notion that Adventists ignore "the evidence" as you claim. You may still claim that it is not today, or ever was an officially recognized papal title, but since the association with 666 apparently first surfaced in 1612, it is no real surprise that Catholics are ignorant of the facts on this matter today, or that the title is denied by Catholic apologists.
>
> The lack of official recognition today, however, does not in any way prove that *Vicarius Filii Dei* is a fantasy or fabrication concocted by Protestantism. The documented evidence I present shows beyond any doubt that *Vicarius Filii Dei* is not, as your article suggests, merely a groundless anti-Catholic invention. On the contrary, it has a very long history of use by the Catholic Church, having appeared in print in the Catholic Canon Law, a respected Catholic encyclopedia and Catholic newspapers. Those are the hard facts, which the Adventists, at least, choose not to ignore.

Hard facts? Mmmm, . . . no. I don't think so. But I will
say this much for our Seventh-Day Adventist friend: He
obviously thought about this matter long and hard before
coming up with the wrong answer.

Now, it's true that over the course of the last two thousand years of Catholic history, a few examples exist of popes
being *described* as the vicar of the Son of God, and some of
these mentions appear in documents that are rightly called
"official." But we are not claiming here that popes have
not been, at one time or another, described that way —
this is not at issue. Rather, the issue is that *Vicarius Filii
Dei* has never been a *name* or an official *title* of the pope.
Seventh-Day Adventists in particular try hard to prove this
fact wrong. In their polemical writings, tracts, "prophecy
seminars" and Internet sites, they go to great lengths to
convince people that the alleged papal title, *Vicarius Filii
Dei,* is a direct fulfillment of the prophecy of the Beast in
Revelation 13.

Lost in a maze of historical details

That same Adventist, in his essay against the papacy,
tried to make his charges stick by offering a series of historical examples of *Vicarius Filii Dei* being used as a papal
title. But before we examine them let's first pause over the
most curious and imaginative of the lot:

> In *Crossing the Threshold of Hope*, by Pope John Paul II,
> in the first chapter, page 3, you will find [this statement]:
> "The pope is considered the man on earth who represents
> the Son of God, who 'takes the place' of the Second Per-
> son of the omnipotent God of the Trinity." If you directly

translate [the phrase] "represents the Son of God" into Latin, the official language of the Church, you get *Vicarius Filii Dei*.

Alas, if only this gentleman's Latin were as good as his imagination. In fact, the phrase "Represents the Son of God," when translated directly into Latin, yields *"Filium Dei Repraesentat,"* not *"Vicarius Filii Dei."* It should suffice to point out that "represents" is a verb. "Vicar" is a noun. But let's not belabor the obvious.

Sometimes an argument that's couched in an appeal to Latin or Greek (like the one above) can appear formidable, especially to Catholics with no familiarity with those languages. But as we can see, invariably these arguments are hollow.

Among the few examples of the use of *Vicarius Filii Dei* that can be dredged up from twenty centuries of Catholic history are *The Decretum of Gratian* and the *Corpus of Canon*. These are the two "examples" most often cited by Seventh-Day Adventists and other purveyors of this particular pope fiction. Perhaps the best-known example of a book that details this argument (along with numerous others against the papacy and the Catholic Church) is *The Prophecies of Daniel and the Revelation,* written by a Seventh-Day Adventist named Uriah Smith.

A lot less there than meets the eye

Uriah Smith was obviously expecting to pull out the history books and have himself a wonderful time, but we're going to have to disappoint him and those who buy into his line of reasoning. As we'll see in a moment, there's a lot less to his argument than meets the eye.

For one thing, those examples of *Vicarius Filii Dei* that are often cited from the *Decretum* and the *Corpus* are actually drawn from the *Donation of Constantine*, a famous forgery. Anyone familiar with medieval Church history will recognize the *Donation* as one of the better known examples of a forged ecclesiastical document and, as such, cannot by any stretch of semantics be regarded as an "official Catholic document."

Another historical document that's sometimes cited by believers in the *Vicarius Filii Dei* scam is Lucius Ferraris's work, *Prompta Bibliotheca*, which also contains an instance of the title in question. But here again, Ferraris's use of *Vicarius Filii Dei* is a description of the role of the pope and is directly based on the *Donation of Constantine* — a bogus document. Ferraris could have been more careful in his use of sources, of course, but nevertheless, this example can in no way be regarded as an instance of *Vicarius Filii Dei* being used in an *official* Catholic document. In fact, regarding Ferraris's scholarship, the *Catholic Encyclopedia* passage that is typically quoted by Adventists reads in full, "This supplement serves to keep up to date the work of Ferraris, which will ever remain a precious mine of information, *although it is sometimes possible to reproach the author with laxism.*" Invariably, Adventists and others who try to use Ferraris as their anti-papal pack mule, neglect to add that last part of the quote from the *Encyclopedia*, but no wonder. Apparently none of them have bothered to *read* the actual passage in the *Catholic Encyclopedia*, which they purport to quote.

They keep coming up empty-handed

Those who perpetuate this myth have obviously trawled carefully through the classic *Catholic Encyclopedia* looking for anything that could be used to bolster their *Vicarius Filii Dei* argument. Unfortunately, they don't bother to read the article in the same Encyclopedia called the "Pope: Primacy of Honour: Titles and Insignia." Under the subsection of "Official Titles of the Pope," the phrase *Vicarius Filii Dei* is nowhere to be found. Why? Because it isn't now nor has it ever been an official papal title. But we shouldn't be surprised that this fact has escaped the notice of those who write books and tracts and articles and fill Web sites with this hokum. Many people make the charge without ever bothering to check the facts.

On any Sunday Visitor

Seventh-Day Adventists and other Protestant groups will sometimes point to a 1915 issue of *Our Sunday Visitor* newspaper, which claimed that the papal mitre is inscribed with the title *Vicarius Filii Dei* in diamonds. I contacted Robert Lockwood, the president of *Our Sunday Visitor*, about this. He had personally gone through the *Our Sunday Visitor* archives and could not find that issue. Evidently, it had been removed. The error on the part of a newspaper staffer (and let's remember, the Catholic Church doesn't claim infallibility for journalists) was caught only after it had slipped into print. Obviously concerned about the blunder being perpetuated, the editor expunged that issue from the archives. Not surprisingly, those who perpetuate the *Vicar-*

ius Filii Dei myth never mention the strong disavowals of this issue made by *Our Sunday Visitor* over the years. For example, in the August 3, 1941 issue, a reader posed this question: "A pamphlet has come to me entitled Mark of the Beast. It identifies the pope with the mark (i.e., 666) referred to in Revelation 13:16–18."

The editor responded:

> The question you ask has been answered many times, although not in recent years, in this paper. If we have recourse to the best biblical scholars or exegetes, we find them applying the text from Revelation to Nero, the arch-persecutor of Christianity in the first century. To give color to their accusation, enemies of the Church publicize something that is not at all true, and that is that the pope's tiara is inscribed with the words, "VICARIUS FILII DEI," and that if the letters in that title were translated into Roman numerals, the sum would equal 666. As a matter of fact, the tiara of the pope bears no inscription whatsoever.

Robert Lockwood has written a letter on behalf of *Our Sunday Visitor* explaining that the 1915 remark regarding the alleged inscription on the pope's mitre was an unintentional and unfortunate error that should not be used as "evidence" to support the *Vicarius Filii Dei* argument. A copy of the letter has been sent to the leadership of the Seventh-Day Adventist church, demanding they stop using this episode as some sort of "proof" to prop up their argument. Let's hope that honesty and a desire to know the truth will compel the Adventists to stop using this illegitimate quote.

Where's the beef?

So, if the very best our Adventist friends can do is point to obscure, erroneous passages from a Catholic newspaper printed nearly a century ago, this demonstrates further the fact that *Vicarius Filii Dei* is not an official title of the pope. If it were, why would Adventists and others have to go through such gyrations to find an example of it? If it were an official papal title, examples would be strewn everywhere (as are occurrences of actual papal titles such as *Vicarius Christi, Servus Servorum Dei,* etc.). In spite of their strenuous efforts at historical sleuthing, the "evidence" these papal critics present is hardly the smoking gun they imagine it to be.

Poof! That part of the question was easy, but some people, especially Seventh-Day Adventists, will ignore the evidence (or lack of it) and hold tenaciously to the notion that "Vicar of the Son of God" *is* an official papal title and therefore identifies the pope as the Beast of Revelation. What else can be said in response? Using the same math exercise we did earlier, point out that the name of the woman who started the Seventh-Day Adventist church, Ellen Gould White, also adds up to 666 in Latin. (L + L + V + L +D + V + V + I = 666). Then ask if this proves that *she* is the Beast. I can assure you that the answer won't be "yes." If the answer is "no," ask how this numbers game could possibly prove the pope or anyone else is the Beast. If you're answered with silence, it's a good bet that you've made some progress with the person.

They can't get no satisfaction

The main fact to impress on someone who uses this argument is that a papal title had to be invented, one that could produce the magic number, in order to give this argument legs.

But we're not quite finished cutting it off at the knees. The charge that the pope is the Beast because he wears a crown, because Revelation 13:1 says the Beast wears crowns and has "blasphemous names" written on his head, must also be answered. This we can do more quickly.

Since about the year 708, many popes have worn — at non-liturgical ceremonial events — a special papal crown called a tiara, but the stylized beehive-shaped papal crown of three diadems that we have come to know as a tiara emerged only in the early fourteenth century. Although it was customary for these tiaras to be encrusted with jewels and precious ornaments, there is no evidence — no statue, bust, painting, drawing, or even written description of any of the many tiaras that were crafted — that any papal tiara never had the name or a title of a pope emblazoned on it.

This is significant, because there have been medieval and Renaissance popes whose extravagant vanity prodded them to have lavishly ornamented, jewel-encrusted tiaras made for themselves. And we possess paintings and statues and other representations of them produced during their lifetimes that show these tiaras. If any popes in history would have been tempted to succumb to the bad taste of spelling out *"Vicarius Filii Dei"* in diamonds across the front of their tiaras, these men would have — but they didn't. No pope did.

One particular anti-Catholic tract I've seen shows a plain

metal tiara with *Vicarius Filii Dei* written in diamonds across it. But it was a *drawing* — not a photograph of a museum piece or even a photo of a painting of a tiara. It had to be drawn, of course, because the "666 papal crown" has never existed except in the minds of those who perpetuate this fantasy.

7

In Revelation, the Whore of Babylon is described as the city that sits on "seven hills" (Revelation 17:9). The seven-hilled city is obviously Rome, headquarters of the *Roman* Catholic Church and the Papacy. It's clear then, that the Whore is Catholicism!

Page through some of the old manuscripts of the Reformation and you'll quickly run across woodcuts and engravings depicting the pope and the Church of Rome as the "Whore of Babylon." This was a very common propaganda ploy used by Protestant polemicists against the Catholic Church and it continues, vis-à-vis this pope fiction, down to our own day.

There's no denying the fact that the city of Rome *is* famous for its seven hills. Nevertheless, as we'll see, this argument doesn't pan out.

To begin with, it makes a huge and unfounded leap. First, the Greek word used in Revelation 17:9 is *óre* (from *óros*), and in Scripture, *óros* usually means mountain. You'll see why this detail is important in a moment.

I have been to Rome many times. I've walked its streets a hundred times, and I know its seven hills well. The main fact that stands out is that most of these hills are so gentle that they barely qualify as "hills." They're certainly not mountains. Granted, two thousand years of development will have had an effect on Rome's hills, effacing them to an extent, but even depictions of Rome that are hundreds of years old — long before the hills endured the onslaught of modern buildings and roads being layered upon them — several of the main hills of Rome are shown to be little more than gentle rises.

Making a mountain out of an Italian mole hill

In a Catholic apologetics tract, the significance of this fact is explained further:

> The mountains [mentioned in Revelation 17] do not even need to be literal, since mountains are common symbols in the Bible. A mountain may symbolize a kingdom. In Daniel 2:35 Christ's kingdom is seen as a mountain. In Psalm 68:15 the kingdom of Bashan is pictured as a mountain. In Obadiah 8–21 the kingdom of Edom is likened to a mountain. In Amos 4:1 and 6:1 the kingdom of Samaria is pictured as a mountain. The "seven mountains" of the whore might be seven kingdoms she reigns over or seven kingdoms with which she has something in common. The number seven may be symbolic, since it often represents completeness in the Bible. If it is symbolic in Revelation 17:9, the seven mountains might symbolize that the whore reigns over all the kingdoms of the earth or (what amounts to the same thing) that she reigns over all the literal mountains of the earth.[1]

_____

[1] "Hunting the Whore of Babylon" tract (San Diego: Catholic Answers).

The conclusion one can draw from all this is that just because Rome — like other famous cities — has been known for seven hills, that fact in itself doesn't necessarily mean that St. John was speaking of the city of Rome in Revelation 17. He could have been referring to a city much closer to his own experience: Jerusalem.

Second, it correctly identifies the Whore of Babylon as a city (cf. Revelation 17:18). Next, it identifies the city with Rome — again, a reasonable (if not sure) assumption. The problem comes in when they jump from the city of Rome to the religion of Catholicism. We see this ill-considered leap in Dave Hunt's *A Woman Rides the Beast*: "Against only one other *city* in history could a charge of fornication be leveled. That city is Rome, and more specifically *Vatican City*" (p. 69).

Whoa. Did you catch that? Hunt clearly equates the city of Rome with the Catholic Church's headquarters, Vatican City. What he fails to mention here is the fact that Rome and Vatican City are two separate and distinct cities.

Hunt's argument is a paper Tiber

He continues, "Numerous churches, of course, are headquartered in cities, but only one city *is* the headquarters of a church . . . [Vatican City] is the heartbeat of the Roman Catholic Church and nothing else" (pp. 69–70). The fundamental flaw with Hunt's argument is the fact that while the city of Rome does indeed sit on the famed seven hills, Vatican city does not. It sits on one hill: Vatican Hill. This would seem to eliminate Vatican City as a candidate for being the Whore of Revelation 17. The seven hills upon which the city of Rome sits are the Quirinal, Aventine, Palatine, Capitoline, Caelian, Esquiline and Viminal. Most people don't realize that Vatican City, built squarely on Vatican Hill, isn't one of the seven hills for which Rome is famous! Unfortunately for the fevered anti-Catholic theories that Dave Hunt and others traffic in, the Catholic Church's headquarters — Vatican City — sits on the other side of the Tiber River, and not on any of the seven hills. The Tiber formed a natural boundary for the city limits of ancient Rome. The seven hills were on one side, snug inside the city walls. Vatican Hill sat across the river, in sight of the old city, but not technically part of it — so close but yet so far.

Some, desperate to salvage this argument, claim that because the cathedral church and official seat of the bishop of Rome is St. John Lateran (which *does* fall within the bounds of Old Rome), the Catholic Church still fits the bill as being based in Rome.

You've got to give these folks an "A" for effort. Even though this variation on the theme fails, too, the people who promote it are nothing if not tenacious. The problem with this argument is that a cathedral is a church building, *not* a city, and the Whore of Babylon (cf. Revelation 17:18) is clearly a city. You can't mix and match biblical symbols to make them fit your own particular interpretative system; that does violence to the text. And, of course, even this last claim still fails to account for the leap from a city to a *religion* (which the identification of Catholicism with the Whore of Babylon *must* make, for it to work).

This road doesn't necessarily lead to Rome

The city of Rome is certainly a viable candidate for the position of the "Great Whore" (and regardless of Dave Hunt, and the many radio and TV preachers who whoop and holler about this passage, no one really knows for sure who the Great Whore is). But it's by no means the only city that could qualify for the job, nor is it necessarily the most likely. The city of Rome may indeed be the location of the "whore of Babylon," but it's futile to insist that it *must* be. Only time will tell.

Jerusalem fits some of the other characteristics of the infernal Whore: It was destroyed in A.D. 70, matching the destruction of the Great City described in the Book of Revelation. It committed "fornication" with the nations, owing to the numerous pagan powers that controlled it and, at times, compromised its religious heritage over the centuries. Both Catholic and Protestant scholars have leaned towards identifying Jerusalem with the Whore, as opposed to Rome. Of course, if Jerusalem *is* the dreaded city, a lot of anti-Catholics will have to rethink their prized argument, and Dave Hunt, his career.

8

The bishop of Rome can not be the "successor to Peter," since Peter was never in Rome. The Bible nowhere says he went there, and Paul, who did go there, never mentions Peter being in Rome. If Peter were the "pope," he certainly would have mentioned it.

There's a cute story floating around the Internet that makes a good point regarding this kind of pope fiction:

A college student was in a philosophy class, which had a discussion about God's existence. The professor presented the following logic:

"Has anyone in this class heard God?" Nobody spoke.

"Has anyone in this class touched God?" Again, nobody spoke.

"Has anyone in this class seen God?" When nobody spoke for the third time, he simply stated, "Then there is no God."

One student thought for a second, and then asked for permission to reply. Curious to hear this bold student's response, the professor granted it, and the student stood up and asked the following questions of his classmates:

"Has anyone in this class heard our professor's brain?" Silence.

"Has anyone in this class touched our professor's brain?"
Absolute silence.

"Has anyone in this class seen our professor's brain?"
When nobody in the class dared to speak, the student
concluded, "Then, according to our professor's own logic,
it must be true that our professor has no brain."[1]

The fact that the Bible doesn't say Peter went to Rome
and died there doesn't mean he didn't. Trying to prove that
St. Peter did not go to Rome and die there is a lot like trying to prove that St. Mark didn't write the Gospel of Mark.
That Gospel, like those of Matthew and Luke, was written anonymously, with no mention of the author's identity.
But that shouldn't trouble us, because the external evidence
(not to mention the internal linguistic evidence), and the
testimony of the early Church, overwhelmingly corroborates the claim that Mark wrote the Gospel attributed to
him.

Similarly, it's true, the Bible nowhere explicitly says that
St. Peter went to Rome. But that shouldn't trouble us either, because the surrounding historical evidence is more
than sufficient to prove that he did.

There's no evidence that he didn't go there

Before we examine that evidence, let's first ask, "If St.
Peter didn't go to Rome, where *did* he go? Where did he
die?" We'd expect to find plenty of evidence in the writ-

---

[1] My apologies for borrowing this perhaps apocryphal anecdote from
its anonymous author, but it's an apt example of how to respond to
fuzzy thinking.

ings of the early Church telling us where this prominent Apostle carried out his final years of ministry, if it were some place other than Rome. The historical record contains no hint that he ended his days anywhere else but Rome. No other city except Rome ever claimed to possess the site of his martyrdom or his tomb (and early Christians were extraordinarily diligent about making and proving such claims). No other city — not even Antioch, where he resided for a time during his apostolate — claimed he ended his days there. No Church Father or Council or any other early Church record indicates that he finished his days anywhere else but in Rome.

That's the "lack of evidence" side of the coin. The flip side is the "mountain of evidence proving he did go to Rome."

Everyone everywhere in the early Church agreed that St. Peter went to Rome, ministered there for over two decades, and suffered martyrdom by inverted crucifixion in A.D. 65, under the persecution of Emperor Nero. Given the grave danger to the early Church from a hostile Roman government, it makes perfect sense that St. Paul would not mention St. Peter's whereabouts in his letters. He didn't want to draw unfriendly attention. It's also possible that St. Peter had not yet arrived in Rome when St. Paul was writing. We even see St. Peter himself making what seems to be a cryptic reference to his presence in Rome when he says "The chosen one at Babylon sends you greetings, as does Mark, my son" (1 Peter 5:13). "Babylon" was a commonly used code word for Rome among Christians, because its pagan decadence and opposition to Christ was reminiscent of the idolatrous wickedness associated with ancient Babylon.

But once St. Peter had been martyred, the testimonies of his sojourn in Rome with St. Paul poured forth in a flood from the early Christian writers. Perhaps the most detailed of these early accounts came from St. Irenaeus of Lyons (d. 200) in his apologetics work *Against Heresies*. He gave a detailed account of succession of the bishops of Rome, from St. Peter down to his own day. He referred to Rome as the city "where Peter and Paul proclaimed the gospel and founded the Church."

Other notable early examples were St. Ignatius of Antioch (d. 107) who referred to the Church at Rome as "the Church of Peter and Paul" (*Letter to the Romans*); St. Cyprian (d. 251), who described Rome as "The place of Peter" (*Epistle* 52); and St. Jerome (d. 420), who called Rome "the See of Peter" (*Epistle 15, to Pope Damasus*). Around A.D. 166 Bishop Dionysius of Corinth wrote to Pope Soter, "You have also, by your very admonition, brought together the planting that was made by Peter and Paul at Rome . . ." (quoted in Eusebius, *Ecclesiastical History*, 2:25).

We've got the bones to prove it

Besides the vast amount of historical evidence showing that St. Peter went to Rome, modern archaeology has cinched the case even more tightly by a definitive scientific demonstration that his bones (studies showed that they are of a powerfully built elderly man who died of crucifixion) are interred directly beneath the high altar in St. Peter's Basilica in Rome, several levels down, where the original first-century Vatican Hill sloped away toward the Tiber River. This was just outside the walls of what was once

Nero's Circus — precisely where all the early Christian and even non-Christian records say St. Peter was crucified and buried.[2]

In his monumental book *The Bones of St. Peter*, author John Evangelist Walsh presents a compelling archaeological case that conclusively demonstrates that the bones of St. Peter are buried below the main altar in St. Peter's. He shows that during the first two centuries after his martyrdom by inverted crucifixion in the nearby Circus of Nero, Peter's modest grave site was venerated and visited as a shrine by Christian pilgrims from across Europe and the Mediterranean world. During the persecution of the Church by Emperor Valerian in the third century, St. Peter's bones were removed by Christians from the grave on Vatican Hill and moved for safekeeping across the Tiber to the Catacombs of St. Sebastian, along the Via Appia Antica. The remains of St. Paul were also brought there, and the bones of the two saints reposed undisturbed in the catacombs for about the next three hundred years. In the sixth century, the bones of St. Peter were brought back to Vatican Hill and interred beneath the main altar in the original Basilica of St. Peter's, built in the early fourth century by the Emperor Constantine to honor the Apostle. The bones are still there, in a stone ossuary about thirty feet below the high altar.

This evidence is important, because it corroborates the constant tradition of the Church and the unanimous tes-

---

[2] For a detailed but very readable analysis of the massive body of historical and archaeological evidence supporting the claim that this spot was the burial site of St. Peter, see John Evangelist Walsh, *The Bones of St. Peter* (Garden City: Doubleday & Company, Inc., 1982).

timony of the early Fathers that St. Peter went to Rome, labored there for many years, and then died a martyr's death.

9

The modern-day papacy, with all its pomp and riches, in no way resembles the simple, humble ministry of Peter and the Apostles, as described in Acts.

I recently received a letter from a Seventh-Day Adventist who made this very claim. He argued that "the attempt to locate an ecclesiastical colossus headed by the papacy at Rome as demonstrated in the New Testament, is an exercise in futility." Catholics can and do agree with him, but not for the reason he might think.

He's right. We shouldn't (and don't) expect to find the full-blown, developed papacy, colossal or otherwise, in the New Testament. Why not? Because the New Testament shows us a picture of the primitive Church, the Church as it was in its infancy, the Church in "mustard seed" form. And Christ Himself promised that His Church, "The Kingdom of God," is an organic entity, one that would grow and develop until it became treelike.

The mustard seed bears no resemblance whatsoever to its mature form. Surely non-Catholics must recognize this and its parallel with the Church (and the papacy). So while it would indeed be futile to attempt to find a fully developed papacy in the pages of the New Testament, it is equally futile for critics to claim that this somehow undermines the Catholic position on the papacy. It doesn't.

A short course on acorns and mustard seeds

It's true that the modern papacy, in many of its external features, does not resemble the apostolic ministry of Peter in the ancient Church. The idea that the modern Church should appear outwardly to be identical to the ancient Church ignores the fact that the Church of the apostolic age wasn't organized as a static entity. It's absurd to expect that the Church won't develop over two thousand years time. It did develop. There are several reasons for this.

First, Jesus Himself predicted His Church would grow and develop:

> Another parable he put before them, saying, "The kingdom of heaven is like a grain of mustard seed which a man took and sowed in his field; it is the smallest of all seeds, but when it has grown it is the greatest of shrubs and becomes a tree, so that the birds of the air come and make nests in its branches."[1]

The term "kingdom of heaven" can mean a couple things in Scripture. Here, however, it refers to the Church. With this in mind, Jesus is describing the growth His Church will undergo over time. Does anyone look at a full-grown oak tree, and see the acorn from which it sprang? Probably not. Yet, nevertheless, that tree *is* exactly the same being as the original acorn that it grew from. The same holds

---

[1] Matt. 13:31–32.

true of the Church. Just as a seed develops into a plant, so too did the early Church become the Catholic Church we see today. When a mustard seed grows, we don't end up with a bigger mustard seed. Rather, in its growth, it changes in appearance and function. It takes someone familiar with botany to identify the seed from the final plant. In like manner, it takes someone familiar with Scripture and Church history to see the clear development of the first-century papacy into the modern papacy.

Indeed, the early Church *was* a seed. Made up of a handful of members, it has since grown to a billion souls worldwide. With this amazing expansion has come necessary changes in the way things are done; the first-century Church wasn't equipped to pastor the needs of one billion people.

The Church grows up, but never grows old

Additionally, two thousand years have passed since the founding of the Church. In that time, our understanding of our environment, not to mention our reality as a whole, has changed. The Faith needs to be lived and expressed in twentieth-century categories. It's impossible to import a first-century mindset into a twentieth-century environment. Hence the way the Faith is lived in modern times will *necessarily* be different. This includes the different ways that authority is exercised.

Despite their loud denials, even the faith of hard-core Fundamentalist Protestants has undergone significant development (as well it should). There are numerous beliefs to which Protestants hold firmly that are the result of centuries of debate and discussion. The Trinity and its nuances, the canon of Scripture and the role of Judaism in the New Covenant are all examples of this. The canon of Scripture — the very foundation of God's revelation for the Protestant — took four centuries to settle. Why is it surprising to the Fundamentalist that the papacy took time as well? Their complaints are inconsistent.

A seed that remains the same year after year is a seed that's long dead. Let's be glad that the mustard seed of the Church is *alive* and has grown and developed into the Church we have today.

Why didn't Christ just say so?

Sometimes, this pope fiction is twisted in a slightly different direction. Rather than arguing against the papacy on the basis of specific Bible verses about the "simple and humble ministry" of Peter and the Apostles that appear to disprove it, some use the "argument from silence." They hope to discredit the papacy by saying that the Bible doesn't say anything about "popes" or "the Vatican" or "papal infallibility," etc. This is an even weaker strain of pope fiction, and is more easily answered.

In a recent written exchange I was involved in on the subject of the papacy, a Protestant writer argued that if Jesus had meant to establish the papacy, He would have said so.

He argued:

If the Lord Jesus Christ had intended to establish the supreme authority of Peter perpetuated in a dynastic line of popes who would enjoy absolute episcopal jurisdiction over the entire world, all logic demands that He would have categorically and intentionally informed his followers in no uncertain terms! But He did not. Other sacred offices of the church are set forth in Holy Writ, yet strange silence prevails with regard to that which is supposedly the highest of them all!

. "Very well." I responded, wanting to subject his argument to a parallel doctrinal situation in a way that would clearly show how unreasonable it is. Let's apply this same principle to the doctrine of the Trinity.

According to this gentleman's skewed logic, if Jesus Christ had meant for Christians to believe in the doctrine of the Trinity (a central tenet of the Christian Faith), logic demands that he would have categorically and intentionally informed his followers *in no uncertain terms.* "Perhaps you could show us in Scripture where, 'in no uncertain terms,' Jesus Christ teaches that God exists in three coequal, co-eternal, consubstantial persons," I asked.

Obviously, Christ nowhere makes any kind of explicit statement like this. And I wish he had! It would have made my job as an apologist so much easier. But God in his wisdom decided not to announce the Trinity doctrine in the pages of Scripture "categorically in no uncertain terms."

Let's be consistent

Unfortunately, the doctrine of the Trinity isn't nearly as clear in Scripture as are other doctrines such as the Holy Eucharist and the primacy of St. Peter. That's why so many non-Christian and quasi-Christian groups like Jehovah's Witnesses, the Mormons, and United Pentecostals appeal to the Bible *itself* to bolster their claims that the Trinity is an "unbiblical" doctrine. The Trinity doctrine is certainly scriptural, as Protestants readily agree, but any systematic biblical defense of this doctrine must be assembled from many verses.

The same can be said of the canon of Scripture.[2] There is no inspired table of contents in the Bible telling us which books belong in it and which books don't. That knowledge is revelation from God. It's preserved in the Church apart from Scripture as part of Sacred Tradition. The irony is that we wouldn't know something as fundamental as what the Bible *is* if it weren't for Sacred Tradition delivering to us the revelation of the canon! So, if even bedrock doctrines like the Trinity and the canon of Scripture are neither mentioned by name nor categorically explained "in no uncertain terms" in the Bible, it's inconsistent and incorrect to demand, on that ground, the same kind of explicit scriptural evidence for the papacy.

What about all that wealth?

But there is a second part to this particular pope fiction — the claim that the papacy is too garish and wealthy. First, we cannot (and should not) try to defend every occurrence of opulence or excess in the history of the papacy. There have been, at times, some truly greedy and corrupt popes, and their materialism is without excuse. However, they've been the exception, not the rule.

---

[2] I.e., the official list of inspired books that make up the Old and New Testaments.

The pope himself isn't wealthy. This is obvious from the relatively sparse papal apartment of John Paul II. It's true, the pope lives inside a magnificent structure, but he doesn't own it; it belongs to the Church. The pope has little or no personal wealth.

There are, however, some opulent trappings associated with the papacy, though not as much as you might imagine. You and I take simple amenities like air-conditioning for granted. But the Vatican, with all its "wealth," doesn't have air-conditioning in most of its offices. When the heat of the Roman summer blankets the city, most Vatican workers continue their work in offices that rely on open windows, not air-conditioners, for relief. A simple thing, yes, but it's revealing about how "opulent" the Vatican really is.

And then there are the magnificent buildings and the precious works of art owned by the papacy. Artisans throughout history have gifted the Church with the fruits of their God-given skills. These gifts are often ornate, and quite valuable. What should the Church do with them? Would it be right to reject these heartfelt expressions of faith and devotion in the name of "humility" or "poverty"?

Sorry, but we need to sell off your parish

Should the pope sell the gifts to give the money to charities? Should he melt down the precious artwork and convert it to hard cash? And when the cash was spent, what then? What if the pope decided to sell off *your* parish church to raise money for some humanitarian project. That idea brings home the reality of the situation. True, in one sense, one might argue that the pope "owns" all the buildings and artwork and possessions of the Catholic Church (technically, the local bishop legally "owns" all the parishes in his diocese, and this line of reasoning can be used to include him). And that means that he "owns" the parish Church you attend, if you're Catholic (if you're a Protestant, you can breathe a sigh of relief here, knowing that the Pope can't reach down from on high and sell off the church building you attend on Sundays). Nobody wants the pope to liquidate *their* local church buildings or church van or bank account in order to help the poor, but many clamor that he should sell off someone else's to do so.

Imagine working for a long time to save the money to give your mom and dad a very expensive Christmas gift for them and the whole family. When you gave it to them, your dad thanked you and then immediately turned around and had the gift appraised for its market value. Then, he sold it to the highest bidder and used the cash for some charitable purpose. In a strict sense, as the father of the family, he would have the right to do so, if he chose. But should he do so? Wouldn't it be an insult to you if he did? Doesn't he have an obligation in charity to accept and cherish the gift you worked so long and hard to give him? Of course.

It's the same with the many gifts of art and land and precious objects that have been given to the Catholic Church and the popes over the centuries. The pope is the recipient and custodian of these treasures, not their "owner." They really belong to the entire Church, to all Catholics, as a patrimony handed down from earlier generations, something for the whole world to treasure and enjoy. The pope gratefully accepts these gifts in the name of the Church. His action is born out of charity, not greed.

10

The papacy is a medieval Roman invention. The early Church knew nothing of a "supreme pontiff." Other bishops didn't regard the bishop of Rome as having special authority to operate the way modern popes do.

Archbishop Fulton Sheen once said, "It is easy to find truth; it is hard to face it, and harder still to follow it." This is certainly true for some when it comes to facing the historical evidence for the papacy in the early Church.

The hard-core purveyors of pope fiction refuse to believe that the papacy was established by Christ. But if the equivalent of the modern papacy was merely a Roman invention of the eighth or ninth century, how do we explain the fact that for the preceding 700 years, the bishops of Rome were regarded (and regarded themselves) as having a special, unique authority and responsibility for the whole Church? Here are a few of the hundreds of examples that could be given.

The earliest account we have of a bishop of Rome exercising authority in another diocese comes from the *Epistle of St. Clement* to the Corinthians. It was written by Clement, bishop of Rome, around the year A.D. 80. In it he responds

to the Corinthians' plea for his intervention. The entire letter is written in a fatherly, kindly way, but it is also clear
that Clement was quite aware he had a special authority.
Two key phrases stand out as testimony of this: "But if any
disobey the words spoken by Him [Christ] through us, let
them know that they will involve themselves in sin and no
small danger"; and "For you will give us joy and gladness
if, obedient to what we have written through the Holy
Spirit, you root out the lawless anger of your jealousy" (59,
63). Clearly, this early bishop of Rome wrote as one who
expected his words to be obeyed.

   Pope Victor I (reigned 189–199) worked to settle a dispute among the bishops of the East and West over when
to celebrate Easter — known as the *Quartodeciman* controversy. The other bishops recognized his unique authority
when they followed his directive to convene local and re-
gional synods to deliberate on the issue. Most of the bishops
decided to adopt his proposal that the whole Church celebrate Easter on the first Sunday after Passover. Those who
didn't he threatened with excommunication. The fact that
no bishop in the world — *not a single one* — disputed his
authority as bishop of Rome to carry out such an excommunication is a powerful piece of evidence that the early
Church recognized the unique authority of the bishop of
Rome. Shortly before his death in A.D. 200, St. Irenaeus of
Lyons wrote a sharp letter of admonition to Pope Victor[1]
criticising his decision and asking him to relent and allow
the Eastern bishops to maintain their celebration of Easter
according to the Hebrew lunar calendar, evidence that he
recognized the pope's authority to threaten excommunica-

----

[1] Quoted in Eusebius, *Ecclesiastical History*, Book 5:24:1–18.

tion. After all, it was Irenaeus who wrote of the Church at Rome: "For with this church, because of its superior origin, all the churches must agree; that is, all the faithful in the whole world, for in her the apostolic tradition has always been preserved for the benefit of the faithful everywhere" (*Against Heresies* 3:3). Interestingly, Pope Victor did relent, and before long, his policy of conciliation paid off. The churches in the East all fell into line with the Roman Easter observance.

Evidence of papal leadership

The Church of Rome, led by the pope, was recognized by the other churches, in the East and the West alike, as having a special primacy. In a letter to Pope St. Damasus,[2] St. Basil recalled with gratitude the guidance and assistance rendered to Eastern Catholics and their bishops by the pope:

> We know, both by the recollection of our forefathers and also by letters which have been preserved among us, how [Pope] Dionysius, that pontiff of blessed memory, who was as illustrious for the rectitude of his faith as for his other virtues, formerly came to the help of our Church of Caesarea; that he consoled us by his letters, sending at the same time persons charged with ransoming our brethren who had been taken captive.[3]

One historian summarized the role of the papacy and the Church of Rome in the early Church:

---

[2] Reigned A.D. 366–383.
[3] Epistle 70, cited in L. Duchesne, *The Churches Separated from Rome*, Arnold Harris Mathew, tr. (New York: Benziger Brothers, 1907), 103.

[A]ll the churches throughout the known world, from Arabia, Osrhoene, and Cappadocia to the extreme west, felt the incessant influence of Rome in every respect, whether as to faith, discipline, administration, ritual [i.e. liturgical matters], or works of charity. She was, as St. Irenaeus says, "known everywhere and respected everywhere, and her guidance was universally accepted." No competitor, no rival stands up against her; no one conceives the idea of being her equal. Later on there will be patriarchs and other local primates, whose first beginnings can be but vaguely perceived during the course of the third century. Above these rising organizations, and above the whole body of isolated churches, the Church of Rome rises in supreme majesty, the Church of Rome represented by the long series of her bishops, which ascends to the two chiefs of the apostolic college; she knows herself to be and is considered by all, the center and organ of unity. Her position is so evident that even pagans themselves remark [about] it. . . .[4]

In the mid-fourth century, Pope St. Julius wrote to a group of Arians, upbraiding them for their neglect of his authority:

Oh beloved! The judgments of the Church are no longer in accordance with the gospel, but are (by you, Arians) to the inflicting of exile and of death. For even though any transgression had been committed, as you pretend, by these men, the judgment ought to have been in accordance with the ecclesiastical rule, and not thus. I behooved you to write to all of us, that thus what was just might be decreed by all. For they who suffered were bishops, and the churches that suffered no common ones, over which

---

[4] Duchesne, 103–104.

the Apostles ruled in person. *And why were we not written to concerning the Church, especially of Alexandria? Or, are you ignorant that this has been the custom first to write to us, and thus what is just be decreed from this place? If therefore, any suspicion fell upon the bishop there, it was befitting to write to this Church.* But now they who acquainted us not, but did what they themselves chose, proceed to wish us, though unacquainted with facts, to become supporters of their views. *Not thus were Paul's ordinances; not thus have the fathers handed down to us; this is another form, and a new institution.* Bear with me cheerfully, I beseech you, for what I write is for the common weal. For what we have received from that blessed Apostle Peter, the same do I make known to you; and these things I would not have written to you, deeming them manifest to you all, had not what has been done confounded us.[3]

Notice that Julius considers it an entirely different "form" of Church governance to bypass the authority of the Roman bishop. Such actions were not consistent with the practice — which Julius obviously considers universal — that the pope is to have authority over issues of orthodoxy and dissent.

Around the same time, the Council of Sardica wrote to the same Pope Julius (the letter is quoted by St. Hilary of Poitiers):

And you, most dearly loved brother, though absent from us in body, were present in mind concordant, and will; and your plea of absence was honorable and required; lest, that is, either schismatical wolves might steal and plun-

---

[3] *Epistle ad Eusebian*, translation by Joseph Berington in *The Faith of Catholics* (New York: Pustet & Company), vol. 2, 67–68 (emphasis mine).

der stealthily, or heretical dogs, smitten with rabid frenzy, might madly bark; or, doubtless that serpent, the devil, scatter the venom of his blasphemies. *For this will be seen to be best, and by far the most befitting thing, if to the head, that is, to the see of the Apostle Peter, the priests of the Lord report from every one of the provinces.*[4]

In the year 382, Pope St. Damasus wrote about his authority as bishop of Rome, anchoring it to the fact that he was the successor to St. Peter. He said the Church at Rome

> has been placed at the forefront, not by the conciliar decision of other churches, but has received the primacy by the evangelistic voice of our Lord and Savior Who says, "You are Peter, and upon this rock I will build My Church, and the gates of hell will not prevail against it; and I will give to you the keys of the kingdom of heaven, and whatever you shall have bound on earth will be bound in heaven, and whatever you shall have loosed on earth shall be loosed in heaven." . . . The first See, therefore, is that of Peter the Apostle, that of the Roman Church, which has neither stain nor blemish.[5]

At the end of the fourth century, Pope St. Siricius writes of his position as bishop of Rome:

> Taking into account my office, it is not for me to choose — on whom it is incumbent that there be a zeal for the Christian religion greater than that of all other persons — to dissemble, and remain silent. I bear the burdens of all who are heavily laden; yes, rather in me that burden is borne by the blessed Apostle Peter, who, we trust, in all

---

[4] Ibid., Fragment 2, *Ex opere Historico*, 68–69 (emphasis mine).
[5] *Decree of Pope Damasus* 2–3.

things, protects, and has regard to us who are the heirs of his government.[6]

In A.D. 404, St. John Chrysostom wrote to Pope Innocent, "I beseech your Charity to rouse yourself and have compassion, and do everything so as to put a stop to the mischief at this point" (*First Epistle to Pope Innocent I*). Note that Chrysostom, the archbishop of Constantinople, a powerful diocese, recognized the need to appeal to the bishop of Rome to resolve a controversy.

At the council of Ephesus in 431, Philip, the papal legate, rose and addressed the council:

> It is a matter of doubt to none, yea rather it is a thing known to all ages, that the holy and most blessed Peter, the prince and head of the Apostles, the pillar of the faith, the foundation of the Catholic Church, received the keys of the kingdom from Jesus Christ our Lord and Savior and Redeemer of mankind. And to him was given authority to bind and loose sins: who even till this present, and always, *both lives and judges in his successors: our holy and most blessed Pope Caelestine, the bishop, the canonical successor and viceregent of this Peter, has sent us a representatives of his person.*[7]

Many other examples of the primacy of the bishop of Rome in the early Church could be added. Even from the earliest years, the bishop of Rome had — and everyone recognized that he had — a special primacy and authority in the Church. Anyone who says the papacy is a "medieval Roman invention," is either ignorant of history or dishonest. Either way, it's a sham argument.

---

[6] *Epistle 1 To Himer* translated by Berington, 74.
[7] *Acts of the Council of Ephesus*, Act 3, Berington, 81.

11

Canon 6 of the Council of Nicea (A.D. 325) decreed, "Let the ancient customs in Egypt, Libya and Pentapolis prevail, that the bishop of Alexandria have jurisdiction in all these, since this is also the custom for the bishop of Rome. Likewise in Antioch and the other provinces, let the Churches retain their privileges." We see, then, that the early Christians recognized Rome as one Church among equals — not as one having greater authority than the other ancient Churches.

This is perhaps the most popular objection made by "scholarly" opponents of the papacy (both Protestant and Orthodox). It's advanced to demonstrate that Roman primacy was a development that occurred in the Middle Ages, not the early Church. To answer this fiction, we need to read canon 6 in context — in light of the rest of the canons *and* with an understanding of the situation behind its promulgation.

First, notice the purpose of the canon: it lays out the jurisdiction of the bishop of Alexandria. Why? *Because*, that's the custom for the bishop of Rome. The validity of

Alexandria's custom is based on the authority of the Roman custom. This alone is a strong indication of the normative nature of Roman tradition.

Despite what some opponents of the Roman Church would like to claim, canon 6 is speaking specifically of Alexandria. It makes no addition or subtraction to Roman authority, and only alludes to the Roman Church to validate the custom of Alexandria. In this way, it isn't limiting or curtailing the authority of Rome. It merely uses Roman tradition as the rule for the church in Alexandria.

But there's another way to look at the words of the canon: Let Alexandria retain its jurisdiction *because it is the custom of Rome for her to have that jurisdiction*. With this understanding, the Roman "custom" referred to is the recognition of Alexandria's jurisdiction.[1]

Precision in language

Recall the reason why this canon needed to be promulgated: the heretic Meletius was usurping the authority of the Alexandrian Patriarch, ordaining bishops and convening synods. This canon was promulgated to reassert the authority of the patriarch of Alexandria.[2] With this in mind, reread the canon. The council's argument (aimed at Meletius) is based on "the custom for the bishop of Rome." For this argument to have any weight, Roman tradition

---

[1] James F. Loughlin makes a compelling case for this interpretation in "The Sixth Nicene Canon and the Papacy," in the *American Catholic Quarterly Review*, v. 5, 1980, 220–239.

[2] Cf. Charles Joseph Hefele, D.D., *A History of the Christian Councils From the Original Documents* (Edinburgh: T&T Clark, 1894), vol. 1, 353.

must be held to be normative and the custom of the Roman bishop must be authoritative. If this weren't the case, Meletius would merely dismiss the pointless reference to a foreign bishop. This is a far more likely interpretation of canon 6. Far from refuting Roman claims of papal primacy, it actually strongly supports them.

But there's more. Have a look at canon 6 in its entirety:

> Let the ancient customs in Egypt, Libya and Pentapolis prevail, that the bishop of Alexandria have jurisdiction in all these, since the like is customary for the bishop of Rome also. Likewise in Antioch and the other provinces, let the Churches retain their privileges. And this is to be universally understood, that if anyone be made a bishop without the consent of the metropolitan, the great Synod has declared that such a man ought not to be a bishop. If, however, two or three bishops shall from natural love of contradiction, oppose the common suffrage of the rest, it being reasonable and in accordance with the ecclesiastical law, then let the choice of the majority prevail.

Just what is the "jurisdiction" mentioned in this canon? Is it absolute authority over all their provinces — hinting at some kind of confederation of equal churches? Not at all. Look at the second half of the canon. The "jurisdiction" refers, primarily at least, to the authority to ordain bishops. In his article, "Ancient Baptists and Other Myths" (*Envoy*, July/August 1998, 37), Fr. Hugh Barbour, O. Praem. notes:

> Notice that after laying out the territory for each of the metropolitans, the canon explains what is to take place within those limits: the selection and ordination of bishops. This point also fits the context of the preceding canons, paraphrased here:

Canon 4: Bishops are to be chosen by bishops of their province, and their choice is then to be ratified by the metropolitan having jurisdiction over that area.

Canon 5: Those excommunicated by one bishop are not to be re-instituted by a bishop of a different territory. Every province should have regular synods to decide these issues.

Canon 6: The metropolitans have jurisdiction over their respective territories. No one is to be made a bishop without their final approval.

Notice the function of canon 6 in context with the preceding two canons: It sets out territorial boundaries for more efficient administration. Recall that the pope is also the bishop of the city of Rome. He has a special administrative jurisdiction over Rome, whereas the bishop of New York has the same jurisdiction over New York, the bishop of Alexandria over Alexandria, etc. But this is not to say the Roman bishop has no authority over the Church; these are two different kinds of jurisdiction.

Canons 4–6 deal with issues in local churches; they have nothing to do with authority in the universal Church. To claim otherwise is to twist the canon, cite from it selectively and ignore its context.

12

The most powerful evidence against the papacy being biblical is the record of the popes themselves. There have been numerous bad popes, men who murdered, stole, were greedy, arrogant, violent and incredibly immoral. This alone disqualifies the papacy as being part of Christ's plan for His Church. There's no way He would have entrusted the "papacy" to sinful men.

Then how do you account for Christ entrusting the office of Apostle to sinful men like Judas? He was one of the Lord's hand-picked protégés. He was a pretty sinful character, yet he was an Apostle! In fact, at one time or another, Scripture tells us that all the Apostles failed to live according to Christ's commands. Though they never appear to have slipped into sexual immorality, the Apostles did blunder their way into plenty of other sins before the New Testament story was finished.

By turns they were violent (Peter cut off the ear of the high priest's servant in the Garden of Gethsemani), vain (they bickered bitterly more than once over which of them would be highest in heaven), lazy ("Can you not stay awake with me one hour?" Christ asked them as they slept during his agony in the Garden), and disbelieving (Christ identified him by name as a "devil," one of those who refused to believe His teaching on the Eucharist in John 6:70–71). The Apostles were cowardly (running away from Christ when he was taken into custody by the Jews). Peter denied three times, once under oath, even knowing his Lord.

Clearly, Christ entrusted the role of Apostle to weak, even at times wicked men. But does that fact somehow disqualify them from fulfilling the purpose for which He called them? Of course not. God's grace is more powerful than man's sin, and the same is true when it comes to the papacy.

The good, the bad, and the ugly

Yes, there have been some wicked popes. Corruption, immorality, even murder, were sins committed by some bishops of Rome. But what does that prove, except that they, like the Apostles, were not always faithful to the graces God gave them? This is true of all of us, to one extent or another. The fact that there have been bad popes — and that's a fact no Catholic disputes — does not disprove the doctrine of the papacy. Why? Because as we've seen, Christ entrusts important work to men who are sinners. He offers them all the grace necessary to be faithful and holy, even though some spurn those graces and choose sin anyway.

Another problem with this fiction is that it seems to assume that *all* the popes have been scoundrels. That's very far from the truth. The fact is, most of the popes have been good — even heroically good — men. They have been, on the whole, good examples of Christian virtue and perseverance in the apostolate. That fact is very easily forgotten by critics of the papacy.

And there's another issue here. Scripture is clear that God can and does confer special teaching authority on men even if they are sinful. One striking example concerns Caiaphas, the high priest at the time of Christ's Crucifixion:

> Caiaphas, who was high priest that year, said to them, 'You know nothing, nor do you consider that it is better for you that one man should die instead of the people, so that the whole nation may not perish.' He did not say this on his own, but since he was high priest for that year, he prophesied that Jesus was going to die for the nation, and not only for the nation, but also to gather into one the dispersed children of God. So from that day on they planned to kill him.[1]

This is a good example of God using a sinful man — a *wicked* man, it seems — to utter inspired prophecy. The Holy Spirit spoke through his lips, in spite of the fact that Caiaphas was actively plotting to kill Jesus.

One bad apple don't spoil the whole bunch

Another episode that illustrates this point, though from a different angle, is found in the Gospel of Matthew. Jesus points to the Jewish leaders and reminds his audience that they possessed a God-given authority to teach. This authority was valid even though many of them were corrupt.

---

[1] John 11:49–55.

Christ later calls them "hypocrites," a "brood of vipers,"
"blind guides," "whitened sepulchers full of dead men's
bones." The Lord made it clear that even though these
men were personally corrupt and unworthy of their position of authority, they nonetheless had that authority:

> Then Jesus spoke to the crowds and to his disciples, say-
> ing, "The Scribes and Pharisees have taken their seat on
> the chair of Moses.[2] *Therefore, do and observe all the things
> whatsoever they tell you, but do not follow their example.*
> For they preach but they do not practice."[3]

In the same way, the Lord commissioned sinful, weak,
impetuous Simon Peter to feed His sheep and tend His
flock, to carry the keys of the kingdom of heaven, to bind
and loose in His name and with His authority, to strengthen
the other Apostles in times of crisis and uncertainty, to be
the rock on which the Church would be built. Peter's successors, the popes, continue in that ministry. Some fulfilled
it poorly, hobbled by the chains of sin and personal failings,
but most carried out the task well, many of them complet-
ing their sacred ministry with martyrdom; their supreme
effort to "strengthen their brothers."

---

[2] The Greek phrase here, *tés Mouséos kathédras*, the chair of Moses, is
the classic Scriptural text that coincides with the Catholic teaching on
the Chair of Peter. This is the source of the Latin term for the pope's
teaching authority: *ex cathedra* (i.e., "from the chair").

[3] Matthew 23:1–3.

13

Papal infallibility is an absurd claim. Given all the lousy decisions different popes have made, there's no way they can be inspired by the Holy Spirit. Christ said the Holy Spirit would guide the Church into "all truth," but clearly, many popes have lived lives that were far from the truth and taught things that were false.

It's amazing just how many Catholics have fallen for this one. Non-Catholics can, perhaps, be excused when they get so fundamental a Catholic doctrine mixed up. But for Catholics, there's not really a good excuse. And if you read this fiction closely, you'll see two, two, two myths in one! The first is the myth that infallibility equals sinlessness (what is sometimes called "impeccability"). The second is that the pope, by virtue of his charism of infallibility, receives inspiration from God. Both notions are untrue.

So, what is papal infallibility? Let's start with a definition. The dogma of papal infallibility was formally promulgated at the First Vatican Council in 1870. The council stated:

> The Roman Pontiff, when he speaks *ex cathedra* — that is, when in discharge of the office of Pastor and Doctor

of all Christians, by virtue of his supreme apostolic authority, he defines a doctrine regarding Faith or Morals to be held by the Universal Church — by the Divine assistance promised to him in Blessed Peter, is possessed of the infallibility with which the Divine Redeemer willed that His Church should be endowed in defining doctrine regarding Faith or Morals; and therefore such definitions of the Roman Pontiff are irreformable of themselves, and not in virtue of the consent of the Church.

What it is — what it does

Papal infallibility wasn't "invented" in 1870, any more than the doctrine of the Trinity was "invented" in A.D. 325 at the Council of Nicea. That was when the Church determined that it should be formally defined, so as to eliminate any ambiguity or error about what, exactly, the doctrine meant.

There are several requirements for a dogmatic, infallible pronouncement:[1]

1. The pronouncement must be made by a lawful successor to Peter — in other words, a pope.

2. The subject matter of the declaration must be in the area of faith or morals. It doesn't fall within the pontiff's ability to make infallible declarations on science, economics, history, etc.

3. The pope must be speaking *ex cathedra,* that is, officially, from the office of Peter. In this way, he must be

---

[1]Cf. Ludwig Ott, *Fundamentals of Catholic Dogma* (Rockford: TAN Books, 1960), 287.

specifically intending to proclaim a doctrine, binding the Church to its assent.

If one or more of these elements is missing, there is no infallible pronouncement. Most "examples" of papal errors offered by anti-Catholics emerge when they ignore the necessity of these three points.

The patristic testimony regarding papal infallibility developed and intensified over time. There are no explicit statements of the pope's infallibility in the first few centuries, though there are many implicit statements and affirmations to that effect. Fr. J. Michael Miller, C.S.B. explains:

> According to the council Fathers [i.e., at Vatican I in 1870], the weightiest argument for their teaching on papal infallibility was the witness provided by ecumenical councils. These references were included in the final version of chapter four [of the council document on papal infallibility, *Pastor Aeternus*]. As proofs for the Church's long-standing teaching on papal infallibility, *Pastor Aeternus* selected statements from three councils: Constantinople IV (869–870), Lyons II (1274), and Florence (1439). Although the Orthodox no longer recognized such councils as truly ecumenical, churches from the East had participated in all three. For the drafters of *Pastor Aeternus*, each one attests to the pope's infallible teaching authority.
>
> As requested by the Roman delegates, the Fathers at Constantinople IV all signed the profession of faith drawn up by Pope Hormisdas (514–523). The pope had sent the text to Constantinople in 515 in order to end the Acacian schism. This statement affirmed that "in the Apostolic See [i.e., Rome] the Catholic religion has been kept unsullied and its teaching kept holy." . . .
>
> Lyons II asserted . . . "And, as she [Rome] is bound

above all to defend the truth of the Faith, so too, if any questions should arise regarding the Faith, they must be decided by her judgment."[2]

Many people misunderstand papal infallibility, thinking it is a sort of dogmatic weapon the pope can wield capriciously against the twin doctrinal rules of Sacred Scripture and Sacred Tradition of the Church.[3] Just the opposite is true. The charism of papal infallibility *protects* the Church, as well as the authority of Scripture and Tradition, by ensuring that the pope is prevented from misusing them and thereby formally teaching error.

Another common misconception confuses infallibility with inspiration. These two charisms are entirely different, though they have, when God willed it, coincided in the same person (e.g., St. Peter, who preached and wrote Scripture infallibly and under the inspiration of the Holy Spirit). The charism of inspiration involves the Holy Spirit providing divine revelation to the recipient. Perhaps the best example of this is found in Scripture. The writers of the Gospels, for example, received in a mysterious way the revelation the Holy Spirit wanted them to set forth with pen and ink. Their human freedom and individual personalities were completely intact, even as God breathed into

---

[2] J. Michael Miller, C.S.B., *The Shepherd and the Rock* (Huntington: Our Sunday Visitor Publishing Co., 1995), 197.

[3] Vatican II's Dogmatic Constitution on Divine Revelation, *Dei Verbum*, explained how the threefold authorities of Scripture, Tradition, and the magisterium function together in the life of the Church. Each needs the others for support and stability. The Greek word (*theopneustos*) St. Paul used in 2 Timothy 3:16 to speak of the inspiration of Scripture, means, literally, "God breathed." A dramatic, real-life example of this "negative protection" aspect of papal infallibility is found in chapter 25.

their minds the revelation He wanted them to communicate. While the sacred writers, then, lent their own natural abilities to the job at hand, obtaining the Gospel message required no effort on their part — that information was given to them directly by the Holy Spirit. That is what we mean by "inspiration."

While inspiration *gives* information, infallibility *protects* information. It doesn't provide the pope with the information he needs to teach (that comes through his own efforts to study and understand the deposit of Faith, just as it does for all other Christians here on earth), but it does make sure that when he does formally teach the doctrines of the Faith, he'll do so without error. And finally, we should note that infallible pronouncements, whether they come from ecumenical councils or popes, never add to the body of revelation that was "Once for all delivered to the saints" (Jude 3), they just make more explicit what is already there.

Misconceptions about papal infallibility

At this juncture, we should also spell out exactly what papal infallibility is *not*. First, it doesn't give the pope the answers to theological questions (as inspiration would), nor does infallibility guarantee that he will be proactive and teach what needs to be taught, when it should be taught, in the way it should be taught. Infallibility doesn't mean that the pope is prompted by God to do or teach something. It doesn't even guarantee that the pope, when he *does* teach, will be as effective or persuasive or clear as he should be in what he teaches. Papal infallibility guarantees none of these things. Rather, it is a guarantee that God the

Holy Spirit will preserve the pope from formally teaching error.

Much like a steel guardrail that lines the outer edge of a twisty mountain road, put there to keep cars from going over a cliff, the gift of papal infallibility is a divine protection against the catastrophe of the Church careening over the precipice of heresy, even if the pope were to drive recklessly, or, as it were, to fall asleep at the wheel.

Infallibility has nothing to do with sin. Unfortunately, not everyone realizes that and therefore some pope fictions you'll run into are off-target simply because they confuse infallibility and impeccability — sinlessness. Take St. Peter, for example. He was, at times, a sinful and weak man, yet he was called by God to teach infallibly, in his preaching and in the Scripture he wrote for the Church. In spite of his personal weaknesses, Peter had the charism of infallibility when he taught the Faith officially. The same is true of his successors.

All popes, even the saintly ones, have been sinners in need of God's mercy and grace. Some, unfortunately, were heavy-duty sinners who seemed to give no thought to the eventual hellfire that awaited them if they refused to repent and change their wicked ways. But even their gross sinfulness didn't change by one fraction the fact that, as popes, they enjoyed the charism of papal infallibility. They may have lived horrible lives, but they were prevented by this grace of the Holy Spirit from formally teaching error to the Church. Amazing, but true; and we should thank God for that kind of armor-plated protection. Even bad popes can't wreck the papacy!

Honestly, though, it would be great if the pope did receive inspiration, direct revelation, from God. It would be marvelous if each pope who has ever sat on the Chair of Peter had been sinless and a model of sanctity for the world. If they had, so many things would have been so much easier! But that kind of tidiness never seems to be part of God's plan. He works best when his grace works through our human weakness and frailty. Sinlessness as a quality of the popes has never happened. Rather, *sinfulness*, to some degree, high or low, has always been and will always be the norm for popes (as with the rest of us).

The fact is, the only pope who was inspired and who received revelation from God to be given to the whole Church was Simon Peter. After he went home to his heavenly reward, all the subsequent popes have had to do their job of teaching and preserving the deposit of faith the old fashioned way: They *learned* it.

14

Catholics claim that the pope is infallible in matters of faith and morals, yet Pope Liberius (reigned 352–366) signed an Arian creed, thereby endorsing a heretical view of Christ. Obviously, then, papal infallibility is a fallacy.

Pope Liberius is the first of the three favorite "heretical" popes used by anti-Catholics to argue against papal infallibility (the other two, Vigilius and Honorius, will be addressed shortly). Allegedly, this pontiff not only held to an erroneous view of Christ, but actually endorsed the error by signing onto a heretical creed. If this is true, how can Catholics claim papal infallibility?

The fourth century was a hard time for the Catholic Church. Despite all hopes of orthodox Catholics, the council of Nicea didn't end the Arian movement. Rather, the Arian bandwagon picked up a good deal of momentum and a lot of new passengers. This was especially the case when the emperor Constantius made it his business to spread Arianism throughout the empire. His efforts brought the emperor into direct conflict with Athanasius, the bishop of Alexandria and a stalwart defender of orthodoxy. Constantius was able to garner strong ecclesiastical support against

Athanasius. Unfortunately for his evil plans, he was unable to sway Pope Liberius, the all-important bishop of Rome. The lengths to which he went to influence Liberius is strong evidence for the obvious importance of the pope, even in the ancient Church.

Pope Liberius, like Athanasius, held strongly to the creed of the council of Nicea. This, for him, was the final test of orthodoxy. Not only did he agree with the great Alexandrian bishop on this point, but he also backed him by upholding a letter — signed by seventy-five Egyptian bishops — that supported Athanasius. In the same way, Pope Liberius rejected a letter sent by the emperor and several heretical bishops urging him to condemn Athanasius. The final straw for Constantius was Pope Liberius's rejection of a large bribe (along with the Arian emperor's concomitant order to "step in line").

Constantius, in a fit of anger, had Liberius arrested and taken to Milan to appear before him in A.D. 357. The emperor tried every means of pressure to force Liberius to comply with his will and to condemn Athanasius, but the bishop of Rome resisted. Finally, having no success, Constantius banished Liberius to live in exile in Thrace.

Did he or didn't he?

Up until this point, most scholars agree on the basic events. Here, however, is where the real questions arise. After two years of imprisonment, exile and harassment, Liberius was released and allowed to return to his see in Rome. Why was he suddenly released? Did he finally cave in and sign a heretical creed, condemning Athanasius? Or did the emperor realize the futility of keeping him captive? There is evidence for both positions.

A number of figures contemporary to the time, St. Athanasius for one, claimed that Liberius did indeed give in and sign the defective creed. But we can't forget that he was under extreme duress, mentally and physically, and was being coerced with the threat of torture and execution if he didn't sign. For this reason alone, Pope Liberius can't be held fully accountable for caving in. True, he could have been braver and stronger, but that's easy to say when one isn't himself in that dire situation. We can't forget this all-important human dimension of this story. In reality, most people imagine themselves being unflinchingly brave in the face of torture or death if their Christian Faith were challenged. But when the time comes, their actual behavior might be very different from what they hoped they would do. And when forced to do something wrong through coercion and threats of violence or death, a person isn't guilty of the deed as he would be if he had total freedom. Pope Liberius was no different.

While Athanasius held firmly to the belief that Liberius caved in and reversed his position, he wasn't in the best position to be able to know all the facts. He was in hiding at the time and didn't have available to him the best information on the subject.[1] Likewise, St. Jerome believed that Liberius bent under the pressure, though his position was based on a series of letters that are now held to be forgeries. Joining Jerome was Philostorgius, an Arian himself. The ancient historian Sozomen claimed Liberius signed a

---

[1] Cf. John Chapman, O.S.B., "Liberius," *The Catholic Encyclopedia* (New York: Robert Appleton Co., 1910), vol. IX, 217–223.

number of creeds, but that none of them were explicitly heretical; at worst, they were ambiguous in their Christology.

One Church historian explains the reasons for believing in Liberius's innocence in regard to this charge:

> It would seem that when St. Hilary wrote his book *Adversus Constantium* [*Against Constantius*] in 360, just before his return from exile in the East, he believed that Liberius had fallen and had renounced St. Athanasius (i.e., the orthodox position); but his words are not quite clear. At all events, when he wrote his *Adversus Valentem et Ursacium* [*Against Valentius and Ursacius*] after his return, he showed the letter *Studens Paci* [*Student of Peace*] to be a forgery, by appending to it some noble letters of the pope. Now this seems to prove that the Luciferians were making use of *Studens Paci* after Rimini, in order to show that the pope, who was now in their opinion too indulgent to the fallen bishops, had himself been guilty of an even worse betrayal of the Catholic cause before his exile. In their view, such a fall would unpope him and invalidate all his subsequent acts. *That St. Hilary should have taken some trouble to prove that the* Studens Paci *was spurious makes it evident that he did not believe Liberius had fallen subsequently in his exile*; else his trouble was useless. Consequently, St. Hilary becomes a strong witness to the innocence of Liberius. If St. Athanasius believed in his fall, this was when he was in hiding, and immediately after the supposed event; he was apparently deceived for the moment by the rumors spread by the Arians.[2]

---

[2] Ibid., 221–222, (emphasis added).

Why the hero's welcome?

While it's possible that Pope Liberius buckled under the pressure of Constantius, we can't ignore this strong evidence that indicates he didn't. Both St. Sulpicius Severus (A.D. 403) and Pope St. Anastasius (A.D. 401) held that Liberius stood strong, refusing to give in.[3] This claim is reinforced by the character of his return to Rome after his exile; he was given a hero's welcome when he entered the city. Indeed, Liberius's return was one of triumph. If he had caved in and signed an Arian creed, surely he wouldn't have been treated in such a way.

Again, a careful analysis of the historical details points away from the common belief that Pope Liberius failed:

> [T]he strongest arguments for the innocence of Liberius are *a priori*. Had he really given in to the emperor during his exile, the emperor would have published his victory far and wide; there would have been no possible doubt about it; it would have been more notorious than even that gained over Hosius. But if he was released because the Romans demanded him back, because his deposition had been too uncanonical, because his resistance was too heroic, and because Felix was not generally recognized as pope, then we might be sure he would be suspected of having given some pledge to the emperor; the Arians and the Felicians alike, and soon the Luciferians, would have no difficulty in spreading a report of his fall and in winning credence for it. It is hard to see how Hilary in banishment and Athanasius in hiding could disbelieve such a story, when they heard that Liberius had returned, though the other exiled bishops were still unrelieved.

---

[3] Ibid.

Further, the pope's decree after Rimini, that the fallen bishops could not be restored unless they showed their sincerity by vigor against the Arians, would have been laughable, if he himself had fallen yet earlier, and had not publicly atoned for his sin. Yet, we can be quite certain that he made no public confession of having fallen, no recantation, no atonement.[4]

The emperor never mentioned it

If the Emperor Constantius had won his battle of wills with the Roman pontiff, why didn't he announce it? One can imagine how he would have exploited such a coup. The ability to trumpet that the pope had given in to his demands would have had enormous P.R. value for the emperor. After all, the whole point of his attempting to force Pope Liberius to sign the heretical creed was so that he could use it as an example for other orthodox Catholic bishops to follow. His goal was precisely to exploit the influence and prestige of the pope.

If Pope Liberius did end up signing the creed, surely Constantius would have shouted this from the rooftops. But there was only silence from the emperor. Neither he nor his government mentioned anything about it. While it's true that this is an argument from silence, it can't be denied that this particular historical fact makes it much more difficult to imagine that Pope Liberius did indeed cave in.

Finally, when Constantius died, Arianism lost its major defender. Orthodoxy returned to the fore, assuming its pre-

---

[4] Ibid.

vious position of strength. Pope Liberius attacked the Arian bishops for their heresy, and required full repentance from them before they were allowed to return to union with the Church. Indeed, they were treated as collaborators with the enemy and betrayers of Christ. How could Liberius act in such a way if he himself had signed the Arian creed? Someone undoubtedly would have pointed out the hypocrisy of such a move. And yet, there was no such outcry.

So as we see, there are arguments for both sides of the issue, with the weight perhaps coming down on the belief that Pope Liberius didn't bend under the pressure brought to bear against him by Constantius. But even if he did, that wouldn't strike a blow against papal infallibility. Assuming the worst case scenario is true, Pope Liberius only signed the heretical creed after two years of harassment, exile and coercion at the hands of the emperor. The alleged signing didn't come about through his own free will. For this reason, papal infallibility isn't an issue, since infallibility requires that the pope be exercising his own free will — apart from any external compulsion. This was clearly not the case if indeed Liberius signed the document. Obviously, then, papal infallibility could not have been in jeopardy.

15

Catholics claim that the pope is preserved from error in matters of faith and morals. But Pope Vigilius (reigned 537–555) approved the views of three heretical Monophysite heretics. Not only that, but he later condemned three Nestorians, then approved them, then condemned them again. Surely, Vigilius, by embracing heresy and flip-flopping on Nestorianism, proves that infallibility is a fallacy.

In the two-thousand-year history of the papacy, you're bound to run across your fair share of wimps. There's no point in trying to claim that every pope was a heroic defender of virtue and orthodoxy. That's simply not true. Sometimes, the bishop of Rome has been an embarrassment to himself, his diocese, and his Church.

Case in point: Meet Pope Vigilius.

This is a complicated story, so settle back and get comfortable. Vigilius actually started off his papal career as an anti-pope, during the reign of the genuine pontiff, Silverius. This was, in large part, due to the influence of the empress Theodora. In exchange for his position, Vigilius was to approve three Monophysites (heretics who believed

Christ had only a· Divine nature), Anthimus, Theodosius and Severus. This he did, to the empress's great pleasure. So while it is true that Vigilius approved the heretics, he only did so as an anti-pope, not an actual pope! Obviously, then, this has nothing to do with papal infallibility.

After Pope Silverius died, Vigilius rose to the position of legitimate bishop of Rome in A.D. 537. When he took that position, he reversed his previous stance on the three Monophysites. Taking up the orthodox banner, Pope Vigilius condemned the three as heretics in letters both to the emperor Justinian and to Menas, the Patriarch of Constantinople. It seems as though the charism of infallibility had seized hold of Vigilius when he became the real pontiff. While there is an alleged letter from the pope to the three heretics, in which he agrees with their heretical views, it is now widely held to be a forgery; one of many attempts to make a pope appear to be sanctioning heresy.[1] By all accounts, Pope Vigilius never endorsed the Monophysite heresy and always held and taught the orthodox position regarding the two natures in Christ.

The Nestorian question

But the Monophysites weren't the only heretics on the scene. They had their opposite extreme: the Nestorians. Nestorians rejected the notion that Christ's human and Divine natures were joined together; in their Christology, Christ did have a human and Divine nature, but they were

---

[1] Cf. J. P. Kirsch, "Vigilius," *The Catholic Encyclopedia* (New York: Robert Appleton Co., 1912), vol. XV, 427–428.

only tenuously connected. In this way, Mary was the mother of Christ's human nature, but not the Divine. There was some question then as to when the Divine nature entered Jesus. Suffice it to say, these views were certainly not in line with orthodox Catholicism. The emperor Justinian, partial to Monophysitism, wanted Vigilius to condemn three Nestorians, hoping to lure the Monophysites back into the Church. The big problem with this situation was that two of the three "heretics" the emperor wanted Vigilius to condemn (Theodoret and Ibas — the third being Theodore) had already recanted of their errors. For this reason, condemning them would have been unjust.

Poultry in motion

Unfortunately, cowardice in the face of threats seems to have been Vigilius's problem. We know that he initially resisted the emperor's wish, refusing to act against the three prelates. For this reason, in A.D. 545, the pope was seized in the middle of celebrating Mass in the church of St. Cecilia in Trastevere. He was brought by force to Constantinople to appear before the angry emperor. While under arrest and the victim of extended duress, Vigilius agreed to condemn the three in 548 — three years after his initial arrest. Three years later, free from the physical compulsion of the emperor, Vigilius reversed his position on the three men, refusing to condemn them. As a final embarrassing flip-flop, in a letter to the Patriarch Eutychius, Pope Vigilius again condemned the three Nestorian bishops and upheld the decision of a Church synod that Justinian had called earlier in Constantinople. This condemnation was repeated in a constitution in A.D. 554.

While Pope Vigilius will never be remembered for his integrity (much less his ability to take a strong stand on such an important issue), his position-shifting raises no doctrinal problem for papal infallibility. The three Nestorians could rightly be condemned for their past errors (including the ones who later rejected their heresies). The two who recanted could also rightly be approved for their turn to Christian orthodoxy. Either position is defensible; the errors were open to condemnation while the individuals could be approved. In this way, Vigilius neither taught error, nor did he ever reverse any earlier doctrinal assertion. His crime was one of weakness and poor leadership, not heresy. Add to this the fact that many of his actions were brought about through intense physical and mental harassment and even coercion (he was, after all, imprisoned for some time over all this). This also goes a long way in explaining, if not excusing, his behavior. In the end, though, we find that this particular pope fiction, like the others, is a flash in the pan.

As a sad side note: after his final concession to Justinian and eight years of forced residence in Constantinople, poor Pope Vigilius was finally released in 555 and allowed to return to Rome. He died on the way.[2]

---

[2] Cf. John Chapman, O.S.B., "Vigilius," in the *Catholic Encyclopedia*.

16

Pope Gregory the Great rebuked John the Faster, archbishop of Constantinople, for his attempt to call himself the "Universal Bishop." Gregory claimed that anyone who called himself this was being impious and blasphemous. So the Catholic claim that the pope is the "Universal pastor" is contrary to the early Church.

This argument is sometimes raised by our Eastern Orthodox brethren, who seek to show that the office of the papacy today — complete with its titles, such as "supreme pontiff," etc. — is inconsistent with the nature of the papacy in the early Church. This episode of Pope St. Gregory the Great criticizing an eastern patriarch, John the Faster, for using the title "universal bishop" seems to be a good tool for debunking Catholic claims.

Well, it's not.

Whenever we're faced with an objection like this, it always benefits us to define terms first. In this case, we need to understand what exactly Pope Gregory was condemning when he forbade John the Faster to use the term "Universal Bishop." Two things can be meant by this phrase. "Universal bishop" can mean either a bishop over the entire Church (universal jurisdiction) while not denying the individual authority of local bishops, or it can imply that the bishop who claims this title sees himself as a bishop of all other bishops — kind of a "superbishop" to whom all other bishops should look to as their bishop. This would imply that the other bishops of the world were not truly bishops in the fullest sense, and that there was a single bishop for the entire world.

The issue of universal jurisdiction

When Gregory attacked the title "universal bishop," the evidence shows that he was condemning the latter definition, not the former. This is clear from his words in *Epistle LXVIII*: "For if one, as [John the Faster] supposes, is universal bishop, it remains that you are not bishops." Gregory was *not* objecting to the term "universal bishop" as if it meant that the pope didn't have universal primacy among the college of bishops. Rather, he was reproaching the arrogance displayed by the then-patriarch of Constantinople.

Not only did Gregory not object to the notion of the pope having universal jurisdiction over the Church, but his own actions show he held to that belief himself. This is evident from his many epistles, in which he admonished, instructed, directed, rebuked, encouraged, and generally guided with a firm but friendly hand the various churches around the world:

Epistle LXXXI — Pope Gregory restored Bishop Maximus back to communion with the Church. Obviously, Gregory had the power to excommunicate other bishops. And the fact that Maximus came back repentant shows that he too recognized the Roman See had that power.

Epistle XVII — Gregory intervened in the affairs of the

church at Firmum, releasing a parishioner from a debt owed to that church. This is evidence that he had jurisdiction over that Church, otherwise he would have had no authority to forgive the debt of someone on the Church's behalf. What's more, his decision was adhered to by that church. If the notion of the pope — the bishop of Rome — having a special authority that extended the borders of his own diocese was truly alien to the early Church, you can be certain that churches like Firmum would have howled to high heavens that the bishop of Rome was overstepping his authority by meddling in their affairs. But that never happened.

Epistle X — He discussed the qualities that made suitable candidates for bishop, and asked his brother bishops to follow those guidelines in their choices. He gave a thumbs down to some candidates and approved others. Obviously, Gregory as pope had a recognized authority regarding policy on who would and wouldn't be raised to the bishopric.

Epistle LXVIII —

And although our most pious Emperor allows nothing unlawful to be done there, yet, lest perverse men, taking occasion of your assembly, should seek opportunity of cajoling you in favoring this name of superstition, or should think of holding a synod about some other matter, with the view of introducing it therein by cunning contrivances — though without the authority and consent of the Apostolic See nothing that might be passed would have any force, nevertheless, before Almighty God I conjure and warn you, that the assent of none of you be obtained by any blandishments, any bribes, any threats whatever; but, having regard to the eternal judgment, acquit ye yourselves salubriously and unanimously in opposition to wrongful aims; and, supported by pastoral constancy and apostolical authority, keep out the robber and the wolf that would rush in, and give no way to him that rages for the tearing of the Church asunder; nor allow, through any cajolery, a synod to be held on this subject, which indeed would not be a legitimate one, nor to be called a synod. . . . For if any one, as we do not believe will be the case, should disregard in any part this present writing, let him know that he is segregated from the peace of the blessed Peter, the Prince of the Apostles.

Here, Gregory showed the authority of the Holy See, which represents "Peter, the Prince of the Apostles." Gregory believed that no canonical law has any validity whatsoever without the "authority and consent of the Apostolic See." The bishop of that see must, then, have some manner of universal jurisdiction over the laws of the Church.

Epistle LIX — Here, Gregory intervened into the affairs of another Church, regarding the disciplining of another bishop:

And it is exceedingly doubtful whether he says such things to us sincerely, or in fact because he is being attacked by his fellow-bishops: for, as to his saying that he is subject to the Apostolic See, if any fault is found in bishops, I know not what bishop is not subject to it. But when no fault requires it to be otherwise, all according to the principle of humility are equal. Nevertheless, do you speak with the aforesaid most eloquent Martin as seems good to your Fraternity. For it is for you to consider what should be done; and we have replied to you briefly on the case, because we ought not to believe indiscriminately men that are even unknown to us. If, however, you, who see him before you in person, are of opinion that anything more

definite should be said to him, we commit this to your
charity, being sure of your love in the grace of Almighty
God. And what you do regard without doubt as having
been done by us.

There are three significant points in this passage: First,
Gregory notes that all bishops are subject to the Apostolic
See. Second, Gregory delegates his authority in the punishment of the erring bishop. And third, Gregory is obviously
seen as holding a higher position than these other bishops,
for the erring bishop appealed to him, and the other bishops await his decision regarding punishment/correction.

Epistle CXI —

This he did as knowing such reverence to be paid by
the faithful to the Apostolic See that what had been set-
tled by its decree no molestation of unlawful usurpation
would thereafter shake. . . . For, though what has once
been sanctioned by the authority of the Apostolic See has
no lack of validity, yet we do, over and above, once more
corroborate by our authority in all respects all things that
were ordained by our predecessor for quiet in this matter.

Gregory claims the non-doctrinal decrees of the Roman
See are unchangeable by others, except, of course, future
popes. They are to be considered the final authority.

Epistle XII — Last, but certainly not least. . . . "*For as to
what they say about the Church of Constantinople, who can
doubt that it is subject to the Apostolic See, as both the most
pious lord the emperor and our brother the bishop of that city
continually acknowledge?* Yet, if this or any other Church
has anything that is good, I am prepared in what is good
to imitate even my inferiors, while prohibiting them from
things unlawful."

According to Gregory, the Apostolic See has authority over all other churches, even Constantinople. There is no hint of equality in authority here. For him, the other churches are the subordinates of the Roman See.

17

Catholics claim that the pope is infallible when teaching on faith or morals. Pope Honorius (reigned 625–638) held a heretical view of Jesus and was later condemned by the Sixth Ecumenical Council (680) as a heretic. Here is a clear example of a pope teaching falsely.

Here we go again. Like most of the historically-based pope fictions, this one can be cleared up by taking a closer look at the events described. All periods of the Church have their prominent heresies. Always have, always will. In the early Church, the Monophysite heresy was prominent. According to the Monophysites, Jesus had only one nature, the Divine. This, of course, contradicted the declaration of the Council of Chalcedon (A.D. 451) which taught that in Christ there are two natures, divine and human.

Out of the Monophysite heresy sprang another (heresies have a nasty habit of mutating into yet more heresies). This error was branded Monothelitism — the belief that in Christ, there is only one will, a combination of the Divine and the human. Sadly, this heresy found its way to some of the highest positions in the Church. Indeed, Sergius, the patriarch of Constantinople, was himself a Monothelite. He sent a letter to Honorius regarding this issue, asking him whether Christ had one "operation" or two.

The language Sergius used was obscure and more than a little confusing. Honorius wrote back condemning both expressions. The problem with his blanket condemnation is that one of the expressions (i.e., Christ having two "operations") can be seen as orthodox. In condemning the expressions, Honorius condemned the concepts behind them.

Additionally, at one point in the letter, the pope seems to favor the heretical view that Christ had only one will, though this section is at best ambiguous. Indeed, John Symponus, the man who composed Honorius's letter, said the pope only meant to condemn the idea that Christ had two *contrary* wills — not the notion that He had two wills in concert with one another. In this way, the condemnation is perfectly orthodox.[1] Nevertheless, Honorius's confusing letter was used by many at the time to buttress the heretical Monothelite position.

Subtleties of language

During the Sixth Council of Constantinople, the Monothelite heresy was openly condemned, along with those who held it. It's true that Honorius was one of the individuals who were declared anathema. But this did not happen with the approval of Pope St. Agatho, as some mistakenly assume. In volume two of his monumental work *A History of Christendom*, historian Warren Carroll explained that Pope

---

[1] Cf. Francis Patrick Kenrick, *The Primacy of the Apostolic See Vindicated* (New York: Edward Dunigan & Brother, 1848), 179.

Agatho never confirmed the council's decrees (including its condemnation of Honorius) because he had been dead several months when the news of the council's action arrived in Rome. His successor, Pope Leo II, confirmed the council's decree but clarified its language regarding Pope Honorius, making it clear that Honorius had *not* endorsed the Monothelitism of Sergius, but had failed in his duty to condemn it. Officially, therefore, Honorius was condemned for his negligence, but not for heresy.

> Writing to the Emperor, almost certainly composing the letter himself in the Emperor's own language, Greek, Pope Leo II wrote that Pope Honorius was condemned because "he permitted the immaculate Faith to be subverted." Writing in Latin to the Spanish bishops, he declared that Honorius was condemned for not at once extinguishing the flames of heresy, but rather gaining them by his negligence. To King Erwig he wrote that Honorius was condemned for negligence in not denouncing the heresy and for using an expression which the heretics were able to employ to advance their own cause, thereby allowing the Faith to be stained. . . .
>
> [T]he fact remains that no decree of a council has effect in the Catholic Church unless and until it is confirmed by the reigning Pope, *and only in the form that he confirms it*. There is no "supreme law" prescribing how the Pope shall designate his confirmation. Pope Honorius, therefore, was never condemned for heresy by the supreme Church authority, but only for negligence [in] allowing a heresy to spread and grow, when he should have denounced it.[2]

---

[2]Warren Carroll, *The History of Christendom,* vol. 2: The Building of Christendom (Front Royal: Christendom College Press, 1987), p. 254; emphasis in the original.

So, despite the claims of those who peddle this pope fiction, Pope Honorius was *not* condemned as a Monothelite heretic. Rather, as we've seen, he was anathematized for allowing the heretical Sergius to put orthodox doctrine alongside heretical. This occurred specifically in Honorius's objection to the heretical claim that Christ had one "operation" and the orthodox assertion that He had two.[3] Honorius had forbade both expressions (one of which was orthodox) and, in that way, failed to promote truth.

In other words, Honorius's crime was not heresy itself, but his refusal to act against heresy when he should have by issuing an authoritative proclamation of the orthodox Catholic Faith, once for all delivered to the saints (cf. Jude 3). This fact is clear from Pope Leo II's letter to the Spanish bishops, wherein he says, "With Honorius, who did not, as became Apostolic authority, extinguish the flame of heretical teaching in its first beginning, but fostered it by his *negligence*."

The article on Pope Honorius in *The Catholic Encyclopedia* summarizes the essential details of this unfortunate moment in papal history:

> It was now for the pope to pronounce a dogmatic decision and save the situation. He did nothing of the sort. His answer to Sergius did not decide the question, did not authoritatively declare the faith of the Roman Church, did not claim to speak with the voice of Peter; it condemned nothing, it defined nothing. Honorius entirely agrees with the caution which Sergius recommends. He praises Sergius for eventually dropping the new expression "one opera-

---

[3] Cf. John Chapman, O.S.B., "Honorius," *The Catholic Encyclopedia* (New York: Robert Appleton Co., 1910), vol. VII, 457–460.

tion," but he unfortunately also agrees with him that it will be well to avoid "two operations" also; for if the former sounds Eutychian, the latter may be judged to be Nestorian.

Another passage is even more difficult to account for. Following the lead of Sergius, who had said that "two operations" might lead people to think two contrary wills were admitted in Christ, Honorius (after explaining the *communicatio idiomatum*, by which it can be said that God was crucified, and that the Man came down from heaven) adds: "Wherefore we acknowledge one Will of our Lord Jesus Christ, for evidently it was our nature and not the sin in it which was assumed by the Godhead, that is to say, the nature which was created before sin, not the nature which was vitiated by sin." Other passages in the letter are orthodox. But it is plain that the pope simply followed Sergius, without going more deeply into the question. The letter cannot be called a private one, for it is an official reply to a formal consultation. It had, however, less publicity than a modern Encyclical. *As the letter does not define or condemn, and does not bind the Church to accept its teaching, it is of course impossible to regard it as an ex cathedra utterance.*[4]

So, while we can certainly criticize Pope Honorius for his failure to act responsibly in his office, his behavior has nothing to do with papal infallibility. He was neither declaring a dogma nor teaching officially. Rather, he condemned two ambiguous theological expressions — one of which can be understood in an orthodox way.

Not careful enough, yes. Heretical, no.

---

[4] Ibid., 453, (emphasis added).

18

In the middle ages, there were often three competing popes reigning simultaneously.

Not exactly. It's true that at different times in Church history, several men simultaneously *claimed* to be the pope, but this is in no way the same as there *being* three popes reigning simultaneously.

Imagine you own a very expensive watch. One day, while walking in a park, you lose the watch. You search everywhere, but in the end, can't find it. Heading home disheartened, you notice two men fighting over something. As you approach them, you see the object of their dispute is the very watch you lost. You go over to claim ownership, but they refuse to give it over. A police officer arrives and begins to deliberate as to the true owner of the timepiece. He finds three claimants to the watch, but knows there can only be one true owner.

So it was with the papacy. Just because two or three individuals *claimed* to be the pope, doesn't mean that they *were* the pope. There can be only one legitimate bishop of Rome; the others are mere counterfeits.

This objection refers to a specific time in Church history: the Great Western Schism. The story begins, surprisingly

enough, not in Rome but in Avignon, France. In 1305,
Pope Clement V was forced to move the papal residence
from Rome to Avignon. At the time, violence was breaking
out among the noble families in the Eternal City. This put
the papacy in physical danger, so the move was an important one.

After seventy years of exile in France, Pope Gregory XI
moved the Holy See back to Rome. When he died in 1378,
it became necessary to choose a pontiff who would be able
to draw both the French and the Roman factions of the
Church together. With this intention, the well respected
Archbishop Bartolomeo Prignano was elected, becoming
Urban VI. It's important to note that his election was supported by all major parties in the Church.

Unfortunately, Urban VI's character soon changed after
his ascendance to the papal throne. He became a difficult
individual to work with, being vocally critical of anyone he
disapproved of. This quickly alienated his former supporters, who then conspired to replace him. Thirteen members
of the Sacred College met in a secret conclave, and elected
another pope, the former Robert of Geneva. After his election, the anti-pope, Clement VII, moved his claimed see
back to Avignon, and reigned in schism there.

Smooth talking antipopes

Sadly, the usurper to the papacy was everything the real
pope wasn't. While Urban VI was brusque, Clement VII
was diplomatic; Urban VI was arrogant, but Clement VII
was endearing. These realities quickly split the allegiance
of the Church. There were mutual excommunications be-

tween the two parties, and the debate as to who was the legitimate pontiff raged throughout the Catholic world. The various powers of Europe got involved, siding with either Rome or Avignon — whichever was more beneficial for them politically.

Eventually, old age caught up to both men, and they died. Their successors — Boniface IX for Urban VI and Benedict XIII for Clement VII — continued the rift, despite several attempts at reconciliation. Boniface IX's reign was short, and he was followed by Innocent II and then Gregory XII. Benedict XIII had, by this time, lost the all-important support of the French royalty. In fact, he spent a good bit of time in their custody, cut off from communication. Nevertheless, this didn't weaken his resolve to be considered the true pope.

This mess got even more confusing when, in 1409, a council convened at Pisa elected yet another antipope, John the XXIII. However, this only served to worsen the matter. Europe was, by this time, sick of the divisions and yearned to be united spiritually once again under a single Roman head.

Their desires were finally realized at the Council of Constance in 1414. Gregory XII abdicated the papacy, while both John XXIII and Benedict XIII were removed from their sees. In their place in 1417, a new pope, agreeable to all, Martin V, was elected. Thus, this sorry chapter in Church history came to an end. There were many other (mostly earlier) antipopes. However, this period saw the most dramatic episode.

The question remains as to who *was* the legitimate pope at this time. Actually, the answer is an easy one: The papacy never left Rome. Even though Urban VI was an unpleasant fellow and, perhaps, a difficult person to work with, he was nevertheless the legitimate successor to Peter. Likewise, his successors, Boniface IX, Innocent II and Gregory XII all had the legitimate title to the papacy. Just because other parties *claimed* to be popes doesn't mean they actually were popes. Recall the example of the watch, given at the beginning of this answer. Even though other people claimed the lost watch was theirs, that didn't make it so. The essential thing is to follow the pedigree of succession. Only then will you be sure to follow the true vicar of Christ.

19

In the middle ages, there was a "Pope Joan," a woman who hid her gender and rose through the ranks of the Church, became a cardinal and was elected pope. No one knew she was a woman until, during a papal procession through the streets of Rome, she went into labor and gave birth to a child. She and the baby were killed on the spot by the mob, enraged at her imposture.

A lot of provocative things are said about "Pope Joan," the alleged medieval female pope. Depending on who is telling the story, she was a courageous feminist, a clever opportunist, and a brilliant scholar who couldn't make it as a woman in a man's world. She is said to have been a wise ruler and an astute theologian, though, oddly, no decree or theological teaching purporting to have come from her has made its way down to our day.

In any case, the fact is there was no Pope Joan. When all the evidence and coincidences are taken into account, it still seems clear that she exists only as pure legend, but one that makes for a sexy story. And when it comes to sexy stories, you know Hollywood will try its hand at making a blockbuster out of this piece of pope fiction. In fact, a major motion picture studio has reportedly bought the movie rights to *Pope Joan*, the best-selling 1996 novel by Donna Woolfolk Cross. Her book is couched as an historical "novel" — embellishing on a grand scale the rather sparse details that have clung to the legend of a brilliant, plain girl who rises to the highest levels in Church service, culminating in her being elected pope by an unwitting college of cardinals. The way the book is written and the way it's being promoted support my concern that it will be seen by most of its historically ignorant readers, not as a novel, a fiction, but as a real biography of the one woman who "made it to the top." When the movie comes out, this problem will certainly grow in proportions.

But what if she was real?

It's important to remember that even if there had been a female impostor pope, this would just mean that an invalid election had taken place, nothing more. Other invalidly elected claimants to the papal office have come and gone over the centuries, and the fact that a woman made that list would simply mean that a woman made that list. She would not have been pope — no one invalidly elected would be. And nothing in the Church's teachings about the papacy would be injured or disproved. This is an important fact for Catholics to keep in mind. Obviously, radical feminists, within and without the Church, would try to use the Pope Joan story as a tool in their efforts to make the Catholic Church change its teaching that the sacrament of holy orders is reserved to men.[1]

---

[1] Cf. Pope John Paul II's letter on this issue, *Ordinatio Sacerdotalis*;

In reality, the "Pope Joan" story is all sizzle and no steak. The basic outline of the main legend (actually, there have been several competing legends over the centuries) says that in the ninth or tenth century, a plain but extraordinarily brilliant young woman contrived to enter the university disguised as a man. Her intellect outstripped that of her male classmates and she shot to the top rank of students. Talk of her prowess in law, science, rhetoric, philosophy and languages was widespread. In another legend, popularized by several thirteenth-century works such as the *Chronicle of Popes and Emperors* by Dominican priest Martin Polonus,[2] the *Universal Chronicle of Metz*, and *Wonders of the City of Rome*, she traveled first to Greece with her boyfriend (why he wanted a girlfriend who disguised herself as a man is anybody's guess), made a name for herself in the university there, and then traveled to Rome.

Making it big in a man's world

Here all the legends converge into the main one that has come down to our day. Once in Rome, Joan managed to enter religious life, although no legend is able to say which order she entered, she was ordained a priest, and earned a high reputation as a skilled notary in the papal court. Eventually, she was noticed by the pope and made a cardinal. You can guess what happens next. She is eventually elected pope, takes the name John, and sets about skillfully ruling the Church. It's at this point that the most dramatic scenes of the story unfold.

English text available online at www.knight.org/advent/docs/jpo2os.htm

[2] Polonus's real name was Martin Strebski, and he was also known as Martin of Troppau (the region of his birth) and Martinus Oppaviensis.

The legends vary as to how Joan's gender and identity were discovered. One holds that she was granted a vision by God in which she was shown two options for her fate, being discovered and disgraced by the world or roasting in hell for her crime. She chose the former. Another version says that she got pregnant by one of her curial advisors and worked to maintain the charade until she gave birth to the baby. At that point her secret was discovered and she was deposed as pope and sent to a convent to do penance for the rest of her life. In this legend, the child she bore went on to become the bishop of Ostia, about twenty miles southwest of Rome and had Joan's body buried there when she died. Of course, no evidence exists to support this.

The main detail these legends have in common is that Joan was discovered because her hanky-panky with a cardinal or secretary resulted in pregnancy, and the childbirth exposed her fraud. The main legend is the most gory on this point. In it, Pope Joan goes into labor while riding in her *sedia gestatoria* — the portable throne in which popes were carried —as her procession passed the Coliseum on its way from St. Peter's Basilica to St. John Lateran Cathedral. The procession halted, the baby was born, and the confused and angry onlookers killed Pope Joan and her baby on the spot.[3] Most accounts say she was killed by stoning, another says she died in childbirth as the mob watching the spectacle shouted and insulted her. Still another says she was dragged to death behind a horse as punishment. Either way, the legends agree that the Romans didn't appreciate the unpleasant discovery.

---

[3]The gender of the mythical baby is not usually specified in the Pope Joan legends, except in the version that says she retired to a convent and her "son" became the bishop of Ostia.

The plot thickens

Several odd historical details gave weight to the legend, including the fact that among the carved busts of the popes in the cathedral of Siena was one of an unnamed woman. No one knows who created it or how it was put there, but when Pope Clement VIII discovered it, he ordered it reworked enough to represent Pope Zacharias, whose image had not previously been included in the collection. This is not surprising, though, given the widespread belief in Europe in the Pope Joan legend during the thirteenth through eighteenth centuries. Versions abounded, and many credulous folks, Catholics included, were sincerely convinced that there had indeed once been a female pope.

But the facts of history show otherwise. The primary proofs that this is all just a fable are these: First, the earliest point that we can trace the legend to is the mid-thirteenth century, but the legend didn't really gain wide currency until the late fourteenth century. No evidence of any kind exists from the ninth century (when Pope Joan was alleged to have reigned), nor do we see any in the tenth through twelfth centuries. None of the annals or acts of the popes that were written between the ninth and thirteenth centuries (and none after that, either) mention her.

Church historian J. P. Kirsch wrote that "Not one contemporaneous historical source among the papal histories knows anything about her; also, no mention is made of her until the middle of the thirteenth century. Now it is incredible that the appearance of a 'popess,' if it was an historical fact, would be noticed by none of the numerous historians from the tenth to the thirteenth century. In the history of the popes, there is no place where this legendary figure will fit in. Between Leo IV and Benedict III, where Martinus Polonus places her, she cannot be inserted. . . ."[4]

The sounds of silence

The 400 years of silence between when Pope Joan is alleged to have lived and the first credible and verifiable mention of her (by Fr. Martin Polonus) is too huge to be accounted for. There is simply no way such a spectacular scandal could have been suppressed everywhere in Europe. The enemies of the papacy and the Catholic Church, and there were many, would have pounced on this juicy episode and propagandized it through the roof. And the papacy would have been powerless to stop it. The papacy was, admittedly, at its low point during the tenth and eleventh centuries. Its temporal influence was vastly circumscribed by rambunctious and powerful European states and, as a result of the debauchery and decadence of some popes and Rome in general during those times, the papacy's moral influence on society was not strong either. So it's clear that the 400-year silence about Pope Joan could not have been the result of a ham-fisted Catholic Church suppressing the story. That would have been simply impossible.

Think about it. The negative P.R. value of Pope Joan, and especially a surprise delivery of a baby on the streets of Rome, would have been incalculably embarrassing to the papacy. Songs would have been written, plays would have been staged, accounts would have been churned out by the dozen, all detailing Pope Joan's life and death — but no one, for 400 years, mentioned it. Why not? Because,

---

[4] "Pope Joan," *The Catholic Encyclopedia*, vol. VIII.

as vivid and widespread as the Pope Joan legend was, she herself wasn't real. Many people, including many Catholics, even clergy, sincerely believed for centuries that she existed. But that sincere, widespread belief doesn't make the story any less false. All the king's horses and all the king's men cannot put the Pope Joan legend back together again.

So where did the legend come from?

Many Catholic apologists have argued that the source of the Pope Joan story was the deceit of Protestant apologists, bent on discrediting Rome. The theory is that nefarious Protestants managed to forge copies of medieval manuscripts, doctoring them to include the story of Pope Joan. That this kind of lowbrow historical revisionism happened, here and there, seems clear (to be fair, we should note that some Catholic polemicists, too, were not above stooping to this kind of sneaky trick themselves in those days). But this theory can't explain the vast amount of Pope Joan literature that was all over Europe at the time of the Reformation and beyond. There is no way, humanly speaking, that so many documents could have been tampered with by unscrupulous Protestants.

The Protestant-forgery theory also fails when we see that verifiable examples of the Pope Joan legend appeared before the Protestant Reformation metastasized throughout Europe in the sixteenth century. Accounts of Joan in the writings of Dominicans Jean de Mailly, Stephen de Bourbon, and Martin Polonus are three such examples.

And you thought those other *popes were bad!*

There are, though, credible ways to account for the legend. The first is that the Roman population became disgusted with the corrupt influence wielded over Pope Sergius (reigned 904–911) by the powerful and wealthy Theodora Theophylact, and more specifically by her young daughter Morozia, a cunning and exceptionally attractive woman. The fabulously wealthy and prestigious Theophylact family wielded immense power in Rome during the tenth century, even, sadly, over several popes. It appears that Morozia was Sergius's mistress and bore him at least one son, the future Pope John XI and, amazingly, was the grandmother, great-grandmother, and great-*great*-grandmother of future popes Benedict VIII (1012–1024), John XIX (1024–1032), and Benedict IX (1032–1048).

This is a sorry episode in the history of the Church, one which displayed a decadence and immorality that even popes, at times, could fall prey to — a reminder to us all that men, even the holiest of men, are not invulnerable to temptation and personal weakness. Despite their sins, Christ's promise that the Church would be protected from error was not, nor has it ever been, broken.

From the details of Sergius III's pontificate, it seems clear that he was a vain, violent and sensuous man. It's quite possible that the disgusted faithful took to mocking him or one of his immediate successors because he was perceived to have been under the influence of the Theophylact women. There is no question that the Theophylact family's (especially Morozia's) corrosive, decadent influence on the papacy — indeed on the whole of Rome at the time — was so scandalous that it was the subject of popular derision and disgust for generations afterward.

Some historians trace the legend of a female pope to Morozia, saying that the people hit upon the phrase "Pope Joan" to mock the weak popes she controlled. The "Theophylact connection" is possible and has been suggested by many respected historians such as Cardinal Caesare Baronius, Ignaz von Dollinger, and Edward Gibbon, best known for his monumental historical series, *The Decline and Fall of the Roman Empire*. Gibbon's complete rejection of the Pope Joan legend as being nonsense is of particular interest here. He was well known as an anti-Catholic agnostic, someone who more often than not was willing to ascribe the most unflattering attributes and motives to Catholics, especially to popes. The fact that such an eminent historian, who was no friend of the Catholic Church, would reject the Pope Joan Legend, is a crucial point.

Other theories

But there are weaknesses to the Theophylact connection theory. For one thing, it's been pointed out that there would have been no need for contemporaries of Morozia and Theodora to mock the pope with a derisive nickname, "Pope Joan." The records of those days make it painfully clear that the Roman citizens of the day did their mocking quite openly. Another possibility is that subsequent generations latched onto the title as a result of a line in some popular tavern ditty, and both the name Pope Joan and her legend eventually took on a life of their own.

Dollinger theorized, improbably, that the Dominican order was to blame for starting the legend as a way to discredit Pope Innocent IV (1243–1254), with whom they were having a squabble over university professorships.[5]

It seems likely that the Pope Joan legend arose, at least in part, from the conduct of the much maligned Pope John VIII (reigned 872–882). He appears to have had a very weak personality, even perhaps somewhat effeminate.

---

[5] In his engaging and well-researched book *The Legend of Pope Joan* (New York: Henry Holt & Company, 1998), Peter Stanford presents a fascinating but ultimately unreasonable account of the theory that the Dominicans, who were embroiled in controversy with several popes, started the Pope Joan myth (pages 141–144). Stanford, whose feminist sympathies are revealed at various points in his book, accepts the myth of Pope Joan as fact, but not without offering some valuable new insights into the history of the legend.

Stanford's analysis of the Pope Joan legend, though engaging and fact-filled, has not met with critical acclaim. For example, *Kirkus Reviews* panned it, saying it was "A flimsy argument for the existence of a female pope in the ninth century." And further that "Stanford too doggedly persists in his determination to see historical evidence for Joan's papacy where almost none exists. His case is built upon circumstances, and he rashly jumps from possibility to fact. . . . Some of this is excusable by Stanford's own obvious enthusiasm for his subject matter; he so clearly wants the reader to believe what he has come to accept as historical truth. . . . This eagerness blinds him to the far more provocative questions he neglects to raise until the conclusion of the book: why is Joan still revered by so many, including proponents of women's ordination, transvestites, and anti-clericalists? What is at stake here for the Catholic Church? Why, despite the weak historical evidence, does the legend of Pope Joan persist? Tenuous, inadequate history that overlooks the more salient issues surrounding Joan's legend." (*Kirkus Reviews*, November 15, 1998, available at www.amazon.com by typing in "The Legend of Pope Joan" in the keyword search window.)

Cardinal Baronius. in his Church history *Annals*, suggests that John VIII's reputation as effeminate gave rise to the legend. Indeed, it would seem that over time, the common folk added more lurid embellishments until the vulgar jokes about the hapless (and certainly male) pope ballooned and metamorphosed into a "papessa."

20

How can the Catholic Church claim infallibility when it officially condemned Galileo for heresy when he declared that the Earth revolves around the sun? Add to this the fact that Galileo was cruelly imprisoned and forced to recant under the pains of torture. Modern science now shows that Galileo was right and the "infallible" pope was wrong.

Many have unwittingly embraced the myth that Galileo Galilei, a seventeenth-century Italian astronomer, discovered the heliocentricity of the solar system and, because his discovery conflicted with Catholic teaching, was tortured until he recanted. It's often said that after recanting Galileo obstinately muttered under his breath, *"E pur si muove"* (Italian: "And yet it does move"). All this is pure fabrication.

Here are the facts. First of all, Galileo was a brilliant physicist and astronomer, but he didn't discover heliocentricity — the ancient Greeks and Romans postulated the theory at least two thousand years before him. We know this because both Aristotle (d. 322 B.C.) and Ptolemy (fl.

ca. A.D. 150), attempted to refute the idea. Aristarchus of
Samos (d. ca. 160 B.C.), Cicero (d. 43 B.C.), Seneca (d. A.D.
65) and Eusebius (died A.D. 339) all discussed the idea in
their writings. This is why the Polish scientist Copernicus (d. 1543), who happened to be a Catholic priest, didn't
fancy himself the "discoverer" of the theory named after
him.

Second, the Catholic Church has never defined (nor could
it ever define) any theory of physical science as a matter of
faith. There never was any "dogma" which said the earth
was the center of the universe or the solar system. The
next time people claim Galileo bravely challenged such a
"dogma," ask them to identify its official name, the name
of the pope who defined it and the date it was defined. If
they can't provide you with this basic information, demand
that they cite the source of their "facts."

Although Galileo's heliocentric theories were contrary
to the understanding of the Church of his day, it wasn't
just with the Church that he found himself at odds. His
ideas were contrary to the Ptolemaic school of thought,
which was accepted by virtually all contemporary scientists. The ideas he pushed had been challenged by such
notable thinkers as Michel de Montaigne (d. 1592), Blaise
Pascal (d. 1662) and Alessandro Tassoni (d. 1635), who said,
"Stand in the middle of a room and look out at the sun
through a window opening toward the south. Now, if the
sun stands still and the window moves so quickly [referring
to the speed at which Galileo theorized the earth rotated],
the sun will instantly disappear from your vision."

Science or religion?

One historian points out that there is current scholarship available that indicates that the source of the Galileo controversy with the papacy may actually have been over something different from what most people think:

> Pietro Redondi, in a widely-discussed recent book, *Galileo Heretic* (1983), argues that the real source of conflict between Galileo and the Church was not the Copernican doctrine, as everyone for centuries has supposed and as the documents seem to attest, but a suspicion of heresy in regard to Eucharistic doctrine. Galileo, like many other natural philosophers of his day, took [the scientific theory of] atomism for granted and made occasional use of it in his theorizing. There was a real doubt on the part of some theologians, however, as to whether atomism could be squared with the doctrine of transubstantiation defined by the Council of Trent. Redondi noticed an unsigned denunciation of Galileo's atomism in the files of the Holy Office; starting from this rather slender clue, he constructed an ingenious and highly readable account of what might really have been going on in 1633.[1]

Protestant critics of Catholicism point triumphantly to the Galileo case, but conveniently forget that ten years before Galileo landed in the ecclesiastical hot seat, his scientific peer, Johannes Kepler (d. 1630), a Protestant, was vehemently condemned by the Protestant faculty at the University of Tübingen for espousing the very same theory.

---

[1] Ernan McMullin, foreword, in Richard S. Westfall, *Essays on the Trial of Galileo* (Rome: Vatican Observatory Publications, 1989), ix.

There's a vast difference between a scientist raising a few eyebrows by postulating unconventional theories and his being persecuted for doing so. One must ask why Galileo was condemned. The answer will surprise and disappoint many anti-Catholics.

The fact is that for many years, Galileo was held in high regard by many Roman hierarchs and was one of the most celebrated members of the scientific Academy of the Lincei. His work in astronomy garnered him high honors from three successive popes: Paul V, Gregory XV and Urban VIII.

Galileo: darling of the curia

Cardinal del Monte, in a letter to the Grand Duke of Tuscany, reveals that far from being persecuted by "anti-science" Catholic churchmen, Galileo,

> during his sojourn at Rome, has been given much satisfaction, and I believe that he has received the same; for he has enjoyed good opportunities to exhibit his inventions, and the best-informed men of the Eternal City regard them as the most wonderful and accurate. If we were living in the olden days of Rome, the worth of Galileo, I think, would be recognized by a statue on the Capitoline.

What, then, caused the row with the Church? The first thing to remember is that Galileo's heliocentric theory, although sternly opposed by theologians who embraced the Ptolemaic model (according to which, all heavenly bodies, including the sun, revolve around the Earth), wasn't the real source of his ecclesiastical difficulties. Rather, the cause of his persecution stemmed from a presumption to teach the sense in which certain Bible passages should be interpreted (using science as the ultimate criterion) and from charges that he claimed God was merely accidental and not substantial.

She blinded him with science

Galileo confused revealed truths with scientific discoveries by saying that in the Bible "are found propositions which, when taken literally, are false; that Holy Writ out of regard for the incapacity of the people, expresses itself inexactly, even when treating of solemn dogmas; that in questions concerning natural things, philosophical [i.e., scientific] should avail more than sacred." Hence, we see that it was Galileo's perceived attack on theology (which is the unique domain of the Magisterium and not of scientists) that elicited the alarmed response from the Church.

In his *Illustrious Italians* (Milan, 1879), the historian Caesare Cantú puts Galileo's claims into perspective:

The earth ceased to be regarded as the largest, warmest and most illuminated of the planetary bodies. It no longer enjoyed a preeminence in creation as the home of a privileged being, but became one of many in the group of unexplored planets and in no way distinguished from the others.

Fearing that science was aggrandizing itself only to war on God, the timid repudiated it. Only later did the better minds understand that the faith fears no learning; that historic criticism can be independent and impartial without becoming irreligious. Then, good sense estimated at their true value the accusations launched against the Church because of the Galileo affair. It distinguished simple assertions from articles of faith, positive and necessary prohibitions from prudential and disciplinary provisions, the oracles of the Church from the deliberations of a particular tribunal.

To such a tribunal [the Inquisition], a denunciation was made that Galileo or his disciples had asserted that God is an accident and not a substance [or] a personal being; that miracles are not miracles at all. Then the pontiff declared that, for the termination of scandal, Galileo should be cited and admonished by the Sacred Congregation.

The Church finally acts

So, we see that it wasn't Galileo's heliocentric theories as such which moved the Church to censure him. In fact, a century earlier, Copernicus dedicated his *De Revolutionibus Orbium Coelestium* [*Revolutions of the Heavenly Orbs*, 1530] to Pope Paul III, saying: "If men who are ignorant of mathematics pretend to condemn my book, because of certain passages of Scripture which they distort to suit themselves, I despise their vain attacks." Although he was opposed by most theologians and fellow scientists for defying the Ptolemaic theory, Copernicus was supported by a number of prelates and was neither prosecuted nor had his theories condemned by the Church.

The Church *did* condemn Galileo after a lengthy investigation into the charges brought against him. In the end, the Holy Office decided against Galileo and pronounced the decision that his theories "were false and contrary to Holy Scripture" and that he was "gravely suspect of heresy."

The Catholic Church doesn't for a moment try to evade

or obscure the fact that Galileo's tribunal erred in its condemnation of heliocentricity (just as Urban VIII did by
ratifying the decision), but as much as critics of "Romanism" would like to imagine the contrary, that error neither
compromises the integrity of the Church nor violates the
doctrine of infallibility.

Church tribunals have juridical and disciplinary authority only, and neither they nor their decisions are infallible. Only a pope (or an ecumenical council) is personally
promised the charism of teaching infallibly. Remember that
in order for a pope to exercise the charism of infallibility,
three conditions must be present: (1) He cannot speak as
a private theologian but in his official capacity as vicar of
Christ and head of the Church; (2) He must officially define a doctrine relating to faith or morals (unfortunately,
the pope is not infallible when it comes to science, politics,
weather and the outcome of sporting events); (3) The pronouncement must not be directed only to a single individual or particular group of people, but it must be promulgated for the benefit of the entire Church.

In the Galileo case, the second and third conditions were
absent and, possibly, also the first condition. At best, one
can make a strong case that the Catholic Church of that
day was under-informed in its views on physical science —
but then so was the rest of the world. In the Galileo affair,
no case can be made which "disproves" papal infallibility.

Was the Church wrong to ban Galileo's writings? A
good case can be made that it was not. Although the bishops who condemned his theories were wrong with respect
to science, they were certainly not in error for wishing
to protect the faithful (most of whom were uneducated
peasants) from what appeared to be a dangerous scientific

theory — dangerous because it was offered in a "package deal" with certain ancillary (and certainly wrong) exegetical principles. Besides, Galileo may have been right so far as the basic scientific theory went, but he got the reasons for it all wrong.

As Frs. Rumble and Carty explain in their three-volume work *Radio Replies*,

> Galileo could not prove it [heliocentricity] and not one of the arguments he advanced for it is accepted today as scientifically demonstrative. All his arguments gave a probability only. In the present state of general education, we all know that there is no doubt on the subject, and that the movement of the Earth is in no way opposed to Sacred Scripture rightly understood. But people did not know that then, and they were not ready for the new knowledge.
>
> Its general publication could result only in widespread disturbance due to a lack of preparatory knowledge. Galileo made the mistake of going outside the realm of science to invade the field of theology. He set himself up as an exegete of Scripture and thus brought upon himself the censures of lawful religious authorities. The conservatism of the Church was prudence itself in the face of these novelties not yet proved.[2]

What about torture?

What about the charge that Galileo was imprisoned and brutally tortured in order to extract a confession from him?

---

[2] Rumble and Carty, *Radio Replies* (Rockford: TAN Books and Publishers, 1979, vol. 2, question 920.)

The astronomer made his first appearance before the Inquisition in 1615 and was neither imprisoned nor tortured but received a mild censure and was sent on his way. By 1633, he was again summoned to Rome to face the charges that he had persisted in promoting his theories as though they were matters of faith and provable by the Bible.

During his second stint before the Inquisition, Galileo was incarcerated, not, as is commonly thought, in some gloomy, rat-infested dungeon, but in the palace of Niccolini, the Tuscan ambassador to the Vatican and an ardent supporter of Galileo. If there had been treachery on the part of the Inquisition, surely Niccolini, one of Galileo's most enthusiastic fans, would have mentioned it.

In a letter of February 13, 1633, to the King of Tuscany, Ambassador Niccolini described the surprisingly benign treatment accorded the astronomer:

> The pope told me that he had shown to Galileo a favor never accorded to another in allowing him to reside in my house instead of the [apartments] of the Holy Office. . . . His Holiness said he could not avoid having Galileo brought to the Holy Office for the examination and I replied that my gratitude would be doubled if he would exempt Galileo from this appearance, but he answered that he could not do so. . . . He concluded with the promise to assign Galileo certain rooms which are most convenient in the Holy Office.

On April 16, Niccolini mentioned, "He has a servant and every convenience. The Reverend Commissary assigned him the apartments of the judge of the tribunal. My own servants carry his meals from my house." Niccolini's June 18 dispatch revealed that, "In regard to the person of Galileo, he ought to be imprisoned for some time because he disobeyed the orders of 1616, but the pope says that after the publication of the sentence he will consider with me as to what can be done to afflict him as little as possible."

In his July 3 missive, after the sentence of censure had been delivered by the Inquisition, Niccolini wrote, "His Holiness told me that although it was rather early to diminish the penance of Galileo he had been content to allow him to reside at first in the gardens of the Grand Duke, and that now he could proceed to Siena, there to reside in a convent or with my lord the Archbishop."

So much for the charge that Galileo was subjected to harsh imprisonment.

But what about torture? While it's true that a decree issued by Pope Urban VIII instructed that Galileo "should be questioned as to his intentions and that he should be menaced with torture," no torture was ever carried out.

It seems that the pope, knowing full well that Galileo had no intention or desire to become a martyr for science, simply wanted the astronomer to be "scared straight."

In the fourth interrogatory, Galileo gave his answer to the charge against him:

> I have not held the Copernican system since I was ordered to abandon it [referring to his censure in 1616]. But I am in your hands. Do with me what you will. For some time before the determination of the Holy Office, and before I received the command [in 1616], I had been indifferent as to the two opinions of Ptolemy and Copernicus, and had held that both were disputable and that both could be true in nature. But after being assured by the prudence of my superiors, all my doubts ceased, and I held, as I now hold, the theory of Ptolemy as true, that is that the earth does not, and that the sun does move.

Most scholars agree that Galileo was never tortured —
there's simply no evidence to support the claim that he was
— nor even that he was shown the instruments of torture.[3]
Galileo had given the inquisitors what they wanted — he
had submitted (although admittedly under coercion) to the
authority of the Church. This being the case, the inquisitors were forbidden by the code of regulations imposed on
them to use torture. The *Directory for Inquisitors* (Venice,
1595), by Friar Nicholas Eymeric, O.P., was the official
guide for the Holy Office and was followed assiduously.
The specific section which deals with torture is part 3, on
the "Practice of the Inquisitorial Office," particularly, the
chapter on "the Third Way of Ending a Trial for Faith."

The official record of the tribunal mentions that in the
fourth interrogatory the judges had "deemed it necessary
to proceed to a rigorous examination, and thou didst reply
like a Catholic" (*respondisti Catholice*). Because of his abju-
ration, Galileo could not be subjected to torture. There is
no mention of maltreatment in any of Galileo's subsequent
letters or essays.

Was the Galileo case an embarrassment to the Church?
Yes. Was the situation rectified later? Yes — in 1825, in an
official document by Dom Olivieri, the General of the Dominican order and commissary of the Holy Office, which
apologized for the condemnation and rehabilitated Galileo
and his work.

The Galileo story, when painted inaccurately in grue-
some hues, seems to stain the credibility of the Catholic
Church. But, understood correctly and in its historical context, the Galileo case really proves nothing, except perhaps

---

[3] Cf. Westfall, 23–24.

that the Catholic Church is very serious (and certain of her members can be overzealous) in her efforts to safeguard the flock from error or scandal.

In 1989, Pope John Paul II discussed the mistakes the Church made in its handling of the Galileo case. He apologized for the Church's handling of the case, largely rehabilitated Galileo's name, and he pointed out once again that the province of the Church is theology and revelation, not science or astronomy. Throughout the Galileo affair, the pope was not acting in his capacity of teacher, but of prudent guardian. Though Pope Urban VIII and his zealous Roman clergy who prosecuted Galileo were dead wrong in their scientific theories regarding the orbits of celestial bodies, and even though their prosecution of Galileo seems to us today to have been heavy-handed and uncalled for, this vexing case doesn't conflict with the Catholic teaching of papal infallibility.[4]

---

[4] This chapter was adapted from an article I wrote (anonymously) in the May 1989 issue of *Catholic Answers* newsletter.

21

How can Catholics call the pope "Vicar of Christ," when it was the papacy that started the bloodbath of the Crusades? Christ would never have done that Himself, nor would He allow His "vicar" to do it in His name. The popes' greed for the Holy Land drove them to order the massacre of millions of Jews and Muslims.

Question: How do you raise the ire of just about anyone opposed to the papacy? Answer: Mention the Crusades. With the possible exception of the Inquisition, there's no more misunderstood event in Church history. The thought of armies of so-called believers raising the sword and spilling blood in the name of Christ is repugnant to most modern people. But in that statement lies one key to understanding the Crusades: violent action on behalf of Christianity is repugnant to most *modern* people. In understanding the Crusades, we must first look at the mindset of the day, and then explore the situation which gave birth to them.

There were, in total, ten general Crusades (though some combine them, reaching a count of seven). Usually, the

Eastern Crusades are the ones objected to, so I'll concentrate on those, treating them like a fluid whole.

Beginning as early as the fourth century, pilgrimages from Europe to the Holy Land were very popular. Believers wanted to maintain some kind of experiential contact with the places in which the Lord had lived. Added to this was the number of alleged relics that were scattered across the lands of the Mediterranean. As Christianity grew increasingly Western and European, it became necessary to maintain ongoing contact with its Palestinian roots.

For the most part, things went smoothly, until the beginning of the eleventh century (A.D. 1009), when Al Hakem, the Muslim Caleph of Egypt, ordered the destruction of the Holy Sepulcher and the removal of the Christian presence in Jerusalem.[1] Needless to say, he was no fan of the Catholic Church. From that point on, the Muslim oppression of Christians (both residents and pilgrims) was nearly constant. Catholics were victims of violence and discrimination. This culminated in the 1071 taking of Jerusalem by the Seldjuk Turks.[2]

The last straw

After being heroically patient in the face of this Muslim onslaught and hoping for a peaceful solution, Pope Urban II could finally take no more of this unacceptable mistreatment of Christians in Palestine. In 1095, he ordered

---

[1] Régine Pernoud, *The Crusades* (London: Secker & Warburg, 1960), 15.

[2] Ibid. 16–17.

the first Crusade, for the protection of all Christians in the Holy Land:

> On beholding the enormous injury that all, clergy or people, brought upon the Christian Faith. . . . At the news that the Rumanian provinces had been taken from the Christians by the Turks, moved with compassion and impelled by the love of God, he crossed the mountains and descended into Gaul.[3]

With the popes' call, Christians from all over Europe set off to rescue the Holy Land from the onslaught of the Muslims. With the threat of Christian extinction in the East, Catholics unified under the banner of the cross. After a number of extended and difficult battles, the Crusaders conquered the Muslim defenders of Jerusalem on July 15, 1099. Tragically enough, when the armies of the West entered the city, they killed every inhabitant they could find.[4] This horrible fact cannot be excused. (We should note here that this kind of atrocity, committed by Catholics in the name of Christ and the Catholic Church, is a sin that the Church deeply regrets and apologizes for. Pope John Paul II has repeatedly asked forgiveness in the name of the Catholic Church for crimes, like this one, committed by Catholics in the name of the Faith.)

After the taking of Jerusalem, garrisons were set up around the Holy Land to protect the area from the inevitable Muslim attacks. Pilgrims were then free to travel to Jerusalem without fear of Muslim oppression, and the

---

[3] Foucher de Chartres, *Histoire des Crois*, as quoted in *The Catholic Encyclopedia*, "Crusades."

[4] Cf. Zoé Oldenbourg, *The Crusades* (New York: Pantheon Books, 1966), 137.

Christian residents of the area were safe from the former Islamic oppression. Despite some truly shameful points along the way, the original intent of the Crusades was an honorable one. Not only that, it was a defensive measure, performed to keep the Muslim majority from slaughtering the Christians in the area and destroying the holy sites. If the West had done nothing, Eastern Christianity would have been eliminated by the Islamic masses.

Good intentions, bad actions

Sadly, though, the original intent of the Crusades was lost on the Crusaders over time. They forgot why they had embarked on this mission in the first place. This became most clear when, in 1204, an army of Crusaders attacked and overtook Constantinople, the then-capital of Eastern Orthodoxy. The city was plundered, the money being split between the armies of the Venetians.[5] Unquestionably, this was one of the darkest days in the history of Christianity, and is a pain that is felt by the Orthodox even to this day. (Catholics should never attempt to deny or sweep under the rug the fact that this and similar sins have been committed by Catholics in the name of the Church. Rather, as a genuine step toward reunion with our Orthodox brothers, we should recognize and grieve with them over these wicked acts, and then seek to heal those old wounds in a spirit of fraternal repentance and forgiveness.)

Pope Innocent III had no part in the attack, nor did he approve when informed of it. It was his desire that the

---

[5] Pernoud, 208–212.

armies would move directly on to the Holy Land without harassing the Orthodox along the way. When he learned of the taking of Constantinople, though, he tried to take advantage of the situation. The pope saw this as an opportunity to install Catholic power in place of the vanquished Orthodox, thereby bringing the residents of the city back to the true Church. For obvious reasons, this attempt was unsuccessful. The residents of the city had only hatred for the Crusaders and their religion.

The impossible dream

Christian control of the Holy Land was doomed from the start. The Crusaders were made up of armies from numerous European countries, each under the rule of a different provincial leader. It's unsurprising, then, that the Crusaders often squabbled and fought amongst themselves. Internal conflict wore down the armies of the West, rendering them impotent in the face of the unending Muslim onslaught.

Finally, after continued Islamic assault, the Christian hold on the Holy Land was lost in July of 1291. There would never again be a significant Christian foothold in the area. There were indeed several Crusades after this point, but their victories were small and short-lived.

A few points about the Crusades need to be made. First, the original intent of this military action was the protection and preservation of Christians in the Holy Land. If you recall, the Muslims were the initiators of the violence. In this way, the Crusades were defensive in nature. However, the noble origins of the Crusades were, at times, ignored.

Instead, personal vendettas were pursued and greed was allowed to hold sway. Additionally, the rage and insanity of warfare gave way to some truly grotesque acts of brutality — things absolutely inexcusable for Christians. However, Jesus did tell us that in the Church, there would be wheat and tares (cf. Matthew 13:24–30). In other words, sinners would stand next to saints in the Faith. It is not our place to try to separate them now; that will be God's job at the end of the age. Nevertheless, we shouldn't be surprised when we see people who claim to be Catholic, and yet perform terrible acts. Jesus said it would happen.

Despite some of the atrocities of the Crusades, there were also some positive aspects. Trade routes between the East and the West were established, helping the citizens of both regions. The West was also exposed to numerous technological advances that had developed in the East. This allowed them to advance dramatically in several scientific disciplines. Most importantly, though, the warfare in the East weakened the Muslim armies significantly, preventing them from an inevitable invasion of the West. Such an invasion would have been absolutely disastrous, very likely resulting in the end of Latin Christianity in Europe.[6] For this last reason alone, it can be said that despite their dark moments, the Crusades were understandable and even necessary.

---

[6] Cf. Louis Bréhier, "Crusades," *The Catholic Encyclopedia* (New York: Robert Appleton Company, 1910), vol. IV, 543 ff.

22

Pope Alexander VI was supremely arrogant and out of line when he imagined he could "divide" the New World between Spain and Portugal. Those lands didn't belong to him or the Catholic Church but to the indigenous peoples who lived there when the explorers arrived.

Pope Alexander VI will very likely never be known as Pope *Saint* Alexander VI. Whether it was his immoral lifestyle or his penchant for nepotism, he was certainly not the holiest pope the Catholic Church has ever had. Nevertheless, that's not to say this pope didn't do some good. As we'll see, he did.

With the discovery of the New World, the Americas were immediate targets for colonization by Portugal and Spain, two dominant powers of the day. As the two nations struggled for control of the newly-found territories, they used the Church as an excuse for their land greed. According to both, they were merely "spreading the gospel" among the inhabitants of the Americas. However, their "evangelization" involved taking over large areas and, in some instances, forcing the indigenous peoples to accept Christianity.

When the pope learned of this, he would have none of it. In the space of four years — from 1493 to 1497 — he released three documents addressing this issue: *Eximiae Devotionis, Inter Caetera* and *Ineffabilis et Summi Patris*. Sadly, these documents have been misunderstood by modern readers, insofar as they seem to divide the New World between Spain and Portugal. Critics charge that, in doing this, the pope was giving away land that didn't belong to him, and was in fact infringing on the rights and property of the peoples who populated the Americas.

It's not what it seems

This criticism, however, misses the mark of what these documents sought to accomplish. Pope Alexander's primary concern wasn't to divide territory between two competing world powers. Rather, his main concern was assigning to Spain and Portugal certain areas in which each would be the primary conveyors of the gospel. It was, in effect, a master plan for evangelizing the New World. His statements in these documents — which are often, today, spoken of as establishing a "line of demarcation," had less to do with property ownership than evangelization. In addition to this fact, the Spanish and the Portuguese were forbidden by the Pope to compel the indigenous peoples to embrace Catholicism. The natives were to be offered the opportunity to do so without coercion. This fact is clear from the pope's letter to King Emmanuel of Portugal, *Ineffabilis et Summi Patris*:

> By the authority granted us by Almighty God in St. Peter and by Apostolic authority, we confirm for you and your

successors dominion over said cities, camps, places, lands and dominions which, as was said before, have had occasion to wish to be subject to you, pay tribute to you and recognize you as their Sovereign.[1]

Notice that the king is granted dominion over those people who "wish to be subject" to him. He may take up lawful dominion, however, as the Pope explains elsewhere, there is to be no coercion or force.

With these documents, Pope Alexander VI not only acted as a restraining force against the land lust of Spain and Portugal, he also made a strong statement regarding the need to respect the rights and free will of the indigenous peoples of the Americas. In a record that is otherwise marred by questionable or outright bad actions, this particular act should stand out as a credit for Pope Alexander.

---

[1] Reprinted in Joel S. Panzer, *The Popes and Slavery* (Staten Island: Alba House, 1996), 14.

23

The pope is grossly hypocritical in his efforts to promote "human rights." The fact is, popes have for centuries profited handsomely from slavery. Popes have owned, bought, and sold slaves. Popes have condoned and even encouraged slavery, especially once European explorers "discovered" and began plundering the "New World" and subjugating its indigenous peoples.

> "Your Holiness, the little matter that brought me here to the furthest edge of your light on earth is now settled. And the Indians are, once again, free to be enslaved by the Spanish and Portuguese settlers."

Those are the words spoken by a Cardinal Altamirano in the movie *The Mission,* as he surveyed the aftermath of his decision to allow the secular powers of Spain and Portugal to have their way with the Indians of Paraguay. Dictating a letter to the pope, the cardinal pauses, decides against that wording, and begins again, this time softening the message and removing the damning words about slavery.

The Mission, starring Robert DeNiro and Jeremy Irons, poses as an accurate account of the situation of the Church

in Paraguay in the eighteenth century. It assures us solemnly
while the final credits are rolling: "The historical events
represented in this story are true." But like most things in
Hollywood, crucial aspects of the "historical events" presented in this movie are pure fiction. And the problem is
that these fictions serve to distort the facts surrounding the
Catholic Church's role in the New World. This movie has
played a major role in shaping popular attitudes in the
West toward the Church and the papacy by portraying the
pope and his quisling emissaries as complicit in the colonial
slave trade.

The stirring music provides a powerful emotional current that runs through the story. The emotional impact of
this movie is strong, hitting you hard with the message that
the white colonial powers, Spain and Portugal, were often
brutal and rapacious in their dealings with the indigenous
peoples of the New World. That much is true, more or
less. The problem is that *The Mission* paints the pope and
his clergy as being squarely in league with the Spanish and
Portuguese slave traders. This part is false.

Unfortunately for this movie's unwary audience, that
isn't the only fabrication passed off as true. In an article critiquing *The Mission*, which was written shortly after
the movie's release, E. Michael Jones offered corrections to
some of the more egregious errors:

> There was a man by the name of Altamirano, but he was
> not a cardinal sent by the pope, he was a Jesuit sent by the
> Jesuits' Superior General in Rome. . . . [He] "represented
> the worst type of court priest. He had been appointed by
> a weak [Jesuit] general to please the King and was given
> absolute authority in all matters concerning the treaty. He
> landed in Montevideo in 1752 along with the Marques de

Valderlirios, the chief boundary commissioner, convinced
that the Paraguay Jesuits were actively opposing the treaty[1]
or at least doing nothing to further its execution. He had
no knowledge of the situation, was too proud to acquaint
himself with it and too imperious to seek advice from his
brethren in the field. When the missionaries pleaded for
time to resettle the Indians, Altamirano interpreted this
as evidence that they were working for a stalemate."[2]

The fact that the real Altamirano was a Jesuit priest, not
a cardinal, was an inconvenient detail for the movie mak-
ers, so they changed it, making him into a Vatican bureau-
crat instead. The movie, as beautiful and moving as it was,
was a propaganda tool for leftist politics in Latin America. It aimed at showing "liberation theology" as the salvation of oppressed people of the Third World. It promoted
an tarnished image of the pope and the Catholic Church
generally as being money-hungry, hypocritical, and utterly
oblivious to human suffering caused by slavery.

The anti-Catholic, anti-European, anti-Capitalist spin

The aftermath of the movie is predictable. "Cardinal"
Altamirano (representing the pope, the movie is at pains to
remind us) sides with the greedy Spanish and Portuguese
slavers, and decides to have the Jesuit *reducciones*, (the rough

---

[1] I.e. Between Spain and Portugal over trade and land ownership
issues.

[2] Jones, quoting here Philip Caraman's *The Lost Paradise* (page 245)
in his article "Mission Impossible: Jesuits At War With the Church"
(*Fidelity*, March 1987, 31).

equivalent of the California Missions) where the newly converted Guaraní Indians lived peaceful, happy lives, destroyed to make way for colonial progress. It does a very effective job of painting the pope as a complete hypocrite: profiting from slavery, but trying to appear aloof from it. This image is wholly false.

At one point, the principal Spanish character, a fat merchant named Don Cabeza, reinforces this illusion, exonerates himself, telling Altamirano with extreme unction:

> Your Eminence! In the territories covered by Spain, there is no slavery. That institution, however, is permitted in the territories of our excellent neighbors, the Portuguese, and is, to my mind, much misunderstood. But in *Spanish* territory, we conduct our plantations in strict accordance with the laws of Spain and the precepts of the Church.

As a propaganda tool, *The Mission* slips here, and actually reveals something critical about the truth behind this Hollywood illusion. The Catholic Church did indeed condemn slavery, otherwise the fictional Don Cabeza would not have been in such haste to point out that Spain observed "in strict accordance . . . with the precepts of the Church."

But our intention here is not pick apart the flaws of *The Mission*. Rather, it's to point out how powerful the media is in its ability to shape and perpetuate negative attitudes toward the papacy.

So what did the popes really say?

The fact is Pope Benedict XIV, who reigned from 1740 to 1758, the time in which *The Mission* is set, issued a strenuous attack on slavery in his 1741 apostolic letter *Immensa Pastorum*. Later, he wrote *Vix Prevenit*, a letter to the Italian clergy warning of the dangers of usury and dishonest profit. He says:

> [I]f everything is done correctly and weighed in the scales of justice, these same legitimate contracts suffice to provide a standard and a principle for engaging in commerce and fruitful business for the common good. Christian minds should not think that gainful commerce can flourish by usuries *or other similar injustices*. On the contrary We learn from divine Revelation that justice raises up nations; sin, however, makes nations miserable.[3]

Can it be shown that the popes condemned slavery at all times? Did they work, using the weight of their office, to eradicate the practice? These are important questions. The *Catechism of the Catholic Church* echoes the age-old teaching of the popes on slavery:

> The seventh commandment forbids acts or enterprises that for any reason — selfish or ideological, commercial, or totalitarian — lead to the enslavement of human beings, to their being bought, sold and exchanged like merchandise, in disregard for their personal dignity. It is a sin against the dignity of persons and their fundamental rights to reduce them by violence to their productive value or to a source of profit.[4]

The Catholic Church's stance toward racial slavery has always been condemnatory. Though there are different forms of slavery, and though many Catholics over the cen-

---

[3] Par. 4.
[4] CCC 2414, cf. Philemon 16.

turies have been involved in it, the popes have always condemned it.

Certainly, there *is* a kind of slavery described and even permitted in the Old Testament. However, this form could best be described as indentured servitude, not slavery in the sense that we today understand the term. This kind of indentured servitude was tightly circumscribed by God, and governed by numerous safeguards designed to uphold the welfare of the servant (cf. Exodus 21:1–11; Deuteronomy 15:12–18).

When the Romans took control of Palestine, they imposed their own form of slavery on the culture. It stood without the positive elements of the Old Testament model; slaves were treated with contempt. Often abused by their masters, their lot was a tragic one. This is the setting in which Jesus and the Apostles spoke in the New Testament. It's often noted that while they didn't endorse the practice of slavery, they did at least allow for it. Peter, for example, gave instructions for slaves to mind their masters, so that their passivity and peacefulness could be a witness to others (cf. 1 Peter 2:18–20).

While the Apostles did indeed allow for the ancient form of slavery, they didn't necessarily approve of the practice; it was a mere cultural reality they had to deal with. In his letter to Philemon, Paul attempts to secure safety for a runaway slave returning to his master. At the end of the letter, however, the Apostle drops a hint that Philemon should "do even more" than he commands — a transparent implication that Philemon should free his slave (cf. Philemon 21).[5]

---

[5] Interestingly, the condemnation of racial slavery is something taught

Things get worse, the popes get tougher

But the already tragic history of slavery was to take a much darker turn in the fifteenth century, with the "discovery" of the New World. The powers of Europe, specifically Spain and Portugal, made haste to enslave the indigenous peoples they encountered in these new lands. Far from endorsing this heinous practice, as anti-Catholics claim, Rome was steadfastly and vocally against it. In fact, in 1435, almost sixty years before Christopher Columbus landed in the Americas, Pope Eugene IV issued a scathing attack on slavery in his papal bull *Sicut Dudum*. In this document, he addressed the situation that was developing in the newly-colonized Canary Islands. He stated in unambiguous terms:

> [The colonists] have deprived the natives of their property or turned it to their own use, and have subjected some of the inhabitants of said islands to perpetual slavery, sold them to other persons and committed other various illicit and evil deeds against them. . .Therefore We. . .exhort, through the sprinkling of the Blood of Jesus Christ shed for their sins, one and all, temporal princes, lords, captains, armed men, barons, soldiers, nobles, communities and all others of every kind among the Christian faithful of whatever state, grade or condition, that they themselves desist from the aforementioned deeds, cause those subject to them to desist from them, and restrain them rigorously. And no less do we order and command all and each of

---

by the Catholic Church as part of Sacred Tradition — Scripture doesn't contain such a prohibiion. Protestants agree with Catholics that slavery is wrong, but they have received this Christian teaching from Tradition — not from Scripture. The understanding that slavery is wrong is embedded in natural law (cf. Jer. 31:33, Heb. 8:10).

the faithful of each sex that, within the space of fifteen days of the publication of these letters in the place where they live, that they restore to their earlier liberty all and each person of either sex who were once residents of said Canary Islands. . .who have been made subject to slavery. These people are to be totally and perpetually free and are to be let go without the exaction of any money. If this is not done, when the fifteen days have passed, *they incur the sentence of excommunication* ipso facto.[6]

Notice that the keeping of taking of slaves by Catholics involves an immediate, automatic excommunication. This is serious business, and the pope was deadly serious in his effort to wipe out the evil practice. Happily, the popes made their case against slavery in the clearest possible terms. Rather than paraphrase what the popes said, it's well worth letting them condemn slavery in their own words. Read on and see what the popes said about the institution of slavery and the slave trade. Judge for yourself if this pope fiction — that the papacy encouraged and profited from slavery — has any inkling of truth behind it.

A *stinging rebuke*

On May 29, 1537, Pope Paul III released *Sublimis Deus,* another powerful condemnation of slavery. The letter is worth quoting here in his entirety:

To all faithful Christians to whom this writing may come, health in Christ our Lord and the apostolic benediction, The Sublime God so loved the human race that He cre-

---

[6]Quoted in Joel Panzer, *The Popes and Slavery,* 77-78, emphasis added.

ated man in such wise that he might participate, not only in the good that other creatures enjoy, but endowed him with capacity to attain to the inaccessible and invisible Supreme Good and behold it face to face; and since man, according to the testimony of the sacred Scriptures, has been created to enjoy eternal life and happiness, which none may obtain save through faith in our Lord Jesus Christ, it is necessary that he should possess the nature and faculties enabling him to receive that faith; and that whoever is thus endowed should be capable of receiving that same faith. Nor is it credible that any one should possess so little understanding as to desire the faith and yet be destitute of the most necessary faculty to enable him to receive it. Hence Christ, who is the Truth itself, that has never failed and can never fail, said to the preachers of the faith whom He chose for that office "Go ye and teach all nations." He said all, without exception, for all are capable of receiving the doctrines of the faith.

The enemy of the human race, who opposes all good deeds in order to bring men to destruction, beholding and envying this, invented a means never before heard of, by which he might hinder the preaching of God's word of Salvation to the people: he inspired his satellites who, to please him, have not hesitated to publish abroad that the Indians of the West and the South, and other people of whom We have recent knowledge should be treated as dumb brutes created for our service, pretending that they are incapable of receiving the Catholic Faith.

We, who, though unworthy, exercise on earth the power of our Lord and seek with all our might to bring those sheep of His flock who are outside into the fold committed to our charge, consider, however, that the Indians are truly men and that they are not only capable of understanding the Catholic Faith but, according to our information, they desire exceedingly to receive it. Desiring to provide ample remedy for these evils, We define and declare by these Our letters, or by any translation thereof signed by any notary public and sealed with the seal of any ecclesiastical dignitary, to which the same credit shall be given as to the originals, that, notwithstanding whatever may have been or may be said to the contrary, the said Indians and all other people who may later be discovered by Christians, are by no means to be deprived of their liberty or the possession of their property, even though they be outside the faith of Jesus Christ; and that they may and should, freely and legitimately, enjoy their liberty and the possession of their property; nor should they be in any way enslaved; should the contrary happen, it shall be null and have no effect.

The Popes leave no wiggle room for slavery

The Holy Father continues:

By virtue of Our apostolic authority We define and declare by these present letters, or by any translation thereof signed by any notary public and sealed with the seal of any ecclesiastical dignitary, which shall thus command the same obedience as the originals, that the said Indians and other peoples should be converted to the faith of Jesus Christ by preaching the word of God and by the example of good and holy living.

The pope wasn't merely condemning the enslavement of Christians, but the enslavement of *anyone*, including all those "outside the Faith."

Some have accused Pope Paul III of being inconsistent, claiming he later endorsed slavery in the city of Rome itself. This is an unfortunate misunderstanding of the facts. The alleged "slavery" he tolerated for a time involved the internment in Rome of Turkish prisoners of war.[7] This was the indentured servitude model of slavery described and allowed in the Bible, and it was a temporary arrangement. Furthermore, the whole concept of prisoners, whether criminals or combatants captured in war, being confined to a work camp is nothing new. The United States and virtually all democratic Western countries (not to mention the rest of the world) have exactly that kind of forced labor at their disposal. There's nothing illegal or immoral about forcing criminals or prisoners of war to work during their internment.

And the beat goes on . . .

Back to the popes. In 1741, Pope Benedict XIV continued the Catholic tradition of opposing and condemning slavery by issuing *Immensa Pastorum*:

> Let it be known that each and every person, both secular and ecclesiastic of whatever status, sex, grade, condition and dignity, even those worthy of special note and dignity, of any Order, Congregation, Society (even the Society of Jesus), Religion, Mendicant and non-Mendicant, monks, Regulars, as well as the Military Brotherhood, even the Hospitalers of St. John of Jerusalem, who contravenes these edicts will incur, *ipso facto*, excommunication *latae sententiae* . . . Those incur this penalty who reduce said Indians to slavery, sell them, buy them, exchange them or give them away, separate them from their wives and

---

[7] Ibid., 27–28.

children, despoil them of their property and goods, lead
or transmit them to other places, or in any manner deprive them of liberty to retain them in servitude; as well
as those who offer counsel, aid or favor to those who do
such things.

On December 3, 1839, Pope Gregory XVI issued his apostolic letter *In Supremo Apostolatus*, in which he condemned
both slavery and the slave trade. He begins by outlining the
theological reasons why all Christians should be opposed
to slavery, but is also candid about the fact that, over the
centuries, there had been many Catholics who owned and
traded in slaves. This sad fact is something Pope Gregory
was willing to include in his letter, not because he sought
to excuse such actions, but rather because he wanted to use
it as a tragic reminder that would impel Christians to shun
slavery. The pontiff also points out the various holy individuals and even religious communities of men that were
formed for the special mission of redeeming the captives
from slavery:

> There were not lacking Christians, who, moved by an
> ardent charity "cast themselves into bondage in order to
> redeem others," many instances of which our predecessor,
> Clement I, of very holy memory, declares to have come
> to his knowledge.

Profiteers beware!

Then the pope turns his guns on the slave traders (including Catholic slave traders), those who made their vast
fortunes buying and selling men, women and children into
the oblivion of slavery.

In the process of time, the fog of pagan superstition being more completely dissipated and the manners of barbarous people having been softened, thanks to faith operating by charity, it at last comes about that, since several centuries, there are no more slaves in the greater number of Christian nations. But — We say with profound sorrow — there were to be found afterwards among the Faithful men who, shamefully blinded by the desire of sordid gain, in lonely and distant countries, did not hesitate to reduce to slavery Indians, Negroes and other wretched peoples, or else, by instituting or developing the trade in those who had been made slaves by others, to favor their unworthy practice.

The pope reiterates the fact that the papacy has always opposed slavery. He even gives a series of specific popes as examples:

Certainly many Roman Pontiffs of glorious memory, Our Predecessors, did not fail, according to the duties of their charge, to blame severely this way of acting as dangerous for the spiritual welfare of those engaged in the traffic and a shame to the Christian name; they foresaw that as a result of this, the infidel peoples would be more and more strengthened in their hatred of the true Religion.

It is at these practices that are aimed the Letter Apostolic of Paul III, given on May 29, 1537, under the seal of the Fisherman, and addressed to the Cardinal Archbishop of Toledo, and afterwards another Letter, more detailed, addressed by Urban VIII on April 22, 1639 to the *Collector Jurium* of the Apostolic Chamber of Portugal. In the latter are severely and particularly condemned those who should dare 'to reduce to slavery the Indians of the Eastern and Southern Indies,' to sell them, buy them, exchange them or give them, separate them from their wives and chil-

dren, despoil them of their goods and properties, conduct
or transport them into other regions, or deprive them of
liberty in any way whatsoever, retain them in servitude,
or lend counsel, succor, favor and cooperation to those so
acting, under no matter what pretext or excuse, or who
proclaim and teach that this way of acting is allowable
and cooperate in any manner whatever in the practices
indicated.

Benedict XIV confirmed and renewed the penalties of
the Popes above mentioned in a new Apostolic Letter addressed on December 20, 1741,[8] to the Bishops of Brazil
and some other regions, in which he stimulated, to the
same end, the solicitude of the Governors themselves. Another of Our Predecessors, anterior to Benedict XIV, Pius
II, as during his life the power of the Portuguese was extending itself over New Guinea, sent on October 7, 1462,
to a Bishop who was leaving for that country, a letter in
which he not only gives the Bishop himself the means of
exercising there the sacred ministry with more fruit, but on
the same occasion, addresses grave warnings with regard
to Christians who should reduce neophytes to slavery.

In our time, Pius VII, moved by the same religious and
charitable spirit as his Predecessors, intervened zealously
with those in possession of power to secure that the slave
trade should at least cease amongst the Christians. The
penalties imposed and the care given by Our Predecessors contributed in no small measure, with the help of
God, to protect the Indians and the other people mentioned against the cruelty of the invaders or the cupidity
of Christian merchants, without however carrying success
to such a point that the Holy See could rejoice over the
complete success of its efforts in this direction; for the

---

[8] I.e., *Immensa Pastorum*.

slave trade, although it has diminished in more than one district, is still practiced by numerous Christians.

This is why, desiring to remove such a shame from all the Christian nations, having fully reflected over the whole question and having taken the advice of many of Our Venerable Brothers the Cardinals of the Holy Roman Church, and walking in the footsteps of Our Predecessors, We warn and adjure earnestly in the Lord faithful Christians of every condition that no one in the future dare to vex anyone, despoil him of his possessions, reduce to servitude, or lend aid and favor to those who give themselves up to these practices, or exercise that inhuman traffic by which the Blacks, as if they were not men but rather animals, having been brought into servitude, in no matter what way, are, without any distinction, in contempt of the rights of justice and humanity, bought, sold, and devoted sometimes to the hardest labor. Further, in the hope of gain, propositions of purchase being made to the first owners of the Blacks, dissensions and almost perpetual conflicts are aroused in these regions.

We reprove, then, by virtue of Our Apostolic Authority, all the practices above mentioned as absolutely unworthy of the Christian name. *By the same Authority We prohibit and strictly forbid any Ecclesiastic or lay person from presuming to defend as permissible this traffic in Blacks under no matter what pretext or excuse, or from publishing or teaching in any manner whatsoever, in public or privately, opinions contrary to what We have set forth in this Apostolic Letter.*[9]

---

[9] The entire English text of *In Supremo Apostolatus* is available at the New Advent Supersite: www.knight.org/advent.

"An evil institution"

In 1890, Pope Leo XIII issued *Catholicae Ecclesiae*, which sought to eliminate entirely the last vestiges of slavery in countries around the world (slavery was in decline already, and the pope wanted to extinguish it permanently). Calling slavery an "evil institution" and a "shameful" and "base dealing," he repeated the traditional teachings of his predecessors. The enslavement of another human went against the dignity which each person has as a creation of God. Once again, the Roman Pontiff was reiterating Catholic teaching, and aiming it precisely at the section of the globe where the slave trade was still in full swing. Again, the document is worth quoting at length to feel the full weight of the pope's opposition to slavery.

To the Catholic Missionaries in Africa. The maternal love of the Catholic Church embraces all people. As you know, venerable brother, *the Church from the beginning sought to completely eliminate slavery*, whose wretched yoke has oppressed many people. It is the industrious guardian of the teachings of its Founder who, by His words and those of the apostles, taught men the fraternal necessity which unites the whole world. From Him we recall that everybody has sprung from the same source, was redeemed by the same ransom, and is called to the same eternal happiness. He assumed the neglected cause of the slaves and showed Himself the strong champion of freedom. Insofar as time and circumstances allowed, He gradually and moderately accomplished His goal. Of course, pressing constantly with prudence and planning, He showed what He was striving for in the name of religion, justice, and humanity. In this way He put national prosperity and civilization in general into His debt. *This zeal of the Church for liberating the slaves has not languished with the passage of time; on the contrary, the more it bore fruit, the more eagerly it glowed.*

A reminder of the facts of history

There are incontestable historical documents which attest to that fact, documents which commended to posterity the names of many of Our predecessors. Among them St. Gregory the Great, Hadrian I, Alexander III, Innocent III, Gregory IX, Pius II, Leo X, Paul III, Urban VIII, Benedict XIV, Pius VII, and Gregory XVI stand out. *They applied every effort to eliminate the institution of slavery wherever it existed.* They also took care lest the seeds of slavery return to those places from which this evil institution had been cut away.

We could not repudiate such a laudable inheritance. For this reason, *We have taken every occasion to openly condemn this gloomy plague of slavery.* We worked toward this goal in a letter sent to the bishops of Brazil on May 5, 1888. In it We rejoiced over their exemplary accomplishments, both private and public, in the area of emancipation. At the same time We showed how much slavery opposes religion and human dignity.

While writing, We were deeply moved by the plight of those who are subject to the mastery of another. We were bitterly afflicted by accounts of the trials which harass all the inhabitants of the African interior. How horrible it is to recall that almost four hundred thousand Africans of every age and sex are forcefully taken away each year from their villages! Bound and beaten, they are transported to a foreign land, put on display, and sold like cattle. These eyewitness reports have been confirmed by recent explorers to equatorial Africa, arousing Our desire to help those wretched men and to alleviate their lamentable condition.

At this point, the pope explains that the main mission and goal of the Church in every age and on every continent is to evangelize. He reminds the Church of the importance of Catholic missionaries bringing the gospel of Jesus Christ to the peoples of the African continent, many of who had still never encountered Christ. Some of these missions, he explains, had been established specifically for the purpose of eradicating slavery. Then he outlines the practical ways the Church will both expand its missionary efforts as well as combat slavery.

> The money collected in the churches and chapels under your jurisdiction should be sent to Rome, to the Sacred Council for the Propagation of the Faith. It will divide the money among the missions which now exist or will be *established primarily to eliminate slavery in Africa.* The money coming from those countries which have their own Catholic missions to free the slaves, as We mentioned, will be given to sustain and help those missions.

Pius X said it long before Malcolm X said it

In 1912, Pope St. Pius X issued *Lacrimabile Statu,* yet another condemnation of slavery of the indigenous people of Latin America:

> Pope Benedict [XIV] complained that although the Apostolic See had done much, and for a long time, to relieve their afflicted fortunes, there were even the "men of the orthodox faith who, as if they had utterly forgotten all

sense of the charity poured forth in our hearts by the
Holy Ghost, presumed to reduce the wretched Indians,
without the light of faith, and even those who had been
washed in the laver of regeneration, to servitude, or to sell
them as slaves to others, or to deprive them of their property, and to treat them with such inhumanity that they
were thus greatly hindered from embracing the Christian
faith, and most strongly moved to regard it with abhor-
rence." It is true that soon afterwards the worst of these
indignities — that is to say, slavery, properly so called —
was, by the goodness of the merciful God, abolished; and
to this public abolition of slavery in Brazil and in other
regions the excellent men who governed those Republics
were greatly moved and encouraged by the maternal care
and insistence of the Church. And we gladly acknowledge
that if it had not been for many and great obstacles that
stood in the way, their plans would have had far greater
success. Nevertheless, though much has thus been done
for the Indians, there is much more that still remains to
be done. And, indeed, when we consider the crimes and
outrages still committed against them, our heart is filled
with horror, and we are moved to great compassion for
its most unhappy race. For what can be so cruel and so
barbarous as to scourge men and brand them with hot
iron, often for most trivial causes, often for a mere lust
of cruelty; or, having suddenly overthrown them, to slay
hundreds or thousands in one unceasing massacre; or to
waste villages and districts and slaughter the inhabitants,
so that some tribes, as we understand, have become extinct
in these last few years? . . .

And now, in order that what you shall do for the benefit of the Indians, whether of your own accord or at our
exhortation, may be the more efficacious by the help of
our Apostolic authority, we, mindful of the example of

our aforesaid predecessor, condemn and declare guilty of grave crime whosoever, as he [Pope Benedict] says, 'shall dare to presume to reduce the said Indians to slavery, to sell them, to buy them, to exchange or give them, to separate them from their wives and children, to deprive them of goods and chattels, to transport or send them to other places, or in any way whatsoever to rob them of freedom and hold them in slavery; or to give counsel, help, favor, and work on any pretext of color to them that do these things, or to preach or teach that it is lawful, or to cooperate therewith in any way whatever.' Accordingly, we will that the power of absolving penitents in the sacramental tribunal from these crimes shall be reserved to ordinaries of the localities.

A consistent track record

An interesting and often overlooked fact is that each of these various papal statements (as well as others not quoted here) includes the pointed reminder that the Catholic Church has *always* vigorously condemned slavery. If that had been a lie or an exaggeration, you can be absolutely sure that the Church's many foes across Europe and the U.S., religious and secular (especially the slave merchants, who had the most to lose from Catholic interference), would have pounced on it. They would have worked hard to show that at some point in its history, the papacy did indeed practice or support slavery. But that sort of rebuttal is conspicuously absent from the arguments raised by Catholic critics each time a pope issued another attack on slavery. Why? Because even her opponents knew the Church's track record against slavery.

While countries everywhere practiced racial slavery, pope after pope condemned the practice as inhuman and unchristian. When some Spanish and Portuguese colonists oppressed and enslaved the indigenous peoples of the Americas, the popes worked against them to bring that atrocity to an end. While Protestant countries such as England and the United States were deeply engaged in domestic slavery and international slave trading, the Catholic Church was speaking out repeatedly to condemn and eradicate the practice. Indeed, the popes have always been champions of human rights, whether as foes of slavery, abortion, forced sterilization, racial intolerance and other evils committed against human dignity, or as defenders of the aged and infirm, the sanctity of the family, and the rights of the working man.

What other institution besides the Catholic Church can claim such a record?

24

Pope Sixtus IV instituted the Spanish Inquisition because he, like many other popes who shared his prejudices, hated Jews, Muslims, and Protestants.

The Catholic Church did not "invent" the inquisition. God Himself did. He imposed on Moses the duty of conducting an inquisition to ferret out and punish those Israelites who had defiled themselves by worshipping the false gods of the pagans (cf. Numbers 25). Similarly, a religious inquisition was commanded by the Lord to be carried out on an ongoing, as needed, basis to "purge the evil from your midst" when there occurred crimes such as sorcery and idolatry, the "heresies" of the People of Israel:

God said:

> If there is found among you, in any one of the communities which the Lord, your God, gives you, a man or a woman who does evil in the sight of the Lord, your God, and transgresses his covenant, by serving other gods, or by worshipping the sun or the moon or any of the host of the sky, against my command; and if, on being informed of it, you find by careful investigation that it is true and an established fact that this abomination has been committed in Israel, you shall bring the man (or woman) who has done the evil deed out to your city gates and stone him to

death. The testimony of two or three witnesses is required for putting a person to death. No one shall be put to death on the testimony of only one witness.[1]

We can see in that passage the essential elements of an inquisition: a) If there is reason to believe that a member of the community is secretly practicing false or heretical religion, you must punish him. b) You must "carefully investigate" the person under suspicion to verify if the charge is true. c) There must be a trial in which witnesses and testimony are brought forth. d) If the person is found to be guilty of this religious crime (i.e., whether guilt has been proved by the "established facts" of the case), the death penalty is to be imposed. And finally, e) this inquisition and punishment is meted out in order to protect the community from being contaminated by the contagion of idolatry and heresy.

An aversion to coercion in the early Church

For roughly the first five centuries, Christians were virtually unanimous in their opposition to the use of force to quell religious problems. The early Church Fathers who commented on the subject typically condemned the use of force in these matters. And that attitude is not surprising, given the fact that for the first three centuries, the Church herself was the object of violent religious persecution. But this attitude began to change once the Church had been established and closely aligned with the state. St. Augustine himself was initially opposed to the force of law being used

---

[1] Deuteronomy 17:2–7.

to deal with heretics, but gradually changed his mind on the subject. Toward the end of his life, he actually recommended that the state deal harshly with Donatist heretics.[2]

Times change, but the Catholic position hasn't

The desire to avoid even the appearance of coercion in the area of religion and personal belief is still very much at the heart of the Catholic Church (cf. Vatican II's decree on religious liberty). There is no fundamental difference between what the early Church believed on this point and what the Church teaches today. Furthermore, even during the eras that saw the use of the Inquisition, the Church

---

[2] "St. Augustine, on the contrary, was still opposed to the use of force, and tried to lead back the erring by means of instruction; at most he admitted the imposition of a moderate fine for refractory persons. Finally, however, he changed his views, whether moved thereto by the incredible excesses of the Circumcellions or by the good results achieved by the use of force, or favoring force through the persuasions of other bishops. Apropos of his apparent inconsistency it is well to note carefully whom he is addressing. He appears to speak in one way to government officials, who wanted the existing laws carried out to their fullest extent, and in another to the Donatists, who denied to the State any right of punishing dissenters. In his correspondence with state officials he dwells on Christian charity and toleration, and represents the heretics as straying lambs, to be sought out and perhaps, if recalcitrant chastised with rods and frightened with threats of severer but not to be driven back to the fold by means of rack and sword. On the other hand, in his writings against the Donatists he upholds the rights of the State: sometimes, he says, a salutary severity would be to the interest of the erring ones themselves and likewise protective of true believers and the community at large" (Joseph Blötzer, "Inquisition," *The Catholic Encyclopedia*, vol. VIII, 27.)

hadn't changed its stance. What was different in those days was the nature of the social order in Europe. All the kingdoms and states in Europe during the late middle ages, and until the Reformation, were thoroughly Catholic. The state so identified itself with the Catholic faith, that religious heresy took on a completely different meaning than it would today or as it did during the time of the early Church. Conditions were so different during the time of the Inquisitions that it can be very difficult for modern-day Catholics and non-Catholics to imagine a situation in which heresy was regarded as a civil crime. It seems strange to us now, but this matter was seen very differently in those days.

By the late middle ages, the Church and state throughout Europe had become so closely aligned that a heretical attack on the Church was perceived by the state to be an attack on society itself. By the time we get to the Spanish Inquisition, the most notorious of the several that were carried out, the religious attacks arrayed against the Catholic Church had taken on a martial quality. Now, as never before, religions such as Islam and Protestantism had the muscle of armies and navies behind them. The threat they posed to the Church wasn't just theological — they could back up that threat with force of arms. And that's exactly what happened in fifteenth-century Spain to prompt the establishment of the Inquisition there.

Defining our terms

What exactly was the Inquisition and how did it come about? One expert explained it this way:

By this term [Inquisition] is usually meant a special ecclesiastical institution for combating or suppressing heresy.
Its characteristic mark seems to be the bestowal on special
judges of judicial powers in matters of faith, and this by
supreme ecclesiastical authority, not temporal or for individual cases, but as a universal and permanent office. . . .
The pope did not establish the [medieval] Inquisition as a
distinct and separate tribunal; what he did was to appoint
special but permanent judges, who executed their doctrinal functions in the name of the pope.

Where they sat, there was the Inquisition. It must be
carefully noted that the characteristic feature of the Inquisition was not its peculiar procedure, nor the secret
examination of witnesses and consequent official indictment: this procedure was common to all courts from the
time of [Pope] Innocent III. Nor was it the pursuit of
heretics in all places: this had been the rule since the Imperial Synod of Verona under Lucius III and Frederick
Barbarossa. Nor again was it the torture, which was not
prescribed or even allowed for decades after the beginning of the Inquisition, nor, finally, the various sanctions,
imprisonment, confiscation, the stake, etc., all of which
punishments were usual long before the Inquisition. The
Inquisitor, strictly speaking, was a special but permanent
judge, acting in the name of the pope and clothed by him
with the right and the duty to deal legally with offenses
against the Faith; he had, however, to adhere to the established rules of canonical procedure and pronounce the
customary penalties.[3]

---

[3] Blötzer, 26.

The enemy of my friend is my enemy

The purpose of the Inquisitions was to protect the Church and state from the danger of heresy. This concept seems bizarre to us now, mainly because we live in a pluralistic society that maintains the posture of allowing all sorts of religious and philosophical systems to coexist and thrive. The United States, for example, was established largely on the principles of equality (I say "largely," because on issues pertaining to race, *inequality* was the institutional position) that sprang from a rejection of the religious turmoil of Europe. Protestant settlers, such as the Pilgrims, wanted to get far away from the inquisitions and persecutions they suffered at the hands of other Protestants, especially those in England.

Before the Protestant Reformation erupted, Europe was entirely Catholic. There was no enforced separation of Church and state the way we know it in the U.S. today. Catholicism was part of the very fabric of society, regardless of the country in which one lived. It was the glue that held medieval European society together. That's why, when the Church was attacked by a heresy (such as the medieval heresies of Catharism and that of the Waldensians), the state perceived *itself* to be under attack as well.

If the Church were thrown into turmoil by a heresy, that meant that all the citizens of the realm were in turmoil, which meant that society, indeed the government itself was in danger. Consequently, the state and Church acted aggressively to repel and extinguish such threats. The two main tools used by all governments in those days to combat crime were torture and capital punishment.

Protestant Inquisitions?

The *Catholic Encyclopedia* explains that

As regards the character of these punishments, it should be considered that they were the natural expression not only of the legislative power, but also of the popular hatred for heresy in an age that dealt both vigorously and roughly with criminals of every type. The heretic, in a word, was simply an outlaw whose offense, in the popular mind, deserved and sometimes received a punishment as summary as that which is often dealt out in our own day by an infuriated populace to the authors of justly detested crimes. That such intolerance was not peculiar to Catholicism, but was the natural accompaniment of deep religious conviction in those, also, who abandoned the Church, is evident from the measures taken by some of the Reformers against those who differed from them in matters of belief. As the learned [Protestant] Dr. Schaff declares in his *History of the Christian Church* (vol. V, New York, 1907, 524),

> To the great humiliation of the Protestant churches, religious intolerance and even persecution unto death were continued long after the Reformation. In Geneva the pernicious theory was put into practice by state and church, even to the use of torture and the admission of the testimony of children against their parents, and with the sanction of Calvin. Bullinger, in the second Helvetic Confession, announced the principle that heresy could be punished like murder or treason.

Moreover, the whole history of the Penal Laws against Catholics in England and Ireland, and the spirit of intolerance prevalent in many of the American colonies during the seventeenth and eighteenth centuries may be cited in proof thereof. It would obviously be absurd to make the Protestant religion as such responsible for these practices. But having set up the principle of private judgment, which, logically applied, made heresy impossible, the early Reformers proceeded to treat dissidents as the medieval heretics had been treated. To suggest that this was inconsistent is trivial in view of the deeper insight it affords into the meaning of a tolerance which is often only theoretical and the source of that intolerance which men rightly show towards error, and which they naturally though not rightly, transfer to the erring.[4]

The practice of punishing, even executing, heretics was not unique to Catholics during the era of the Inquisitions. Even Protestants regularly meted out death sentences to their theological foes. Clearly, this fact in no way mitigates, much less excuses any Catholic atrocities that were committed in the name of Christ and the papacy, but it does put the whole tragic issue into clearer perspective.

Many imagine that the Catholic Church was alone in carrying out inquisitions. This notion is false. One of the most noted examples of Protestant inquisitions and subsequent executions for "heresy" is the case of John Calvin and Michael Servetus. In 1553 Calvin had Servetus, a fellow Protestant, arrested on charges of heresy. After a sham trial, Servetus was convicted, and Calvin ordered him to be burned at the stake for his crime. Servetus wasn't the only one who suffered such punishment at the hand of Protestant inquisitors such as Calvin.

Historian William Barry provides a glimpse into a few

---

[4] Blötzer, 36.

episodes in which Protestant Reformers punished men who
dared to disagree with their interpretations of Scripture:

> In November, 1552, the Council declared that Calvin's *In-
> stitutes* were a "holy doctrine which no man might speak
> against." Thus the State [i.e. the Protestant government in
> Geneva] issued dogmatic decrees, the force of which had
> been anticipated earlier, as when Jacques Gouet was im-
> prisoned on charges of impiety in June, 1547, and after se-
> vere torture was beheaded in July. Some of the accusations
> brought against the unhappy young man were frivolous,
> others doubtful. What share, if any, Calvin took in this
> judgment is not easy to ascertain. The execution, how-
> ever must be laid at his door; it has given greater offense
> by far than the banishment of Castellio or the penalties
> inflicted on Bolsec — moderate men opposed to extreme
> views in discipline and doctrine, who fell under suspi-
> cion as reactionary. The Reformer did not shrink from
> his self-appointed task. Within five years *fifty-eight sen-
> tences of death*[5] and seventy-six of exile, besides numerous
> committals of the most eminent citizens to prison, took
> place in Geneva. The iron yoke could not be shaken off.
> In 1555, under Ami Perrin, a sort of revolt was attempted.
> No blood was shed, but Perrin lost the day, and Calvin's
> theocracy triumphed.

"I am more deeply scandalized," wrote [the historian]
Gibbon "at the single execution of [Michael] Servetus than
at the hecatombs which have blazed in the [Catholic] autos-
da-fé of Spain and Portugal". He ascribes the enmity of
Calvin to personal malice and perhaps envy. The facts of
the case are pretty well ascertained. Born in 1511, perhaps
at Tudela, Michael Served y Reves studied at Toulouse and
was present in Bologna at the coronation of Charles V. He

---

[5] Emphasis added.

traveled in Germany and brought out in 1531 at Hagenau his treatise *De Trinitatis Erroribus*, a strong Unitarian work which made much commotion among the more orthodox Reformers.

He met Calvin and disputed with him at Paris in 1534, became corrector of the press at Lyons; gave attention to medicine, discovered the lesser circulation of the blood, and entered into a fatal correspondence with the dictator of Geneva touching a new volume *Christianismi Restitutio*, which he intended to publish. In 1546 the exchange of letters ceased. The Reformer called Servetus arrogant (he had dared to criticize the *Institutes* in marginal glosses), and uttered the significant menace, "If he comes here and I have any authority, I will never let him leave the place alive." The *Restitutio* appeared in 1553. Calvin at once had its author delated to the Dominican inquisitor Ory at Lyons, sending on to him the man's letters of 1545-46 and these glosses. Hereupon the Spaniard was imprisoned at Vienne, but he escaped by friendly connivance, and was burnt there only in effigy.

Some extraordinary fascination drew him to Geneva, from which he intended to pass the Alps. He arrived on 13 August, 1553. The next day Calvin, who had remarked [on] him at the sermon, got his critic arrested, the preacher's own secretary coming forward to accuse him. Calvin drew up forty articles of charge under three heads, concerning the nature of God, infant baptism, and the attack which Servetus had ventured on his own teaching. The council hesitated before taking a deadly decision, but the dictator, reinforced by Farel, drove them on. In prison the culprit suffered much and loudly complained. The Bernese and other Swiss voted for some indefinite penalty. But to Calvin his power in Geneva seemed lost, while the stigma of heresy; as he insisted, would cling to all Protestants, if

this innovator were not put to death. "Let the world see"
Bullinger counseled him, "that Geneva wills the glory of
Christ."

Accordingly, sentence was pronounced 26 October, 1553,
of burning at the stake. "Tomorrow he dies," wrote Calvin
to Farel. When the deed was done, the Reformer alleged
that he had been anxious to mitigate the punishment, but
of this fact no record appears in the documents. He disputed with Servetus on the day of execution and saw the
end. A defense and apology next year received the ad-
hesion of the Genevan ministers. Melanchthon, who had
taken deep umbrage at the blasphemies of the Spanish
Unitarian, strongly approved in well-known words. But a
group that included Castellio published at Basle in 1554 a
pamphlet with the title, "Should heretics be persecuted?"
It is considered the first plea for toleration in modern
times. Beza replied by an argument for the affirmative,
couched in violent terms; and Calvin, whose favorite disciple he was, translated it into French in 1559. The dialogue, "Vaticanus", written against the "Pope of Geneva"
by Castellio, did not get into print until 1612. Freedom of
opinion, as Gibbon remarks, "was the consequence rather
than the design of the Reformation."

Another victim to [Calvin's] fiery zeal was Gentile, one
of an Italian sect in Geneva, which also numbered among
its adherents Alciati and Gribaldo. As more or less Unitarian in their views, they were required to sign a confession drawn up by Calvin in 1558. Gentile subscribed
it reluctantly, but in the upshot he was condemned and
imprisoned as a perjurer. He escaped only to be twice incarcerated at Berne, where in 1566, he was beheaded.[6]

---

[6] William Barry, "John Calvin," *The Catholic Encyclopedia* (New
York: Robert Appleton Co., 1908), vol. 3, 197.

So with all of that information in mind, and recognizing that the idea of an inquisition was not at all foreign to European society for the last thousand years, let's look more closely at the Spanish Inquisition in particular and see why it's useless as an argument against papal infallibility.

The so-called "Black Legend" of the Spanish Inquisition, like most of the other pope fictions, must be examined in its historical context to get a full understanding of what really went on.

Fifteenth-century Spain was a kingdom (actually, several allied kingdoms) threatened by powerful outside forces. The most formidable enemy it faced was Islam. For centuries, the Mediterranean world, including Spain, had been the scene of great struggle between Christian Europe and the Muslims in Arabia, Asia Minor, and Northern Africa.

Under siege for 700 years

Spain had been at war with Muslim powers — known generally as the Moors — for over 700 years. Imagine what it would be like to live in a country that had been at war for so long. That kind of never-ending stress is bound to take its toll on a nation, and it certainly did take one on the Spaniards. They had lived for so long under the Muslim threat of violence, and even the annihilation of their Catholic Faith, that the fabric of Spanish culture was embroidered with deep fear of invasion, subterfuge, and deceit aimed at overthrowing their way of life. They were acutely aware of the history of the area and knew well how the Catholic Church had fared under the sword of Islam in Northern Africa and the Eastern Mediterranean. They knew that in other regions where Islam had conquered decisively (as it tried for 700 years to conquer the Iberian Peninsula), Christian culture had been all but obliterated and nothing discernibly Catholic left standing. It wasn't until the Spanish monarchs Isabella and Ferdinand ascended the throne in 1489 that the Moorish occupiers were finally driven out.

Indeed, in 1480, Muslim Turks attacked and captured the Italian city of Otranto and executed half its population — some *twelve thousand* people perished under the sword, including all the Catholic clergy the Turks could lay their hands on.[7] The poor archbishop of Otranto suffered a particularly cruel fate: While very much alive and awake, he was held down and sawn in half. Many of those who were killed had first been offered their lives if they would convert to Islam. The souls of many unknown martyrs for Christ ascended to glory that day. Those who survived the slaughter weren't in a pleasant situation either. All ten thousand inhabitants of the city who escaped death were herded aboard Turkish ships and taken away to be sold into slavery.

Clearly, Islamic aggression was a threat not only to the bordering kingdoms of Europe, but to Western Christianity itself. The Faith in the East had already been devastated by Muslim armies, and it appeared that the same might be in store for the West. This fear, and the imminent threat of Islamic attack, formed much of the basis for the Spanish Crown petitioning the pope to allow the implementation of the Inquisition in Spain.

In Spain at the time, were numerous "conversos": Mus-

---

[7] Ibid., 199.

lim and Jewish converts to Christianity. The problem was that among the genuine converts there were those who continued to practice their old religions. Essentially, their alleged embrace of the Catholic Faith was a false one. For this reason, owing to the very real threat of internal collaboration with the invading Muslims, it became necessary to distinguish the true Catholics from the treasonous false Catholics. Being a "false" Catholic was a capital crime under Spanish law in those days.

How do you tell friend from foe?

Catholic historian Warren H. Carroll describes the problem:

> The Spanish Inquisition was established to deal with the special problem created in Spain by the very large numbers of its citizens known as conversos. These were people who had converted from Islam or Judaism to Christianity, either recently in person or as a result of the conversion of their forebears within three or four generations. Many of these conversions were genuine, or had become so with the passage of time and generations. But many others had been stimulated by ambition and greed — only Christians were allowed to hold high public office and obviously only they could hold positions in the Church, which were very influential — or by fear, particularly when there was large-scale mob violence against non-Christians. And once an individual was baptized, he was not permitted to return to Judaism or Islam.
> There is convincing, indeed overwhelming evidence, which even the most critical modern historians have acknowledged, that tens of thousands of false conversos, who

did not believe in the Christianity they professed, continued to live secretly by the teachings and rites of their or
their forebear's former religion. Many had risen high in
Christian society, even in the Church; some were priests
who mocked the Mass as they said it. While most of the
reports of conversos engaging in satanic rites and crucify-
ing children were probably false, it would be rash to say
that all of them were; for the worst passions in human
nature feed on the kind of situation in which the false
conversos found themselves.[8]

Carroll goes on to describe the thorny dilemma that the
conversos posed to the Spanish state. They were regarded as
"potential traitors," people who were likely to side with the
Muslims during an attack. It was feared that these "false"
conversos would use subterfuge and collusion to help the
Turks invade Spain. The problem was that it was impossible to tell who would be a traitor and who would be loyal.
Outwardly, conversos appeared to be regular Catholics. But
there was enough evidence to show that some secretly plot-
ted against the government, using their outward "Catholicism" as a disguise to shield them from suspicion. And this
was the double-edged sword that cut to the heart of the
problem. The Spanish government very much wanted to
be able to identify and prosecute these traitors, but it also
saw its duty to protect innocent people from being wrongly
accused by their enemies of being "false conversos." How
would one know one from the other?

---

[8] Warren H. Carroll, *The Glory of Christendom* (Front Royal: Christendom College Press, 1993), 607.

Call in the experts

King Ferdinand and Queen Isabella realized very quickly that neither they nor their government had any expertise in this area. Without some way to investigate and discover the theological facts in a given situation, guilty parties could remain hidden and innocent parties could be wrongfully accused of heresy. So the monarchs did what they thought prudent. On November 1, 1478, they officially petitioned Pope Sixtus IV to allow the establishment of the Spanish Inquisition to help them solve the problem.

> [Queen] Isabel saw the Inquisition as necessary to preserve the national security and to promote the spiritual and social unity of Spain. In deeply Catholic Spain, people who pretended to be Catholic but were not could never be trusted. Such deceivers must be exposed, then reconciled if possible, or forced to leave if they could not be reconciled. If stubborn and beyond any reclamation in their hostility, as a second conviction by the Inquisition would indicate [i.e., a repeat offense], she believed they had to be executed. She regarded this as her duty, an essential part of the administration of justice to which she had devoted most of her energies. . . . Justice was also the shield of the innocent. Those falsely accused of hidden heresy, of not being genuine Christians, deserved and would receive full vindication from a court uniquely competent to determine whether such accusations were true, whose judgments were accepted as definitive by the great majority of the nation.[9]

---

[9] Ibid., 609–610.

Another historian pointed out that,

The Spanish Inquisition was mainly a state affair, ruled over by the sovereigns of that nation. The pope was a distant overseer — a court of final arbitration when insoluble disputes over procedure or verdict arose. One such example occurred when two Dominicans, Miguel de Morillo and Juan de San Martin were accused of excesses in their roles as inquisitors, the pope admonished them and threatened the pair with deposition, should their behaviors not change.[10]

On the testimony of two or three witnesses . . .

By the standards of the day, the court of the Inquisition was, in almost all instances, a very fair one. Testimony was carefully weighed; the biases of potential witnesses were taken into account. Accusations of heresy were investigated, most being dismissed early in the proceedings. Those who were found to be heretics were punished, the seriousness of the infraction determining the degree of the punishment.

English historian Edward Burman, a non-Catholic critic of the Inquisition, offers a correction to those who (incorrectly) assume that the Spanish Inquisition was uniquely ruthless and bloodthirsty in its time:

It must be remembered that the Spanish Inquisition was certainly no worse than contemporary secular courts in other countries — including England — and no more vicious in its application of torture than the Inquisition in

---

[10] Cf. Blötzer, 26–38.

earlier centuries in France and Italy. The record is bi-
ased by seventeenth- and eighteenth-century works with
titles such as *A Review of the Bloody Tribunal or the Hor-
rid Cruelties of the Inquisition, The Inquisition Revealed*, or
the more blatantly propagandistic titles like *The History
of Romanism* and *A Master Key to Popery*. Similar books
inspired and elaborated a legend of violence and torture
far worse than the reality of the Inquisition.[11]

Much is often made about the executions carried out by
the Inquisition. This is a partial truth. First, the ecclesiastical officials executed no one. Rather, those found guilty
were turned over to the civil officials, who then carried out
their own punishments. Second, contrary to popular myth,
the number of executions was relatively low — probably
around two thousand.[12] This is still a tragically high number, obviously, but it's far from the grotesquely exaggerated
claims of some anti-Catholics.

For example, Protestant writer Arthur Maricle rants:

Catholic apologists attempt to downplay the significance
of the Inquisition, saying that relatively few people were
ever directly affected. While controversy rages around the
number of victims that can be claimed by the Inquisition,
conservative estimates easily place the count in the millions.
This does not include *the equally vast numbers of human
beings slaughtered in the various wars and other conflicts in-
stigated over the centuries by Vatican political intrigues.* Nor
does it take it account the Holocaust wrought upon the

---

[11] Edward Burman, *The Inquisition, Hammer of Heresy* (New York:
Dorset Press, 1992), 150.
[12] ZENIT news agency interview with Dr. Jose Ignacio Tellechea,
November 2, 1998. Full text available at www.ZENIT.org.

Jews by the Nazis, led by Roman Catholics who used their own religious history to justify their modern excesses.[13]

The body counts differ dramatically, depending on who is recounting the Black Legend, but they all have one thing in common: they vastly overstate the number of those who perished as a result of being tried by the Inquisition. One particularly outlandish example of exaggeration, sometimes found in Protestant anti-Catholic propaganda is the claim that over the years *fifty* million people were killed by the Inquisition! When you think about this, the absurdity of such a figure becomes clear. In order to kill fifty million people (or thirty million, or twenty million), the Catholic Church would have had to have killed every single man, woman, and child in Europe and then imported millions more, just to kill them.

Maintaining a sense of historical perspective

But the fact remains that there were serious problems with the Inquisition. While it is true that torture was used in some instances, critics forget that whether we moderns like it or not, torture was an accepted practice in medieval society. We need to maintain a sense of perspective here. We recoil from the idea of torture (as well we should), but even in the United States, until recently, torture was an accepted form of interrogation used by law enforcement officers on uncooperative suspects. Colloquial American phrases such as giving someone the "third degree" or

---

[13] *The Inquisition: A Study in Absolute Catholic Power*, (San Diego: Mission to Catholics, www.mtc.org/~bart/), emphasis added.

the "rubber hose treatment" stem from the actual fact of violent interrogation methods used by police officers. This kind of "torture" was legal in this country until just a few decades ago.

The records of the Spanish Inquisition show repeated incidents of Church officials intervening on behalf of an accused, when they learned of excesses or cruelty in interrogations.

There were some good things to come out of the Inquisition. First, it did uncover numerous pseudo-Catholics — individuals who were masquerading as members of the Church in order to disrupt it from within. As a result, opportunities for Muslim invasion and takeover were significantly reduced. Additionally, the Inquisition provided a sober, generally fair legal system. In fact, as Carroll points out, "the Inquisition was one of the fairest, most honest courts in Spain. Men preferred to have their cases brought before it wherever possible, or transferred to it from other tribunals."[14] When paranoia over alleged witchcraft swept Europe in the sixteenth and seventeenth centuries, Spain was largely spared that convulsion. This was due, in no small part, to the calm and considered investigative procedures of the Inquisition; when several cases of alleged witchcraft were investigated and found to be without merit, the hysteria dissipated.[15]

When the Inquisition was finally abolished in Spain, in the nineteenth century, it was found to be a mixture of success and failure: a success in its general aims and ac-

---

[14] Warren Carroll, *Reasons for Faith*, (Front Royal: Christendom College Press, Jeff Mirus, ed., 1984), 202.
[15] Ibid., 204.

complishments, a failure in many of its actions to achieve
those aims.

Weighing the good and the bad

In addressing the vexing issue of the Spanish Inquisition,
two extremes must be avoided. First, we must not make the
mistake of condemning the institution out of hand. Indeed,
there were good and positive things that both occurred in
and came out of the Inquisition. Any serious appraisal of
the situation will reveal that.

On the other hand, we must not fail to recognize the
reality of terrible abuses that went on as well. These things
cannot be defended, and we don't seek here in any way to
excuse or minimize the evil actions that were carried out
during the various Inquisitions in the name of the papacy
and the Church itself. Rather, what we seek to do here is
to show that the Inquisition — in particular the Spanish
Inquisition — while flawed does not injure or disprove the
Catholic teaching on the infallibility of the popes.

Why doesn't it? Because papal infallibility falls strictly
into the province of teaching doctrine, while the Inquisition was concerned with discipline: the civil and legal issues
revolved around heresy. Or, to put it another way, papal
infallibility only comes into play when the pope is formally
teaching doctrine to the whole Church in his official capacity as supreme pontiff. The Inquisition was merely a
legal entity that acted in the name of the pope to determine
how well or poorly the people accused of heresy followed
those teachings.

By the standards and practices of the day, the Spanish

Inquisition operated in a fair and reasonable way. By our standards today, it is portrayed as being an out of control, bloodthirsty, anti-heresy machine. The truth is that it was a useful and legitimate tool that was sometimes misused. It would be wrong, of course, to attempt to excuse the excesses of the Inquisition by pointing out that human beings do sinful things, intentionally or otherwise, in the name of the Church. While that may be true, it doesn't undo or make more palatable the sins committed by Catholics in the Inquisition.

It's enough to admit that, yes, during the Spanish Inquisition, terrible things were done by Catholics in the name of the pope and the Church itself. But as bad as things were (and they were not always bad) that admission doesn't damage the fundamental issue here: The popes are not infallible in their application of ecclesiastical discipline. They can and do at times make mistakes in judgment when it comes to how to deal with a problem in the Church.

Papal infallibility, once again, involves only the formal teaching office of the papacy. It has nothing to do with how popes govern the affairs of the Church.

25

The Catholic myth of papal infallibility was debunked once and for all when Pope Sixtus V issued a botched revision of the Latin Vulgate Bible. This edition was so filled with errors, so riddled with omissions and deformities of the text, that it was hastily recalled after his death by embarrassed Roman cardinals. But the damage was done. Sixtus V had formally taught that the defective edition was to be the only Bible used for the entire Catholic Church. If that isn't a perfect example of a pope fulfilling all the necessary ingredients for teaching "infallibly," nothing else in papal history is. The pope clearly taught error.

~

Sixtus V reigned as pope for just five years (1585–1590). By the accounts of his contemporaries (friends and foes), he was a hurricane of activity and reform. Besides being a brilliant leader in the political and ecclesiastical arenas, he proved to be a tireless innovator in the fields of agriculture, engineering, law and industry. He did much to benefit the citizens of the papal states, especially in and around Rome, by enacting and enforcing laws that effectively eradicated highway robbers. He created an impressive system of aqueducts that delivered fresh, clean water to the city of Rome, and presided from a distance over the defeat by Catholic warriors at Lepanto of the Turkish-Muslim navy that threatened Christian Europe with invasion. He followed in the footsteps of his illustrious predecessor, Pope Saint Pius V, in his efforts to reform the clergy and the Church's liturgical customs. He abolished the scandalous practice of simony among the clergy, enacted decrees aimed at reforming lax monastic orders (and was largely successful in doing so!), and reinstituted the ancient practice of regular *ad limina* visits for bishops — the regular official visits of bishops to the bishop of Rome. He took an intense interest in the foreign missions, especially Jesuit missions to Japan, China, Mexico, South America, and the Philippines and he allocated large sums from his treasury for their upkeep.

Similarly, when it came to building projects and patronage of public works, Sixtus was no slouch. He masterminded the huge aqueduct project, he had swamps near Rome drained and cultivated to eradicate the scourge of malaria, he spent large sums on charitable works and feeding the poor and, in addition to many other building projects, he oversaw the completion of the dome on St. Peter's Basilica. In short, Pope Sixtus V packed an immense amount of energy and good work into his brief pontificate.

The Vulgate revision

Unfortunately, this towering pontiff also seems to have had a towering ego, and it got him into serious trouble over the incident of his "revision" of St. Jerome's Latin Vulgate edition of the Holy Bible. If ever a pope subscribed to the "if you want something done right, do it yourself" school of thought, it was Sixtus V.

Before we can properly dispatch this particular pope fiction, it's important to give some brief background to the controversy. First, let's consider the importance of the Latin Vulgate translation of Scripture. Historian Francis Gasquet explains the background of the Vulgate:

> The Latin text of the Sacred Scriptures had existed from the earliest times of Christianity. The translator or translators were unknown to St. Augustine and St. Jerome; but the former says that the old Latin version had certainly come "from the first days of the Faith", and the latter that it "had helped to strengthen the faith of the infant Church." Made and copied without any official supervision these western texts soon became corrupt or doubtful and by the time of St. Jerome varied so much that that doctor could declare that there were almost "as many readings as codices." It was this that as Richard Bentley, writing to Archbishop Wade, declares, "obliged Damasus, then Bishop of Rome, to employ St. Jerome to regulate the last revised translation of each part of the New Testament to the original Greek and to set out a new edition so castigated and corrected. . . .
>
> At the present day, scholars are practically agreed as to the competence of St. Jerome for the work given him by Pope St. Damasus. He, moreover, had access to Greek and other manuscripts, even at that time considered ancient, which are not now known to exist; he could compare dozens of important texts, and he had Origen's "Hexapla" [an ingenious edition of six major Bible versions shown in columns, side by side across the pages. This format made the scholarly comparison of texts a much easier task. —

AU.] and other means of determining the value of his material, which we do not possess. It is obvious that the pure text of St. Jerome must form the basis of any critical version of the Latin Bible, and, what is more, that it must be taken into account in any critical edition of the Septuagint Greek version of the Old Testament and the various Greek texts of the New Testament, no manuscript copies of which are older than St. Jerome's Latin translation made on then ancient copies.[1]

What were the pope's reasons?

We must also remember the political and theological forces that helped shape Sixtus's brief but robust pontificate. For the entire century, political earthquakes rumbled across the kingdoms of Europe. Alliances were shifting, new states emerging and old ones dying off. The exploration and colonization of the Americas by European powers, and the ensuing influx of gold, spices, and other new riches, drastically bolstered the power of states such as Spain and Portugal. All these things altered the political landscape that surrounded the Holy See.

The cyclone of Protestantism had been loosed on Europe some seventy years earlier. The gale winds that were howling across Europe at the time that Sixtus ascended the throne of Peter had been steadily gathering momentum. The entire social order was shifting in France, Germany, England, Scotland, Prussia, and the Low Countries. Most

---

[1] Francis A. Gasquet, "Revision of Vulgate," *The Catholic Encyclopedia* (New York: Robert Appleton Co., 1913). Available in electronic form at www.newadvent.org.

ominous of all, though, from a religious standpoint, was the rise of Huguenot Calvinism in France. France had always been a bulwark of Catholicity in the heart of Europe, and as such was extremely important to the safety of Catholicism across the continent. The possibility of it turning into a Protestant state as a result of the Calvinist onslaught was alarming in the extreme to the papacy.

Pope Sixtus V recognized the grave threat Protestantism posed to the Church in Europe. He realized that in order for the Church to be most effective in its efforts to win back the souls of those who had left the Faith, it needed the very best biblical tools it could muster if it was to properly engage the mainly biblical arguments being used by Protestant critics of Rome. Unfortunately, there were many editions of the Vulgate then in circulation, many of which were deficient and unsuitable. So the pope felt a great urgency for providing the Church with the very best, most accurate Scripture translation possible.

Nor was Sixtus V alone in feeling that urgency. His immediate predecessors, Pius IV, Pius V, and Gregory XIII, had each intended to carry out the revision of the Vulgate, but none were able to get the project launched. Finally, when Sixtus V came on the scene with his astonishing capacity for organization and management, the revision project became a reality. He assembled a team of scholars and linguists, headed by Cardinals Allen, Bellarmine, and Caraffa, which located and compiled as many Greek manuscripts as they could find (a vast amount) and began the revision process.

James Broderick, S.J. described the promising situation in the wake of the first revision carried out by this commission:

The commissioners took the well-known and deservedly popular Louvain Bible of the Dominican scholar Hentenius as their starting point, and wrote in between the lines of its text, or in the ample margins, the corrections they deemed advisable. Their work, to which they had brought immense erudition and the greatest possible devotion, was finished towards the close of 1588, and the revisers began to dream with pardonable pride of the immortality that must surely be the crown of their efforts. But they received a rude awakening when the pope examined the ten thousand variant readings they had diligently and eruditely chosen. He became so angry at the sight of them that he drove Cardinal Caraffa from his presence with harsh words and forthwith cashiered the commission. He would revise the Vulgate himself.

In the bull which he drafted subsequently to introduce his work to the Christian world, he declared, "We, weighing the importance of the matter, and considering carefully the great and singular privilege we hold of God, and our true and legitimate succession from Blessed Peter, Prince of the Apostles . . . Are the proper and specially constituted Person to decide this whole question."[2]

He was unequipped for the task

This pompous and unrealistic attitude regarding his own intellectual abilities was, unfortunately, a grave flaw in Sixtus's pontificate. It proved to be the undoing in his revision as well. He scrapped the work performed by Caraffa, Bellarmine and the commission and set to work on it himself.

---

[2]James Broderick, S.J., *Robert Bellarmine, Saint and Scholar* (Westminster, Newman Press, 1961), 113.

His abilities to translate, edit, and supervise such a gigantic project of textual analysis and revision were nowhere near up to the level necessary to do the job well. So the result was no surprise to anyone: eighteen months later, in early 1590, Pope Sixtus V unveiled the revision to his cardinals. It was filled with errors. Mistranslated passages, omitted passages, passages added that didn't belong — many such flaws riddled the "revised" version.

News of this problem spread quickly. Cardinal Bellarmine and another Jesuit scholar, Fr. Toledo, who were not directly involved in the project but were close enough to know the situation, expressed fears

> that by such mutilation he [Sixtus] was laying himself open to the attacks of the heretics, and was giving more serious scandal to the faithful than anything else the pope could do. . . . Bellarmine spoke in similar terms in the time of Gregory XIV: there is reason to fear, he said, that the Protestants will avail themselves of the changes made by Sixtus V to prove that the pope has falsified Holy Scripture with his own hand. A more effective means of disturbing Catholics and consolidating the work of the heretics could hardly be imagined than this work; they would now have a strong and manifest proof of their old contention that the pope made himself the equal of God, if they could show that the pope had assumed authority over the Word of God, and thus attempted to correct the Holy Spirit Himself.[3]

A serious danger to the Church indeed. But in answering this particular pope fiction, the question boils down to tim-

---

[3] Quoted in Ludwig Freiherr von Pastor, *History of the Popes* (St. Louis: B. Herder Book Co., 1932), vol. 21, 213.

ing. It is quite true, as Cardinal Bellarmine would shudder later, remembering the situation: Pope Sixtus nearly drove the Catholic doctrine of papal infallibility right over the cliff with his error-laden revision of the Vulgate. But the amazing, happy truth is that he didn't quite make it to the edge.

If ever in the life of the Catholic Church there was a "close call" regarding papal infallibility, this was it. If the pope had formally promulgated this botched version, a very strong case could be made that the doctrine of papal infallibility had been proven false. Sixtus fulfilled the requirements for teaching infallibly: a) He was acting in his formal capacity as pope; b) He was planning to officially promulgate a version of Scripture for the whole Church, indeed the whole Christian world; and c) What he intended to promulgate was squarely in the category of faith and morals.

Pope Sixtus relents (barely)

Luckily, the weight of opposition to the release of the botched revision from Robert Bellarmine and other prominent theologians and scholars was enough to stay the pope's hand:

> [H]e could not shut his eyes or fail to see that his work could not be imposed under the gravest penalties of the Church as the one and only approved text of the Vulgate. He therefore abandoned his original plan at least so far as not to publish the bull which had long been prepared, with its grave enactments concerning the exclusive au-

thenticity of the Sixtine text, with those formalities which
were necessary to give it the force of law. . . .
The Sixtine bull on the Vulgate naturally shared the
fate of the Sixtine Vulgate itself. Its being printed at the
beginning of the new Vulgate made it to a great extent
public [insofar as advance copies had already been circulated unofficially]; but the note concerning its promulgation which is to be found in the original of the bull was
omitted, as evident proof that this solemn promulgation
never took place.[4]

Pope Sixtus was busily engaged in correcting typograph-
ical errors in the first edition, preparing to release a revised
version and solemnly promulgate it by the bull, when the
Holy Spirit seems to have intervened. Fr. Broderick describes the endgame of this bizarre episode:

> Publication of the long-expected volume was deferred
> from day to day and month to month, though the bull
> which was to introduce it to the Christian world had been
> drafted, printed, and made ready for posting upon the
> doors of St. Peter's and the Lateran Basilica, much earlier.
> In it Sixtus said: "By the fulness of Apostolical power, We
> decree and declare that this edition . . ., approved by the
> authority delivered to Us by the Lord, is to be received,
> and held as true, lawful, authentic, and unquestioned in
> all public and private discussion, reading, preaching, and
> explanation."[5]

By now, expectation was at a boiling point. The news
in Rome had it that the official promulgation would happen any day. Advance copies of the new Vulgate had been

---

[4] Ibid., 215, 218.
[5] Ibid., 115.

bound and delivered to all the cardinals in Rome along with advance copies of the bull officially publishing it. Everything was ready for the pope to promulgate the new version. Nothing could stop him. All he had to do was take that last fateful step.

And then he died.

On August 27, 1590, Pope Sixtus V died after a very brief illness. He had been in excellent health, and was one of the most vigorous and active pontiffs in the history of the papacy. But at the last moment, it seems the Holy Spirit fulfilled, once again, Christ's promise that He would guide the Church into all truth. Advance copies of the version were quietly withdrawn by the cardinals. The bull announcing it was never issued. At the request of the new pope, Gregory XIX, under Cardinal Bellarmine's supervision, a new commission was formed to carry out the revision of the revision. Before Pope Gregory could release it, he died, and his successor, Pope Clement VIII had that honor. The version released by Clement bore the name of Pope Sixtus V. The new pope, Cardinal Bellarmine and others, who were directly involved in the project, wanted, out of charity, to preserve the good name of Pope Sixtus V and decided that the corrected version would be issued in his honor.

Only God knows if Sixtus V's sudden death was a dramatic proof of divine intervention — the evidence that papal infallibility isn't just a Catholic pipe dream but that God Himself will prevent, by death if necessary, the pope from teaching an error formally to the Church. What we do know, is that the mighty Pope Sixtus V didn't live long enough to cross that line.

26

In defining papal infallibility, the First Vatican
Council (1870) declared dogmatically that Peter is
the rock of Matthew 16, and that the Council's
interpretation of the passage has "always been understood" and held by the Christian Church. However, when we take a look at the early Church Fathers, we find that very few of them believed Peter
was the rock of Matthew 16. This means that the
so-called "infallible declaration" of Vatican I was
just plain wrong.

Like so many of the preceding pope fictions, this one has
a multi-part answer. First, a careful reading of the relevant
portions from council document *Pastor Aeternus* shows the
objection is fundamentally flawed. Here is the definition
referred to:

   1. We teach and declare that, according to the gospel evidence, a primacy of jurisdiction over the whole Church of
God was immediately and directly promised to the blessed
Apostle Peter and conferred on him by Christ the Lord.
   2. It was to Simon alone, to whom he had already said
"You shall be called Cephas," that the Lord, after his confession, "You are the Christ, the son of the living God,"

spoke these words: "Blessed are you, Simon Bar-Jona. For flesh and blood has not revealed this to you, but my Father who is in heaven. And I tell you, you are Peter, and on this rock I will build my Church, and the gates of the underworld shall not prevail against it. I will give you the keys of the kingdom of heaven, and whatever you bind on earth shall be bound in heaven, and whatever you loose on earth shall be loosed in heaven."

3. And it was to Peter alone that Jesus, after His resurrection, confided the jurisdiction of supreme pastor and ruler of His whole fold, saying: "Feed my lambs, feed my sheep."

4. To this absolutely manifest teaching of the Sacred Scriptures, as it has always been understood by the Catholic Church, are clearly opposed the distorted opinions of those who misrepresent the form of government which Christ the Lord established in his Church and deny that Peter, in preference to the rest of the Apostles, taken singly or collectively, was endowed by Christ with a true and proper primacy of jurisdiction.

5. The same may be said of those who assert that this primacy was not conferred immediately and directly on blessed Peter himself, but rather on the Church, and that it was through the Church that it was transmitted to him in his capacity as her minister.

6. Therefore, if anyone says that blessed Peter the Apostle was not appointed by Christ the Lord as prince of all the Apostles and visible head of the whole Church militant; or that it was a primacy of honor only and not one of true and proper jurisdiction that he directly and immediately received from our Lord Jesus Christ Himself: let him be anathema.

Doctrine not exegesis

Notice first that the dogma being defined here is Peter's primacy and authority over the Church — *not* a formal exegesis of Matthew 16. The passages from Matthew 16 and John 21 are given as *reasons* for defining the doctrine, but they are not themselves the *subject* of the definition. As anyone familiar with the dogma of papal infallibility knows, the reasons given in a dogmatic definition are *not* themselves considered infallible; only the result of the deliberations is protected from error. It's always possible that while the doctrine defined is indeed infallible, some of the proofs adduced for it end up being incorrect. This doesn't touch on the doctrine itself, though. For this reason, the perpetuator of this pope fiction is guilty of misreading the Vatican I documents.

But what about the issue of the Early Church Fathers rejecting the idea that Peter is the rock of Matthew 16? Often, anti-Catholics will rely on secondary material for this claim, either unwilling or unable to research the material themselves. Sadly, this leads to numerous historical blunders on their part. Some of Protestant writer James White's writings against the Catholic Church are unfortunate examples of this problem. In his book, *The Roman Catholic Controversy*, he quotes Anglican controversialist George Salmon, who quotes a Jesuit priest named Maldonatus to come up with the following beauty:

> There are among ancient authors some who interpret "on this rock," that is, "on this faith," or "on this confession of faith in which thou hast called me the Son of the living God," as Hilary, and Gregory Nyssen, and Chrysostom, and Cyril of Alexandria. St. Augustine, going still further

away from the true sense, interprets "on this rock," that is, "on myself Christ," because Christ was the rock. But Origen "on this rock," that is to say, "on all men who have the same faith."[1]

This quote is followed by the cheery assertion: "Was Maldonatus correct? Most definitely so." Here we have a perfect example of what happens when a self-styled "scholar" doesn't check his references. Unwitting readers are taken in by this type of shoddy "scholarship," lulled into thinking that, simply because such an assertion is made, it must be true. Well, this particular example is not true. Let's take a look at each Father, and see if Maldonatus really is "most definitely" correct in his claims.

Did St. Hilary consider Peter the rock of Matthew 16? In his work, *The Trinity*, he wrote of "blessed Simon, who after his confession of the mystery was set to be the foundation-stone of the Church, and received the keys of the kingdom of heaven" (6, 20). Here, he obviously held that Peter is the foundation upon whom the Church is built — and he links it, with the mention of the "keys," to Matthew 16:18–19, the passage where Christ names Simon "rock" and says that He will build His Church on that rock. It seems this Protestant writer was unaware of St. Hilary's teaching here.

Turning to a contemporary, good friend, and close collaborator of Gregory of Nyssa, St. Gregory of Nazianzen, we find a view of Peter at variance with White's claim:

"Seest thou that of the disciples of Christ, all of whom were great and deserving of the choice, one [i.e., Simon

---

[1] James White, *The Roman Catholic Controversy* (Minneapolis: Bethany House, 1996), 121.

Peter] is called rock and is entrusted with the foundations of the church."[2] So, according to St. Gregory, Simon Peter is the rock that forms the foundation of the Church.

St. John Chrysostom, the great patriarch of Constantinople, also considered Peter the rock foundation of the Church:

> Peter himself the head or crown of the Apostles, the first in the Church, the friend of Christ, who received a revelation, not from man, but from the Father, as the Lord bears witness to him, saying, "Blessed art thou, etc." This very Peter — *and when I name Peter I name that unbroken rock*, that firm foundation, the great Apostle.[3]

In Cyril of Alexandria's *Commentary on John*, he is even clearer about Peter's role as the rock of Matthew 16:

> He suffers him no longer to be called Simon, exercising authority and rule over him already as having become His own. But by a title suitable to the thing, He changed his name into Peter, from the word *petra*; for on him He was afterwards to found His Church.[4]

Origen, too, considered Peter the rock upon which Christ built His Church, writing,

> Look at the great foundation of the Church, that most solid of rocks, upon whom Christ built the Church! And

---

[2] *T.i. Or.* XXVI., translated in Right Rev. Msgr. Capel, D.D., *The Faith of Catholics* (New York: Fr. Pustet & Co., 1885), vol. 2, 21.

[3] *Concerning Almsgiving and the Ten Virgins* (Homily 3, 20), cited in *St. John Chrysostom on Repentance and Almsgiving* (Washington, D.C.: Catholic University of America Press), 39, translated by Gus George Christo.

[4] *IV Commentary on John*.

what does the Lord say to him? "Oh you of little faith,"
He says, "why did you doubt!"[5]

Did Augustine change his mind?

Finally, we get to Augustine, the famed bishop of Hippo,
in North Africa. While the saint did teach that Peter was
the rock of Matthew 16 throughout most of his career, he
also advanced another interpretation of that passage toward
the end of his life. This is not to say that he ever denied
the reality or legitimacy of the papacy itself, as some non-
Catholics wish to infer from his writings. Far from it. In
his *Letter to Generosus*, he wrote:

> If the very order of episcopal succession is to be considered,
> how much more surely, truly, and safely do we number
> them from Peter himself, to whom, as to one represent-
> ing the whole Church, the Lord said, "Upon this rock I
> will build my Church, and the gates of hell shall not con-
> quer it." Peter was succeeded by Linus, Linus by Clement,
> Clement by Anacletus. . . .

We see here that Simon Peter himself, as far as St. Augustine is concerned, "represents the whole Church," and this
unique representation is passed on to his successors. In one
of his better-known sermons, he said in regard to the Pela-
gians, "Two councils have already been sent to the Apostolic See; and from there, rescripts have also come. The
matter is at an end; if only the error too might sometime
be at an end" (*Sermon 131*, 10). Based on St. Augustine's
remarks in this sermon, an oft-quoted Latin dictum was

---

[5] *Homilies on Exodus*, 5, 4.

derived, "*Roma locuta est, causa finita est*," which translates roughly as, "Rome has spoken; the case is closed." The moral to this particular story: St. Augustine was clear in his belief that the pope, the head of the Church of Rome, had the final authority to decide matters that affected the entire Church. When a controversy arose and was submitted to Peter's successor for a decision, that decision, when rendered, was final and binding. One can almost hear the exasperation in St. Augustine's voice as he wonders when the parties to the controversy will get the point and realize the issue is over and done with.

So, while St. Augustine may have proposed more than one teaching about who or what is the rock of Matthew 16:18, Augustine certainly never gave up his belief in and respect for the papacy that was foretold in that passage. And the fact that this great Catholic bishop offered more than one opinion on how to understand a given Scripture verse shouldn't surprise us. The understanding that Sacred Scripture contains in itself a fourfold sense (literal, allegorical, anagogical, tropological) is part of the ancient Christian tradition of Biblical interpretation.

The failure (or unwillingness) of some non-Catholic apologists to check up properly on their sources points to two possibilities. Either the writer is ignorant of the evidence that runs counter to his claims (in which case he is certainly no scholar), or the second possibility is worse: The writer has deliberately concealed important evidence that would undermine his criticism of the papacy, thereby intentionally misrepresenting the facts, misleading his audience, and subverting the truth. Either way, it's not a pretty picture.

27

The myth of papal infallibility was effectively demolished at Vatican I by Bishop Joseph Strossmayer in his famous speech to the council. Strossmayer urged the assembled bishops to reject Pope Pius IX's call for a declaration of papal infallibility on the grounds that the notion of infallibility, even the papacy itself, was an unbiblical Roman tradition: "Now, unless I have failed of reading the New Testament from beginning to end, I declare to you before God, lifting my hands toward yonder great crucifix, that I find in its pages no trace of the papacy as it now exists." In spite of the Catholic Church's strenuous efforts to suppress Strossmayer's speech, it was translated into English and other languages and has been widely circulated, showing that at least one Catholic bishop had the courage to reject this papal claim.

If it weren't for an insidious effort by anti-Catholics to purposefully misrepresent him[1], Bishop Josip Juraj (Joseph

---

[1] Some critics of the papacy know that the famous "Strossmayer

George) Strossmayer, Bishop of Croatia, would have faded into happy obscurity long ago. Let's start our discussion with a brief sketch of Bishop Strossmayer's life. He was born to German parents in 1815 in Croatia, was ordained a diocesan priest in 1838, made bishop of Diakovár in 1849, and elevated to archbishop by Pope Leo XIII in 1898. He was widely respected as an academic, theologian, and champion of the Slav language and culture. He died in 1905 at the age of 90.

Strossmayer is remembered chiefly for his involvement — real and imagined — at the First Vatican Council of 1870. He was one of the main and, by all contemporary accounts, the most articulate, opponents of the Vatican Council's intention to define papal infallibility as a dogma of the Catholic Faith. Drawing on various scriptural and patristic quotations, he delivered in impeccable classical Latin a lengthy intervention [i.e., formal remarks addressed to a plenary assembly of the council fathers] in which he argued against the doctrine of papal infallibility and urged his brother bishops to resist the effort to dogmatize it.

The Council had been convened by Pope Pius IX against the backdrop of the growing political and social turmoil in Europe, especially in Italy. The process of Italian unification being effected by King Victor Emmanuel included an inexorable absorption of the papal states.

Speech" is a fake, but continue to use it. Others are simply unaware it is a fraud and unwittingly perpetuate this pope fiction. Examples of citing the full "text" of the bogus Strossmayer Speech abound in anti-Catholic writings. Among the more well-known examples are: Henry T. Hudson, *Papal Power* (Hertfordshire: Evangelical Press, 1981), 117-133; Bartholomew F. Brewer, *The Bishop Strossmayer Speech*, (El Cajon: Mission to Catholics, Intl.), undated pamphlet.

What really happened at Vatican I?

The full text of the actual speech (translated from the Latin original by the late Fr. William G. Most) cannot, for reasons of space, be printed here, but we can summarize it by saying that Bishop Strossmayer opposed any definition of papal infallibility on four principal grounds:

a) *Practical and pastoral concerns*: He argued that a solemn definition of papal infallibility would lead inevitably to a confusion of jurisdictions and an undermining of the authority and autonomy of bishops. He warned that two jurisdictions "in one place and exercised in the same respect will mutually impede one another. And in the natural course of things one either impedes or altogether takes away the other, to the great detriment of the common good."

b) *Patristic evidence*: He argued, citing St. Cyprian, St. Vincent of Lerins, and other Church Fathers, that the early Church did not hold or teach the doctrine of papal infallibility in the formal sense that it was being expressed in the doctrinal schema at Vatican I. Strossmayer asserted,

> Whoever knows the development of this controversy, knows that at least in the third century after Christ nothing was known about the personal and absolute infallibility of the Roman Pontiff. . . . Therefore, this light (i.e., St. Cyprian), not only of the African Church but of the whole Church, at his time, saw that there was nothing [in Catholic doctrine] about the absolute and personal infallibility of the Roman Pontiff, but there was [teaching] about the infallibility of the Pontiff joined together with the rest of the Church in a close and inseparable bond.

c) *Conciliar integrity*: Strossmayer believed that if papal infallibility were defined as dogma by the First Vatican

262 Pope Fiction

Council, it would, ironically, have the effect of subverting the authority of general councils. His speech endeavored to convince the assembled bishops that a definition of papal infallibility (indeed the doctrine of papal infallibility itself, which Strossmayer rejected as a "novelty") would seriously render general councils superfluous.

d) *Ecumenical complications*: Given the geographical location of his see (Bosnia/Croatia) and his friendly links with members of the Orthodox hierarchy and with bishops of various Eastern Catholic Churches, Bishop Strossmayer was keenly sensitive to the tension between Orthodoxy and the Catholic Church over the issue of papal primacy. He believed that a formal definition of papal infallibility by the Catholic Church would further injure ecumenical progress between Rome and Constantinople and her sister churches in Orthodoxy.

It's crucial to add here that Bishop Strossmayer in no way opposed either the Catholic doctrine of papal primacy or the Catholic Church's emphasis on the unique teaching prerogatives of the pope (though this is exactly what foes of the papacy who perpetuate the forged "Strossmayer Speech" would have you believe). In his intervention during the council, he repeatedly linked that special teaching authority of the pope always and *only* to the general councils of the Church:[2]

---

[2] A clear manifestation of Gallicanism, an erroneous theory regarding papal authority that was widespread among many European bishops and clergy during the late nineteenth century. "Gallicanism," as bishop Strossmayer detailed in his Vatican I intervention, held that the supreme teaching authority in the Catholic Church was the general councils, not the pope personally. *The Catholic Encyclopedia* describes Gallicanism as: "This term is used to designate a certain group of religious opinions for

We certainly attribute the fullness of power equally to Blessed Peter and to his successors and as it is known that there was a discussion of this matter at the Council of Trent, but the Supreme Pontiff exercises this fullness of power among other things, on various occasions. He exercises it by most solemnly convoking general councils. He exercises it by presiding over them; he exercises it by confirming the decrees and the canons and by these adding to it a divine unbreakable character.

Obviously, the Council Fathers at Vatican I did not adopt Bishop Strossmayer's singular views, nor did they give them a warm reception when they were delivered at his intervention. On July 13, the council voted on the constitution. Bishop Strossmayer voted against it. Most of the Council Fathers voted to affirm it, and so Vatican I formally defined papal infallibility (cf. *Pastor Aeternus*). The emaciated "Gallican" view of papal authority, very popular in some episcopal circles in Europe at that time, went down

---

some time peculiar to the Church of France, or Gallican Church, and the theological schools of that country. These opinions, in opposition to the ideas which were called in France 'Ultramontane,' tended chiefly to a restraint of the pope's authority in the Church in favor of that of the bishops and the temporal ruler. It is important, however, to remark at the outset that the warmest and most accredited partisans of Gallican ideas by no means contested the pope's primacy in the Church, and never claimed for their ideas the force of articles of faith. They aimed only at making it clear that their way of regarding the authority of the pope seemed to them more in conformity with Holy Scripture and tradition. At the same time, their theory did not, as they regarded it, transgress the limits of free opinions, which it is allowable for any theological school to choose for itself provided that the Catholic Creed be duly accepted" (The full text of the article on "Gallicanism" is available in electronic form at www.knight.org/advent/cathen/06351a.htm).

in flames. That position was rejected by the majority of assembled bishops as being inconsistent with the ancient history of the authority of the bishop of Rome. The "ultramontanist" view prevailed. Ultramontanists were those who looked "over the mountains," to Rome, to the final authority of the bishop of Rome. While the ultramontanist model of authority is closer to the orthodox Catholic teaching than Gallicanism, it nevertheless falls short of complete accuracy due to its tendency to downplay the role of bishops and councils in order to exalt the unique teaching prerogatives of the papacy. Both elements are crucial, and the Church always seeks to preserve and strengthen the special role of councils, bishops and the pope without distortions.[3]

The bishops returned to their dioceses, charged with the

---

[3] Catholic ecclesiastical historian Msgr. Umberto Benigni describes ultramontanism as, "A term used to denote integral and active Catholicism, because it recognizes as its spiritual head the pope, who, for the greater part of Europe, is a dweller beyond the mountains (*ultra montes*), that is, beyond the Alps. The term "ultramontane", indeed, is relative: from the Roman, or Italian, point of view, the French, the Germans, and all the other peoples north of the Alps are ultramontanes, and technical ecclesiastical language actually applies the word in precisely this sense. In the Middle Ages, when a non-Italian pope was elected he was said to be a *papa ultramontano*. In this sense the word occurs very frequently in documents of the thirteenth century; after the migration to Avignon, however, it dropped out of the language of the Curia. In a very different sense, the word once more came into use after the Protestant Reformation, which was, among other things, a triumph of that ecclesiastical particularism, based on political principles, which was formulated in the maxim: *Cujus regio, ejus religio.* Among the Catholic governments and peoples there gradually developed an analogous tendency to regard the papacy as a foreign power; Gallicanism and all forms of French and German regalism affected to look upon the Holy See as an alien power because it was beyond the Alpine boundaries of

task of promulgating the newly defined dogma. Stross-mayer delayed doing so for over a year, after which he submitted wholeheartedly and without reservation, having the pertinent acts of the council published in his diocesan newspaper.[4] But his submission to the Church's decision angered foes of the papacy.

It's all just fun until someone loses an eye

It's at this juncture in the drama where things started getting ugly. The good bishop was horrified to learn that his name was attached to an anti-Catholic propaganda piece that argued strenuously against not just papal infallibility, but the papacy itself as well as most of the rest of the Catholic Faith. It is laced with anti-Catholic invective and

---

both the French kingdom and the German empire. This name of Ul-tramontane the Gallicans applied to the supporters of the Roman doc-trines — whether that of the monarchical character of the pope in the government of the Church or of the infallible pontifical *magisterium* — inasmuch as the latter were supposed to renounce "Gallican liberties" in favor of the head of the Church who resided *ultra montes*. This use of the word was not altogether novel; as early as the time of Gregory VII the opponents of Henry IV in Germany had been called Ultramontanes (*ultramontani*). In both cases the term was intended to be opprobrious, or at least to convey the imputation of a failing in attachment to the Ultramontane's own prince, or his country, or his national Church." Benigni's complete explanation of this trend is found in *The Catholic Encyclopedia* (New York: Robert Appleton Company, 1912), vol. XV, 125–127. The electronic form of this article is available at the New Advent Supersite: www.knight.org/advent/cathen/15125a.htm.

   [4] The diocesan paper *Diakovár Glasnik* in editions 1 and 2 (1873) pub-lished, by order of Bishop Strossmayer, the Constitution *Pastor Aeternus* from the first Vatican Council.

heavy with the standard Protestant arguments against the papacy.

This document is known as the infamous "Strossmayer Speech," an outrageous and blatant forgery that, even today, is used by anti-Catholics to "prove" that even Catholic bishops can't in good conscience accept the doctrine of papal infallibility. It is commonly used as "evidence" against the Catholic Church in various Protestant polemical writings.

The "Strossmayer" we encounter in the forged speech is a flaming Protestant, as anti-Catholic as can be imagined, one who rejects and denounces practically all major elements of the Catholic Faith. Among other things, this "Strossmayer" urged the assembled council bishops to reject Pope Pius IX's call for a declaration of papal infallibility on the grounds that the notion of papal infallibility, even the papacy itself, is an unbiblical Roman "tradition": "Now, unless I have failed in reading the New Testament from beginning to end, I declare to you before God, lifting my hands toward yonder great crucifix, that I find in its pages no trace of the papacy as it now exists" (Strossmayer Forgery). The forged speech is so riddled with Protestant anti-Catholic rhetoric, it is so transparently bogus, that it boggles the mind that one could assert with a straight face that a highly esteemed bishop of the Catholic Church could have spoken those words.

In the century since Vatican I, many anti-Catholic books which touch on the subject of papal infallibility quote from, in whole or in part, the forged speech. Notable examples of books that perpetuate this myth are Henry T. Hudson's classic anti-Catholic tome, *Papal Power*,[5] and the ran-

---

[5] Hertfordshire, U.K.: Evangelical Press, 1981.

cid landmark polemic book, *Roman Catholicism* by Loraine Boettner ("godfather" of modern anti-Catholics).[6]

Bart Brewer, an ex-Catholic priest turned professional anti-Catholic, is an example of Protestant attempts to embarrass the Catholic Church with the Strossmayer forgery. On his Web site (www.mtc.org) Brewer writes:

> For Roman Catholics who question the genuineness of the following message by Roman Catholic Strossmayer, there is grave need to consider the following information: *The Catholic Encyclopedia* (©1913 Vol. XIV p. 316) gives an account of Bishop Josip Strossmayer (1815–1905) at the Vatican I Council of 1870, from which we quote: "At the Vatican Council he was one of the most notable opponents of papal infallibility, and distinguished himself as a speaker. The pope praised Strossmayer's 'remarkably good Latin.' A speech in which he defended Protestantism made a great sensation. . . . After the Council Strossmayer maintained his opposition longer than all the other bishops and kept up a connection with Johann J. Ignaz von Dollinger the greatest Roman Catholic historian in Germany. His books commanded universal respect. This was 'until October 1871. Then he notified von Dollinger and Reinkens that he intended to yield "at least outwardly."'"

Selective quoting

Brewer engages in some of his own sleight of hand to make that partial quote from the *Catholic Encyclopedia* appear as damaging to the Catholic Church as possible. First, he added a phrase which is not in the *Catholic Encyclopedia*: "Johann J. Ignaz von Dollinger *the greatest Roman*

---

[6] Phillipsburg, N.J.: Presbyterian and Reformed, 1962.

Catholic historian in Germany. His books commanded univer-sal respect." Why did Brewer add this? To make it appear that even "great," widely respected "Roman Catholic historians" agreed with the anti-Catholic claims contained in the forgery.

Brewer also intentionally left out (indicated by the ellipsis in the extract above) the following pertinent material:

> Afterwards another speech, delivered apparently on 2 June, 1870, was imputed to him. It is full of heresies and denies not only infallibility but also the primacy of the pope. The forger is said to have been a former Augustinian, a Mexican named Dr. José Agustín de Escudero.

And this is what followed his quote:

> Finally, on 26 December, 1872, he published the decrees of the council in his official paper. At a later date he repeatedly proclaimed his submission to the pope, as in his pastoral letter of 28 February, 1881, on Sts. Cyril and Methodius, expressing his devotion to the papal see at times in extravagant language.

Of course Brewer's omission of these relevant sections of the *Encyclopedia* article is understandable, if not defensible, since they undercut the negative impression he wanted to make on his reader.

The Strossmayer strikes back

Naturally, Bishop Strossmayer himself and other Catholics who knew the truth of the matter, made strenuous efforts to expose the forged speech as a fraud and to suppress it where possible. Regrettably, it was not possible to suppress it. The speech was translated into English and other languages and has been widely circulated, all in an effort to embarrass the Catholic Church by showing that one of its most esteemed bishops had rejected the papacy.

The forgery was composed by a disgruntled ex-priest named José Augustín de Escudero who, on his deathbed, confessed his role as forger, and begged Strossmayer for forgiveness. The forgery surfaced first in Italian in 1871 under the title *Papa e Vangelo* (*The Pope and the Gospel*), and soon was spread throughout Europe. From there, it reached the United States, and was used far and wide by enemies of the Church (liberals, Protestants, schismatic Catholics).

Witnesses who had attended the council, including Bishop Ketteler (a German bishop who was with Bishop Strossmayer in Rome) publicly repudiated the document as a forgery, but this didn't keep people from propagating it. In fact, even to this day, there are those who ignore the facts and claim the speech was legitimate. Protestant writer Robert Zins claims in his tactfully titled 1994 book, *Romanism: The Relentless Roman Catholic Assault on the Gospel of Jesus Christ!*: "Evidently, the verdict is still out on whether Strossmayer actually spoke what the infamous pamphlet attributed to him! We grant that Catholic historians are convinced enough to claim it a forgery. But is it?"

(Sigh.) Yes, Mr. Zins, it *is* a forgery. And it's regrettable that you didn't bother to do your homework on the subject, or you wouldn't have asked such an absurd rhetorical question.

Since the world's greatest expert on what Strossmayer said was Strossmayer himself, it's best to simply quote him, from a letter of 18 March, 1872, to Bishop Joseph Fessler of St. Pölten, Germany:

You know, as do all those who attended the Council, that I never gave such an Address as was falsely attributed to me. My principles are totally different from those that come into play in the aforesaid Address. I am aware of never having said anything which could actually weaken the authority of the Holy See or in some way wound the unity of the Church. I authorize you, Most Reverend Sir, to make whatever use you like of this Clarification of mine.

On March 25, 1872, Bishop Fessler himself wrote publicly in response:

In order to witness openly to the truth against falsehood and forgery, I believed this clarification from the letter to me of Bishop Strossmayer, whose name is shamefully misused by the enemies of the Church, should be made public. The handwritten letter of Bishop Strossmayer is in my keeping and remains there for anyone's inspection.[7]

The slippery Dr. Escudero

On August 18, 1876, Fr. P. Stollenwerk, a Vincentian Priest ministering in Buenos Aires, Argentina, wrote in German to Bishop Strossmayer (my thanks to Fr. Ronald Tacelli, S.J. for his translation into English):

Your Grace! Allow me to send you an issue of [a magazine] appearing here, *America del Sud* [i.e., South America]. It contains under the title *La Verdad en el Vaticano*

---

[7] This letter and the *real* speech given by Bishop Strossmayer were printed in the German newspaper *Neue Tiroler Stimmen*, no. 78, April 6, 1872.

[The Truth in the Vatican] the confession of a man who has done you a grave injustice, in that he, on the occasion of the Vatican [Council] published under your name an address which has recently been disseminated afresh by Protestants. As a result of this, he has named himself as the author, and thereby at least somewhat made up for the scandal. Although I have no connection with the author, I know that he wants his retraction to be widely known in Europe.

Dr. José Agustín de Escudero is a Mexican, was an Augustinian [priest] there, left his order without authorization, bummed around in Spain, France, and, at the time of the Council, Italy. He became a Protestant, a Freemason, a Carbonaro, a Preacher, even a Protestant bishop, and as such gave further scandal in Brazil and Montevideo. Here in Buenos Aires he was reconciled with the Church and, after his ordination was declared null in Rome, married. At the time of the enclosed retraction, he was a contributor to *America del Sud*, of which he is now editor. Is his conversion sincere? God alone knows. I doubt it. Should Your Grace want more information, I place myself gladly at your service and so enclose also my address.

The forgery attributed to Archbishop Strossmayer dogged him to the end of his days. He spent decades trying strenuously (and futilely) to expose it as a fraud and to demonstrate his attitude of humble submission to the Catholic Church's teaching on papal infallibility. His actions with regard to this doctrine, both during the council and afterward, were honorable, honest, and thoroughly Catholic in their spirit of humility.

The facts of history prove that the alleged "Strossmayer Speech" is bogus. Unfortunately, many anti-Catholics continue to ignore those facts.

28

The See of Peter is currently vacant and has been for quite awhile. Pope Pius XII was the last validly elected pope of the Catholic Church, and all other claimants to the papacy that have succeeded him are just impostors.

[Announcement made October 24, 1998:]

> I announce to you a great joy. We have a pope! The Most Reverend Father Lucian Pulvermacher, O.F.M., Cap., priest of the Holy Catholic Church, born April 20, 1918 and ordained on June 5, 1946, who takes to himself the name Pius XIII.

This astonishing announcement can be found on one of the many Web sites run by sedevacantist groups. "Sedevacantism" comes from a combination of two Latin words: *sedes* = chair, and *vacans* = (what else?) vacant. Sedevancantists are those Catholics who argue that, since the death of Pius XII, there has been no legitimate pope elected to the throne of Peter; the throne is empty. Or at least it was until October 24, 1998 when the new "pope" was elected.

Sedevacantists argue that Popes John XXIII, Paul VI, John Paul I and John Paul II are all antipopes — invalidly elected pretenders to the Chair of Peter. Obviously, this isn't what you might call a "mainstream" view, but it does have enough sympathizers among disaffected Catholics that it needs to be analyzed.

(The real) Paul is dead

To make such a seemingly ludicrous claim, Sedevacantists must surely have strong evidence to support their contention that the Chair of Peter is empty, right? Wrong. It seems they have lively imaginations, but they come up empty-handed when it comes to the hard facts needed to make their case. Colorful fantasies are about all the Sedevacantists can muster to support their claims. For example, there's the widespread conspiracy theory that Pope John XXIII was a secret Rosicrucian Mason! And then there is the even wilder charge that the *real* Pope Paul VI (that's right, as opposed to the *fake* "Pope Paul VI" who stepped into the role and impersonated him for years) was killed and replaced with a look-alike liberal who managed to fool the world and the entire Roman bureaucracy *and* hijack the Church by allowing the Second Vatican Council to continue. The fake Pope Paul was responsible, so some Sedevacantists tell us, for all that's wrong in the Church today. After the real pope was disposed of, the look-alike impostor was able to swing the wrecking ball of Modernism from inside the Catholic Church itself.

The most popular sedevacantist argument against the papacy goes something like this: Canon 188 of the Catholic Church's *Code of Canon Law* lists several ways in which an episcopal office can be rendered vacant. The fourth reason is brief: "if a cleric has publicly lapsed from the Catholic

Faith." St. Robert Bellarmine, a cardinal and Doctor of the
Church, wrote similarly on this theme, postulating:

> The fifth opinion [regarding the hypothetical situation of
> a heretical pope] therefore is true; a pope who is a mani-
> fest heretic by that fact ceases to be pope and head [of the
> Church], just as he by that fact ceases to be a Christian and
> a member of the body of the Church. This is the judgment
> of all the early Fathers, who teach that manifest heretics
> immediately lose all jurisdiction.[1]

St. Robert Bellarmine against the pope?

The Sedevacantists seize upon this teaching of St. Robert
Bellarmine and turn it against the papacy — the very institution the good Jesuit saint lived and died defending.
According to the Sedevacantists, Pope John XXIII perpetuated heresy after heresy, especially with his "modernist"
Second Vatican Council, which "contradicted" numerous
past Church dogmas. For this reason, he vacated the papacy, according to Canon 188. The "conciliar" Church that
emerged in the wake of Vatican II was *not* the Catholic Church, Sedevacantists contend, but rather, it is a
cheap imitation, a hybrid of Modernism, Indifferentism,
and Catholicism. The "popes" of *that* Church have no validity. The papacy, then, is vacant.

Non habemus papam!

A position paper put out by one schismatic group of
"Marian" sedevacantist priests puts it more starkly:

---

[1] *De Romano Pontifice*, 10.

It must be concluded that the modern hierarchy who have approved and implemented the errors of Vatican II no longer represent the Catholic Church and her lawful authority. This most certainly includes the ones who have confirmed, approved, decreed, and implemented these heretical teachings, namely Paul VI (Montini) and John Paul II (Wojtyla). Furthermore, John Paul II, by his own repeated convocations of and participation in ecumenical religious services with non-Catholic and non-Christian religions, has become suspect of heresy. Despite the lack of canonical warning and formal declaration of loss of office, his repeated acts of ecumenism, his enforcement of the heresies of Vatican II, and his promulgation of a new code of Canon Law injurious to faith and morals are manifestations of his pertinacity in heresy. . . . Further, since John Paul II has manifestly taught heresy, promoted ecumenism and fostered interfaith worship, he clearly cannot be recognized as a successor of St. Peter in the primacy.[2]

We see here a hint of another "proof" often advanced by Sedevacantists. They argue, rightly, that the charism of papal infallibility entails that the pope will be prevented from officially teaching error (as, perhaps, Pope Sixtus V discovered). However, according to them, John XXIII, Paul VI and John Paul II taught many errors and heresies, including those issued by Vatican II, in which they were all deeply involved. Therefore, these men couldn't have been the legitimate successors to Peter!

It's outside the range of this book to answer every charge of alleged heresy the Sedevacantists make against Popes John Paul II, Paul VI, and John XXIII, but we can at least address their primary argument, one that shows up again

---

[2] "Theological Position," posted on the Web site of The Religious Congregation of Mary Immaculate Queen, available at www.cmri.org.

and again in their literature. That is, the question of "religious freedom" as taught by Vatican II. Those who claim the council fell into heresy point to statements by earlier popes on the issue of religious liberty. For example, Pope Gregory XVI wrote:

> We now continue with a most fertile cause of evils by which we deplore that the Church at present is being afflicted, that is, Indifferentism, or that evil opinion. . . . that by any profession of faith whatsoever, the eternal salvation of the soul can be attained, if morals are kept to the norm of the right and good. . . . And from this most putrid font of Indifferentism flows that absurd and erroneous view or rather insanity, that liberty of conscience should be asserted and claimed for just anyone.[3]

In Pius IX's *Syllabus of Errors*, he condemned the idea that, "Each one is free to embrace and profess that religion which, led by the light of reason, he thinks is true" (DS 2915).

The *Declaration on Religious Liberty* from Vatican II seems to contradict these earlier Church teachings:

> The Vatican Council declares that the human person has a right to religious freedom. Freedom of this kind means that all men should be immune from coercion on the part of individuals, social groups and every human power so that, within due limits, nobody is *forced* to act against his convictions nor is anyone to be *restrained* from acting in accordance with his convictions in religious matters in private or in public, alone or in associations with others.[4]

While a first appearance gives the impression of a reversal in Church teaching, a closer look reveals this isn't the

---

[3] *Mirari Vos*, DS 2730.
[4] *Dignitatis Humanae*, 2, (emphasis added).

case. Notice the *Declaration* endorses not a general freedom to believe whatever you want, but rather, a freedom from being *coerced* into believing something. In other words, no one is to be *forced* to submit to the Catholic Faith, or forcefully restrained from believing something else. The document does *not* advance religious relativism — the notion that all faiths are somehow equal. In fact, the Council was clear on this point, underlining the distinction between relativism and freedom from coercion:

> So while the religious freedom which men demand in fulfilling their obligation to worship God has to do with *freedom from coercion* in civil society, it leaves intact the traditional Catholic teaching on the moral duty of individuals and societies towards the true religion and the one Church of Christ.[5]

All humans have a moral obligation to seek the truth in Catholicism, but they cannot be coerced into embracing it. Forced faith is no faith at all.

No inconsistency

But what about Pius IX's statement condemning the notion that "one is free to embrace and profess that religion which, led by the light of reason, he thinks is true." This statement condemns relativism, not the freedom from coercion advocated by Vatican II. It's true, no one has the right to believe in and follow a false religion; all rights come from God, and He doesn't endorse error. This fits perfectly with the *Declaration*'s statement on the "moral duty" of people to pursue the "true religion and the one

---

[5] Ibid., 1, (emphasis added).

Church of Christ." In the pursuit, however, no one is to be forced against his free will. They must embrace the truth of their own accord.

This point was taught clearly by Pope Leo XIII (a pontiff the Sedevacantists would accept) in his *Immortale Dei*:

> The Church is accustomed to take care that no one be forced to embrace the Catholic Faith when unwilling, as Augustine wisely reminded: "A person cannot believe if he does not do it willingly" (DS 3177).

We see, then, that not only does the *Declaration* not contradict earlier teachings, but its main points were held by earlier popes as well. There was no change in Church teaching.

The idea that the papacy could be vacant for an appreciable amount of time (excluding the obvious period between a pope's death and the election of a new pontiff) goes against the scriptural teaching on the continuation of the Church. If indeed the pope is the earthly head of the Church — a point with which Sedevacantists agree — then the Church couldn't continue without that head. In Matthew 16:18, Jesus promised that the "gates of Hades" would never overcome the Church He was to build on Peter. If indeed Pope John XXIII slipped into heresy, lost his place on the Chair of Peter and vacated the office, then the gates of Hades *did* overcome the Church. When Jesus promised to be with the Church "always to the close of the age," He allowed no exceptions. There would never be a point when the Lord would fail to guide His Body, the Church.

Sedevacantism is essentially just another form of Protestantism, but with holy water, rosary beads and no effort to change Catholic teaching on the sacraments. Those who adhere to this position do so through personal interpretation of both the Scriptures and the teachings of the Church. They reject the current pope by misinterpreting the teachings of pontiffs past. Instead of listening to the Magisterium of Christ's Church, they've constructed their own teaching office — that of their own fallible opinions.

29

Modern day Roman Catholic apologists suffer from the "Peter Syndrome" when they use Scripture and the Fathers. This refers to the tendency they have to read the papacy anachronistically back into the Bible and the writings of the early Christians. Every praise of Peter found therein is taken to be a reference to the bishop of Rome. But this consistently twists the real meaning of the passages used.

The first problem with this objection is that it's an instance of what the famed Anglican convert John Henry Newman called "poisoning the well." That is, it rejects out of hand any evidence the Catholic apologist might bring up, by virtue of the fact that it's offered by a Catholic apologist (all of whom allegedly suffer from the spiritually fatal "Peter Syndrome"). Instead of actually dealing with the specific material advanced to support the papacy, the objector can simply brush it aside, assuming it to be invalid or slanted. It's certainly an easy escape hatch for the Protestant who has no other answer to the verse or Church Father cited.

Not only that, but this charge can only be made and

defended in *specific* examples. In this way, it's absolutely impossible for the Catholic to refute this blanket indictment of Catholic apologetics. Intellectual honesty, therefore, makes it incumbent upon the non-Catholic to back up his charge. If he cannot or will not do that, his claim for the "Peter Syndrome" is an empty one — a bit of unscholarly bravado intended to sway those with little familiarity with the scriptural and patristic material.

If the shoe fits, throw it at the other guy

It's funny that the very Protestants who make this kind of charge against Catholics suffer from a more insidious form of anachronism themselves. While trying to find their distinctive Reformation doctrines in Scripture and the early Church, they read their own relatively modern beliefs back into ancient Christianity.

For example, some Protestant critics of Catholicism have made quite a splash by combing through the writings of St. Athanasius and pulling out every praise of Scripture found therein. As a true Catholic, the Alexandrian saint's writings are *full* of such references. Unfortunately, the Protestants then hold up those praises as evidence that Athanasius believed in *sola scriptura* (Latin: by Scripture alone). Ignored are the references Athanasius made to the authority of the Church and the existence of Sacred Tradition. Through selective quotations, this particular Father can be made to look awfully Protestant. This isn't, however, a fair way to approach the subject, and is a fine example of anachronism.

The very nature and antiquity of the Catholic papal claims, on the other hand, fall well outside the limits of anachronism. Catholics since the earliest centuries have been clearly repeating these alleged "anachronisms." Is it reasonable to believe in the existence of a nearly two-thousand-year-old anachronism — especially one originated by those existing in the time period itself? Obviously not.

Protestant doctrines, on the other hand, find their first expression around the fifteenth-sixteenth centuries. Nowhere are these doctrines found in the early Church. It's revealing that even Jehovah's Witnesses could claim greater antiquity than this — they could point to the fourth century heretic Arius as an early proponent of the same warped theology. Protestants can do nothing of the kind.

Bogus assumptions, bogus conclusions

The "Peter Syndrome" objection is also based on an unestablished premise. That is, it's based on the assumption that the bishops of Rome are *not* successors to the ministry of Peter. With this erroneous presupposition, it's possible to make the objection that a description of Peter's ministry has nothing to do with the papacy. The "Peter Syndrome" claim, then, begs the question. "Grant me," it claims, "that there's no connection between Peter and the bishops of Rome and I'll prove that your citations of the Fathers's descriptions of Peter have nothing to do with the bishops of Rome." That's a logical fallacy through and through, folks. The papacy debate *centers* around the question of whether or not there's a connection between Peter and the popes. To approach the question with the presupposition that there is no such connection is not to address the issue honestly.

There's another problem with this Protestant objection. Often, people who make this charge are building a "straw man" argument (where a person misrepresents someone else's argument, purposely making it weak so that it can be more easily refuted). They'll take a passage intended by a Catholic to establish the primacy of Peter in the Church and will respond with a quick, "That doesn't prove the papacy!" The Catholic, of course, wasn't claiming that passage *alone* demonstrated the papacy. Rather, the scriptural and Patristic case for the papacy must be established using several steps, one of which — one of the early ones, mind you — is to prove the primacy of the Apostle Peter himself. It's patently dishonest for a Protestant to interrupt the argument at its first step, and then complain it never reaches its conclusion.

Finally, the "Peter Syndrome" objection offers no coherent answer for the abundant and early patristic evidence that speaks about the essentials of the Catholic Faith (e.g., Sacraments, the Mass as a sacrifice, prayers to the saints and Mary, the authority of the bishop of Rome, purgatory, etc.). In the overwhelming number of patristic statements about the Catholic Faith of their era (and we are speaking of thousands of passages here), most never mention Peter. How can it be that Catholics are guilty of the so-called "Peter Syndrome" for citing evidence that doesn't even mention Peter?

What are we to make of Pope Clement's powerful *Epistle to the Corinthians*, written around A.D. 80? What about Irenaeus's appeal to Pope Victor not to excommunicate the Eastern church over the Easter controversy? What of St. Irenaeus's teaching about the *Roman* Church being the Church with which all should be in agreement? Try as they might, our non-Catholic friends simply can't dismiss these facts with the broad, clumsy strokes of their futile "Peter Syndrome" objection.

30

Pope Pius XII was silent in the face of Nazi atrocities against the Jews during World War II, and that silence led to the deaths of many innocent people. If he, as pope, had exercised his moral leadership and denounced Hitler, many lives would have been saved.

Wrong. When World War II came to an end and the horrors of the Holocaust came to full light, Pope Pius XII was exalted around the world as a hero. According to the witnesses of the day, including many Jews and other non-Catholics, through his efforts, *hundreds of thousands* of Jewish men, women and children were saved from the brutality and certain death the Nazi extermination machine had planned for them. Especially after his death in 1958, praises for his efforts on behalf of the Jews poured in from all corners of the world.

When he died, the whole world knew and acknowledged that Pope Pius XII had done everything he could to defend and protect the Jews. He had done far more than the governments of the United States, England and other countries had done to protect them. According to his quiet but immensely effective strategy, this pope had done far,

far more than any Protestant, Muslim or other religious
leader or denomination had done during those harrowing
years. But this widespread recognition of the pope's efforts
on behalf of the Jews during World War II underwent a
dramatic change a mere five years after the pontiff's death.

A lie is born

Historical revisionism is alive and well. Amazingly, the
undeniable, verifiable facts surrounding Pope Pius XII's
persistent efforts on behalf of the Jews were forcibly am-
putated from the public consciousness. In place of the facts,
a sinister myth was grafted in, and it quickly took root,
choking out the truth. The seeds of this lie about Pope Pius
XII were planted, in all places, in the form of a third-rate
play.

In 1963, a young German playwright named Rolf Hochhuth wrote his now obscure but still poisonous play, *The
Deputy*. In it, he alleged that Pope Pius XII, through his
"silence" about the extermination of European Jews, was
directly complicit in the horror of Nazism. Hochhuth's erroneous attitude spread quickly among critics of the Catholic Church, particularly in secular and political circles.[1]

While Hochhuth's personal pope fiction portrays Pope
Pius XII as a cowardly collaborator with the Nazis, the
facts show otherwise. As a cardinal and papal nuncio to
Germany, Monsignor Eugenio Pacelli, the future Pope Pius
XII, distinguished himself over many years of service to

---

[1] For a fuller discussion of Hochhuth's corrosive "contribution" to
this issue, see "Judging Pope Pius XII," *Inside the Vatican*, May-June
1997, 12–26.

the Holy See as a vocal opponent of the racial policies of the National Socialist Party, the Nazis.

On the strength of his long experience in Germany, it was Pacelli who personally wrote the draft of Pope Pius XI's 1937 encyclical against the Nazi Reich, *Mit Brennender Sorge* (With Burning Anxiety), a vigorous and direct condemnation of anti-Semitism. The only encyclical ever to be issued first in German, it took the dramatic step of identifying Catholics as "spiritual Semites."

But for Hochhuth, this reality didn't matter. His

> condemnation of the "silence" of Pius XII was not ameliorated by his awareness of countervailing arguments. For example, in Hochhuth's 60 pages of supporting documents, he quotes a Nazi defendant at Nuremberg who testified that a direct papal condemnation of Hitler would have driven Hitler to more horrors. "The Pope did not protest" [publicly], this man testified, because he "quite rightly" said to himself, "If I protest, Hitler will be driven to madness; not only will that not help the Jews, but we must expect that they will be killed all the more." Apparently Hochhuth was unpersuaded by such Nazi testimony. For him, Pius should have made a powerful statement even if such a statement would not have helped the Jews, *even if more of them would have been killed as a result.*[2]

Nothing would have been good enough

Regardless of what the Monday-morning quarterbacks say as they second-guess Pope Pius XII, the fact remains

---

[2]Ibid., 18-19, emphasis added.

that he did the right thing in the way he handled his pro-
Jewish, anti-Nazi diplomacy.

> Of course, no one will ever know what would have hap-
> pened had Pius taken the course Hochhuth, and others
> since, would have had him take. But there is ample evi-
> dence that protests incited Hitler to fury and that exter-
> mination campaigns could always be intensified, even by
> a nation fighting enemies on many fronts.[3]

Even in 1937, before he had been elected to the papacy,
even before Adolph Hitler had fully plunged Germany
into its nightmare of self-destruction, Eugenio Pacelli, the
future Pope Pius XII, spoke out fearlessly against Nazi
anti-Semitism. He did so as a priest, as a bishop, as papal
nuncio to Germany during the 1920s. The most important
example of his behind-the-scenes efforts can be glimpsed
in *Mit Brennender Sorge*, the encyclical letter he composed
in German (a language in which he was fluent) for then-
reigning Pope Pius XI:

> We have weighed every word of this letter in the balance
> of truth and love. *We wished neither to be an accomplice to
> equivocation by an untimely silence, nor by excessive severity
> to harden the hearts of those who live under Our pastoral
> responsibility*; for Our pastoral love pursues them none the
> less for all their infidelity.[4]

This was a careful way of saying that the Pope knew he
was walking a tightrope with the Nazis. On one hand, he
refused to be silent on this issue, but on the other hand, he
recognized that his condemnations of Nazi anti-Semitism

---

[3] Ibid., 18.
[4] Ibid., 41.

could easily provoke a deadly backlash against the Jews, the very people he sought to protect. It was precisely this dilemma that shaped the way Pope Pius XII approached the problem during his pontificate.

Mit Brennender Sorge gives us a blueprint of the Church's actions, carried out largely by Eugenio Pacelli while he was papal nuncio to Germany. A few particular passages are worth noting here:

> When, in 1933, We consented, Venerable Brethren, to open negotiations for a concordat, which the Reich Government proposed on the basis of a scheme of several years' standing; and when, to your unanimous satisfaction, We concluded the negotiations by a solemn treaty, We were prompted by the desire, as it behooved Us, to secure for Germany the freedom of the Church's beneficent mission and the salvation of the souls in her care, as well as by the sincere wish to render the German people a service essential for its peaceful development and prosperity. Hence, *despite many and grave misgivings*, We then decided not to withhold Our consent for We wished to spare the Faithful of Germany, as far as it was humanly possible, the trials and difficulties they would have had to face, given the circumstances, had the negotiations fallen through. It was by acts that We wished to make it plain, Christ's interests being Our sole object, that the pacific and maternal hand of the Church would be extended to anyone who did not actually refuse it.[5]

Second,

> The experiences of these last years have fixed responsibilities and laid bare intrigues, which from the outset only

---

[5] Ibid., 3.

aimed at a war of extermination. In the furrows, where We tried to sow the seed of a sincere peace, other men — the "enemy" of Holy Scripture — oversowed the weed of distrust, unrest, hatred, defamation, of a determined hostility overt or veiled, fed from many sources and wielding many tools, against Christ and His Church. They, and they alone with their accomplices, silent or vociferous, are today responsible, should the storm of religious war, instead of the rainbow of peace, blacken the German skies.[6]

As we know, Hitler and his "accomplices" did blacken all of Europe with war, and suffering, and death. We know that Pope Pius XI warned the German bishops that it was about to happen, and that the future Pope Pius XII played an important role in crafting that warning.

Hitler didn't like what he saw

When Eugenio Pacelli was elected pope in 1939, the Nazi government, remembering his opposition to their policies while he was papal nuncio to Germany, was greatly agitated by the new turn of events. *Das Schwarze Korps*, the official publication of the German SS, stated mockingly:

> We do not know if Pius XII, though young enough to see the new developments in Germany, is intelligent enough to sacrifice many old things of his institution. As nuncio and secretary of state, Eugenio Pacelli had little understanding of us; little hope is placed in him. We do not believe that as Pius XII he will follow a different path.[7]

---

[6] Ibid., 4.
[7] Cited in Margherita Marchione, *Yours is a Precious Witness: Memoirs of Jews and Catholics in Wartime Italy* (Paulist Press, 1997, 138).

Das Reich, another official organ of the Third Reich, growled that "Pius XI was a half-Jew, for his mother was a Dutch Jewess; but Cardinal Pacelli is a *full* Jew."[8]

In another jab, the Nazis observed: "In a manner never known before . . . The Pope has repudiated the National Socialist New European Order [i.e., the Nazi party] . . . It is true, the Pope does not refer to the National Socialists in Germany by name, but his speech is one long attack on everything we stand for . . . Here he is clearly speaking on behalf of the Jews."[9]

The Nazis' anxiety over Pacelli's election was well founded. As papal nuncio, he had openly opposed their racial policies at every turn. They knew he would be an even more formidable opponent now that he was pope, with the full weight of the Catholic Church at his disposal. And so it happened. Pius XII worked tirelessly behind the scenes to secure the safety of the oppressed Jews. Just a few examples should suffice to demonstrate this.

In his article, "The Real Story of Pius XII and the Jews," author James Bogle describes an important event:

> In August 1943, Pius XII received a plea from the World Jewish Congress to try to persuade the Italian authorities to remove 20,000 Jewish refugees from internment camps in Northern Italy. "Our terror-stricken brethren look to Your Holiness as the only hope for saving them from persecution and death," they wrote. In September 1943, A. L. Easterman on behalf of the W.J.C. reported to the

---

[8] Thomas Craughwell, "Pius XII and the Holocaust," *Sursum Corda*, Spring 1998.

[9] Gestapo report on Pope Pius XII's 1942 Christmas sermon to the world, quoted in *Inside the Vatican*, June 1997, 12.

Apostolic Delegate in London . . . that the efforts of the
Holy See on behalf of the Jews had been successful.[10]

The Vatican intervenes

Thomas Craughwell describes another such action:

On June 15, 1940, about 500 Jews embarked at Bratislava
for Palestine. They were refused entry there and at every
other port they tried. After four heartbreaking months,
the ship was captured by an Italian patrol boat and es-
corted to the Italian-occupied island of Rhodes. Here the
Jewish passengers were imprisoned until they could be
turned over to the Germans.

Herman Herskovich, the son of one of the refugees,
made his way to Rome where he requested and was
granted audience with Pope Pius. When Pius heard Herskovich's story, he contacted the Italian authorities, won
the release of the refugees and oversaw their transfer to a
hastily erected settlement camp in southern Calabria. Pinchas Lapide of the 178th Transport Company of the 8th
British Army and later Israel's consul in Milan recalled:
"That is where we found most of them, sound and thankful, on December 23, 1943, the day after our Palestinian
unit landed at Taranto."

A few days later, Lapide and the 178th were greeted
at Ferramonti-Tarsia near Cosenza by 3,200 Jews — the
entire population of another settlement camp operated by
the Vatican. The residents were refugees from Austria,
Czechoslovakia and Hungary, who had been saved by
Pius XII's intervention. Their camp was under the pro-

---

[10] James Bogle, "The Real Story of Pius XII and the Jews," *Catalyst*,
December 1996.

tection of two papal emissaries who had set up a kosher kitchen for the residents and established a school for the children.[11]

By October 1943, the German forces occupying Rome were apprehending Jewish people in Rome for deportation. Pius XII negotiated with the German ambassador at length, saving the lives of eight thousand Jews.[12]

At the time of the German occupation, the pope commanded that all convents, monasteries and houses of study in Italy be opened to hide the Jewish population from the Nazis.[13] Thousands of Jews were hidden and saved through this action.

Why didn't Pius issue a public condemnation?

It's often alleged by critics of the papacy that Pius XII should have made a loud, specific, public condemnation of the Nazi atrocities. Such a claim sounds good at first — that is, until it's weighed against the reality of the time. Any vocal public stand by the pope would have resulted in horrible reprisals against the Jews and Catholics under German control. During an address to the College of Cardinals on June 2, 1943, the pope cautioned "every word on our part, addressed on this subject to competent authorities, every public allusion, has to be seriously weighed and measured by us, *in the interest of the suffering* [people] *them-*

---

[11] Cf. Craughwell.
[12] Marchione, 16–17.
[13] Ibid., 24.

selves, so as not to render their lot still graver and more unbearable."[14]

This fact was not lost on the Jewish community of that day, either. Carlo Sestieri, a Jewish writer who was given sanctuary personally by Pope Pius XII and hidden from the Nazis in one of the Vatican's properties, noted that

> Thousands of Roman Jews would have been captured by the Nazi troops on October 16, 1943, had it not been for the prudent politics of the Vatican. . . . Perhaps only the Jews who were persecuted understand why the Holy Father, Pope Pius XII, could not publicly denounce the Nazi-Fascist government. . . . Without doubt, it helped avoid worse disasters.[15]

"The Pope's message"

On December 25, 1941, a *New York Times* editorial praised the pope's efforts on behalf of the Jews. Specifically, the editorial commented on an address the Holy Father had given. Here is the complete text of both editorials — read them and ask yourself if the pope fiction is true that Pius XII was "silent" in the face of the Nazi atrocities:

> The voice of Pius XII is a lonely voice in the silence and darkness enveloping Europe this Christmas. The Pope reiterates what he has said before. In general, he repeats, although with greater definiteness, the five-point plan for peace which he first enunciated in his Christmas message after the war broke out in 1939. His program agrees in fundamentals with the Roosevelt-Churchill eight-point

---

[14] Ibid., 54.
[15] Ibid., 65.

declaration. It calls for respect for treaties and the end of the possibility of aggression, equal treatment for minorities, freedom from religious persecution. It goes farther than the Atlantic Charter in advocating an end of all national monopolies of economic wealth, and so far as the eight points, which demands complete disarmament for Germany pending some future limitation of arms for all nations.

The Pontiff emphasized principles of international morality with which most men of goodwill agree. He uttered the ideas a spiritual leader would be expected to express in time of war. Yet his words sound strange and bold in the Europe of today, and we comprehend the complete submergence and enslavement of great nations, the very sources of our civilization, as we realize that he is about the only ruler left on the Continent of Europe who dares to raise his voice at all. The last tiny islands of neutrality are so hemmed in and overshadowed by war and fear that no one but the Pope is still able to speak aloud in the name of the Prince of Peace. This is indeed a measure of the "moral devastation" he describes as the accompaniment of physical ruin and inconceivable human suffering.

In calling for a "real new order" based on "liberty, justice and love," to be attained only by a "return to social and international principles capable of creating a barrier against the abuse of liberty and the abuse of power," *the Pope put himself squarely against Hitlerism.*[16] Recognizing that there is no road open to agreement between belligerents "whose reciprocal war aims and programs seem to be irreconcilable," he left no doubt that the Nazi aims are also irreconcilable with his own conception of a Christian peace. "The new order which must arise out of this war,"

---

[16]Emphasis added.

he asserted, "must be based on principles." And that
implies only one end to the war.

"The Pope's verdict"

The following year, again on Christmas Day, the *New
York Times* editorial revisited the theme of Pope Pius XII's
efforts on behalf of the Jews:

> No Christmas sermon reaches a larger congregation
> than the message Pope Pius XII addresses to a war-torn
> world at this season. This Christmas more than ever he
> is a lonely voice crying out of the silence of a continent.
> The Pulpit whence he speaks is more than ever like the
> Rock on which the Church was founded, a tiny island
> lashed and surrounded by a sea of war. In these cir-
> cumstances, in any circumstances, indeed, no one
> would expect the Pope to speak as a political leader, or
> a war leader, or in any other role than that of a preach-
> er ordained to stand above the battle, tied impartially,
> as he says, to all people and willing to collaborate in any
> new order which will bring a just peace.
>
> But just because the Pope speaks to and in some
> sense for all the peoples at war, the clear stand he takes
> on the fundamental issues of the conflict has greater
> weight and authority. When a leader bound impartially
> to nations on both sides condemns as heresy the new
> form of national state which subordinates everything
> to itself: when he declares that whoever wants peace
> must protect against "arbitrary attacks" the "juridi-
> cal safety of individuals:" when he assails violent
> occupation of territory, the exile and persecution of
> human beings for no reason other than race or polit-
> ical opinion: when he says that people must fight for

a just and decent peace, a "total peace" — the "impartial judgment" is like a verdict in a high court of justice.

Pope Pius expresses as passionately as any leader on our side the war aims of the struggle for freedom when he says that those who aim at building a new world must fight for free choice of government and religious order. They must refuse that the state should make of individuals a herd of whom the state disposes as if they were a lifeless thing.[17]

The sad fact is that most people today have no idea that Pope PIus XII's contemporaries — Jews, Nazis,and the rest — openly recognized his strong, if often hidden, efforts to rescue his Jewish brothers and sisters as well as the many Catholics and others who were being ground beneath the boot of the Third Reich. A collective amnesia has set in. We as a society are no longer aware of what happened a mere fifty years ago.

Why? What caused this strange amnesia? It seems clear that revisionist historians, like Rolf Hochhuth and his sympathizers, have labored to obscure the facts about the pope and shape public opinion in a wholly different direction than the facts warrant. For whatever reason, perhaps out of a deep, if unspoken, anti-Catholicism, there has been a consistent effort to paint Pope Pius XII as a "Jew hater," an "anti-Semite," a "Catholic bigot" who sat back and did nothing as the Nazis did the dirty work for him. That kind of thinking is not simply contrary to the overwhelming facts that disprove that notion, it is a poisonous and extremely powerful form of anti-Catholicism.

---

[17]Both of these editorials are available at the Catholic League's Internet site: www.catholicleague.org.

Old prejudices die hard — old lies never die

As the old saying goes, "If you tell a lie long enough, loud enough, and to enough people, that lie will soon become the 'truth.' " The Pius XII slanderers know this well, and they exploit it to maximum advantage in their efforts to smear the papacy and the Catholic Church. Regardless of the facts, they *want* you to believe their pope fiction — that Pope Pius XII was "silent" in the face of Nazi atrocities against the Jews. In one sense, the pope was "silent." He learned the savage lesson of what would happen to the Jews when the Catholic bishops of Holland took the heroic but ultimately disastrous course of public confrontation with the Nazis. Pius wisely elected not to pursue a strategy of aggressive *public* harangues against Hitler and his war machine. Instead he carried on a tireless and extremely effective behind-the-scenes operation to shield Jews from the German extermination effort.

Still, the Pope's detractors insist he did nothing to help the Jews.

Tell that to Pinchas Lapide, a Jew and a former Israeli diplomat. He quotes one of the Jews he knew in Nazi-occupied Rome during World War II: "None of us wanted the Pope to speak out openly. We were all fugitives, and we did not want to be pointed out as such. The Gestapo would only have increased and intensified its inquisition. . . . It was much better the Pope kept silent. We all felt the same, and today we still believe that."[18] The truth of this statement was demonstrated tragically in Holland, when in July

---

[18]Pinchas Lapide, *Three Popes and the Jews* (New York: Hawthorne Books, 1967).

1942, the Dutch Catholic hierarchy publicly condemned the deportation of Dutch Jews to German and Polish concentration camps.

> All leaders of the churches — Calvinists, Lutherans and Catholics — agreed to read a public protest against the deportation of Jews on a certain Sunday. The plan came to the attention of Dr. Karsten, head of the Gestapo in Holland, who made it clear to all the heads of the churches that, if the protests went forward, the Germans would deport not only Jews who were so by blood and religion but also the Jews who had converted to Christianity and been baptized. Faced with this threat, all the heads of the churches backed down except those of the Catholic Church. In all the Catholic churches of Holland a letter of protest was read. As a consequence, the deportation of Jews of blood and religion was accelerated, and the baptized Jews were also deported, including Edith Stein and her sister. Thus, as a result of the intervention of the Dutch bishops who refused to retreat before the Nazi threat, Edith Stein, her sister, and many other Jewish converts were deported and killed.[19]

Their protest, heroic as it was, was met immediately by fierce Nazi reprisals against both Dutch Jews and Catholic — with special attention given to those Jews who had converted to Catholicism. Saint Edith Stein, the great Carmelite nun and renowned writer, was one such convert from Judaism. She was deported, along with tens of thousands of Jews, ending up in Auschwitz, one of Hitler's most malignant death camps. After a horrifying stint there,

---

[19]Peter Gumpel, S.J., quoted by Antonio Gaspari, "Justice for Pius XII!" *Inside the Vatican*, June 1997, 23-24

the young woman was executed along with 300 others in a Nazi crackdown against "unruly" prisoners.

The diary of Anne Frank

Anne Frank, the gifted Jewish teenager who perished in 1945 in the Nazi death camp Bergen-Belson, was another victim of this Nazi reprisal against Dutch Jews. Millions around the world have read *The Diary of Anne Frank,* her poignant memoir which ends abruptly just before she was sent to the death camp. Her story is filled with haunting details of her experience of being literally *sealed* into a secret apartment in Holland with her family and another family. Her poignant account of that suffocating existence (never once being able to go outdoors into the sunlight!) is as riveting as it is tragic. Yet, even that hidden, stifled existence, as terrible as it was, would have been infinitely better than the fate that awaited Anne Frank.

All hell broke loose when the Dutch Catholic bishops issued their public condemnation of the Nazi atrocities against the Jews. As we know, the Third Reich was enraged at such an open act of defiance and its response was swift and devastating.

A pale green horse rampaged through Holland. Its rider was named Death, and hell accompanied him.[20] Storm troopers smasher through Amsterdam, Rotterdam and other major Dutch cities in search of all hiding Jews. And they found thousands of them. Anne Frank and her family were discovered. This sweet, intelligent young girl was

---

[20]Cf. Rev. 6:8.

swept into the maw of the Nazi death machine and disappeared into the oblivion of the camps.

She left this earth through a crematorium smokestack.

Clearly, if *that* was how the Nazis reacted to a public condemnation of their depredations by the Dutch Catholic bishops, any thinking person can imagine the ferocity they would have unleashed against the Jews of Europe if Pope Pius XII himself had followed suit and issued a similar public condemnation. Many, *many* more Jews would have been killed as a result.

Pius XII knew this and he agonized daily over it. The irony is that the rest of the world knew he knew it and people near and far praised him repeatedly for his careful but relentless efforts on behalf of the Jews. Pope Pius XII wanted with every ounce of his being to stand at the balcony of St. Peter's and cry out to humanity at the top of his lungs against the Nazi horror of the *Shoah* (the Holocaust). The plight of his Jewish brothers and sisters trapped behind Germany's wall of death weighed on him each day of his pontificate.

The personal toll on the pope

Though Pius XII was not personally suffering the crushing weight of Nazi anti-Semitism that was devouring thousands of his fellow human beings, he felt their suffering as keenly as if he had been in Dachau or Auschwitz with them. And he did his best to offer his personal sacrifices as an act of solidarity before God with them.

One Vatican associate who worked daily with the Holy Father during those dark days recalled the various simple and hidden ways the pope would offer penances to the Lord on behalf of his brothers and sisters. For example, he loved to drink coffee, especially in the morning as he attended to his office work. One day, he announced to his household that he would no longer be drinking-coffee. "My brothers in the camps are not able to drink coffee, so I will not drink coffee." And that was that. For the duration of the war, Pius XII abstained from his favorite beverage as a personal act of solidarity with the Jews and others being persecuted by the Germans, especially those trapped in the death camps. He was also known to perform other acts of private mortification on their behalf: fasting, sleeping on the bare floor at night, working at his desk until the early morning and allowing himself only a few hours sleep before he rose to begin again.

Clearly, there can be no one-to-one comparison whatsoever made between the excruciating suffering the Jews underwent at the Nazis' hands and the hidden, private mortifications Pope Pius XII embraced out of solidarity with them. No sort of objective comparison could possibly be made. Rather, it's important to recognize here the humanity of Pope Pius XII, the aching compassion he felt for the suffering that was compounded by the maddening frustration of not being able to directly intervene on their behalf. His private fasts and modest sufferings were objectively nothing compared to what those in the camps suffered, but still the Pope yearned to offer to the Lord even the little suffering he could, as an offering of love and solidarity for them.

During World War II, the pope, though technically a "free man," was in reality a prisoner in the Apostolic Palace in the Vatican. He understood that he could spiritually enter into deeper solidarity with the suffering Jews in more ways that just his actions on their behalf. Simple things like his fasting, giving up coffee, and denying himself much needed sleep and recreation, were in themselves insignificant when compared to the daily anguish the Jews and Catholics and others in the death camps were experiencing. But the fact remains that Pius wanted to suffer with them. He wanted to offer his private mortifications to the Lord both in intercession for his suffering brethren, and as a hidden act of solidarity with them. During his pontificate, only a few close personal associates knew about these penances.

By the time the United States had entered the fray, the pope was acutely aware that, at this point in the war, public protestations on his part would only inflame Hitler's blood lust and result in an even more frenzied slaughter of Jews, Gypsies, Catholics and other *miserábles* in his grip. Jewish leaders in Europe and the United States knew this too.

When the war ended, Pope Pius XII's behind-the-scenes efforts on behalf of European Jews were warmly recognized. Rabbi Abraham Zolli, the chief Rabbi of Rome, was so moved by the pope's defense of his people that he felt compelled to investigate the Catholic Faith that animated this great man. He began to study Catholicism and eventually converted to the Catholic Faith, taking Eugenio — Pope Pius XII's own name — as his baptismal name. He chose that name in honor of the good pope who worked so tirelessly for the Jewish people. What could be stronger evidence that Pope Pius XII was not, as his critics allege, "silent and immobile" in the face of Nazi persecution of Jews?

Jewish gratitude after the war

Let's up the ante. Most people don't realize that shortly after World War II ended, the World Jewish Congress sent two million lire as a gift of gratitude to the Vatican, saying their "first duty was to thank him and the Catholic Church for all they had done to rescue Jews."

Isaac Herzog, the chief rabbi of Jerusalem, noted similarly: "The people of Israel will never forget what His Holiness and his illustrious delegates, inspired by the eternal principles of religion which form the very foundations of true civilization, are doing for our unfortunate brothers and sisters in the most tragic hour of our history, which is living proof of divine Providence in this world."[21]

The great Jewish scientist Albert Einstein published in *Time* a statement of admiration for the efforts of the Catholic Church to help the Jews. This statement appeared on December 23, 1940, *during World War II* — exactly the time frame during which the pope's critics claim that he and the Church had been "silent."

> Being a lover of freedom, when the revolution came in Germany, I looked to the universities to defend it, knowing that they always boasted of their devotion to the cause of truth; but no, the universities immediately were silenced. Then I looked to the great editors of the newspapers, whose flaming editorials in days gone by had proclaimed their love of freedom. But they, like the universities, were silenced in a few short weeks.
>
> Only the Church stood squarely across the path of Hitler's campaign for suppressing truth. I had never any

---

[21] Ibid.

special interest in the Church before, but now I feel a great affection and admiration because the Church alone has had the courage and persistence to stand for intellectual truth and moral freedom. I am forced thus to confess, that what I once despised, I now praise unreservedly.[22]

In 1958, when Pope Pius XII died, the first official dignitary to react was Golda Meir, delegate to the United Nations and the future prime minister of Israel. She said in her public message:

We share in the grief of humanity at the passing away of His Holiness, Pope Pius XII. In a generation afflicted by wars and discords he upheld the highest ideals of peace and compassion. *When fearful martyrdom came to our people in the decade of Nazi terror, the voice of the Pope was raised for its victims.*[23]

It was estimated by the newly created government of Israel that Pope Pius XII's policy of quiet but intense behind-the-scenes effort had saved over *800,000* Jewish lives during the Holocaust — more than all other relief organizations combined.[24] James Bogle points out the fact that

---

[22]Albert Einstein. *Time,* December 23, 1940, 40. Quoted in *Inside the Vatican* June 1997, 23.

[23]Ibid., 57, emphasis added.

[24]Robert Graham explains in his book *Pius XII and the Holocaust,* "After the war, the Jewish organizations themselves publicly acknowledged the sympathy and cooperation they received from the Holy See. Volume 10, however, provides more graphic substance to these acknowledgements in the precise narration, day by day, month by month, of the Holy See's correspondence with the most active international Jewish organizations. Among the more important of these are the Emergency Committee to Save the Jewish People of Europe, the World Jewish Congress, the American Jewish Congress, Agudas Israel World Or-

the government of Israel officially approved the creation of a memorial forest with the planting of 800,000 trees in the Negev desert, southeast of Jerusalem, to stand as a perpetual monument to the heroic efforts of a truly great man and a true friend of the Jews, Pope Pius XII.[25]

---

organization, Vaad Hahatzala of the Union of Orthodox Rabbis of the United States and Canada, Hijefs *(Schweizerischer Hilfsverein fur Judische Fluchling im Ausland),* the Jewish Agency for Palestine and the American Jewish Committee. In 1944, the War Refugee Board came into existence and represented, in fact, the united effort of the various American Jewish organizations. During and after the war, the War Refugee Board publicly acknowledged its close relationship with the Holy See, as well as the services rendered to the cause by the Holy See. The documentation also includes correspondence from eminent rabbinical leaders who made special appeals to the Holy See; among them are the Grand Rabbi of Jerusalem, Dr. Isaac Herzog, the Grand Rabbi of the British Empire, Dr. Joseph Hertz, and Rabbi Abraham Kalmanowitz, leader of the rabbinical school of Mir, in Lithuania."

[25] I highly recommend to the reader the detailed evidence on behalf of Pope Pius XII that is assembled at the Catholic League's Internet site: www.catholicleague.org.

Conclusion

Down through the ages, many people have opposed the papacy. The idea that the bishop of Rome represents the visible unity of the Catholic Church is offensive to many. To call him the "vicar of Christ" is particularly annoying for some.

"Why must you Catholics place all this emphasis on Peter and the popes?" some say in disgust. "Why can't you just concentrate on *Jesus* and his gospel?" The answer to both questions is simple: We believe in the papacy because Christ instituted it. The evidence, both scriptural and historical, proves beyond reasonable doubt that the Galilean fisherman, Simon Peter, was the first in a two-thousand-year line of bishops of Rome who stand at the center of the Christian Church. In a sense you can say the popes *are* its center.

Unlike any other institution on earth, the papacy has survived against all odds. It has withstood the test of time like nothing before or since. The papacy existed when the last Apostle, John, at the end of his long life, put down his pen and died. The popes strengthened and ministered to the flock during the long, horrible night of pagan persecution under the Romans. The "Dark Ages" weren't nearly so dark as they would have been, had it not been for the bright light radiated by saintly pontiffs such as Leo I (440–461), Gregory I (590–604), and Nicholas I (858–867), each known to Christians the world over as "The Great."

It keeps going, and going, and going . . .

The papacy has seen the rise of all the heresies that have ever come against orthodox Christianity. It has vanquished most of them. Those that still linger will, in due time, pass away like the others, and the papacy will still be there. The papacy had existed for 600 years before Muhammed traversed the burning deserts of Arabia in search of followers for his new religion.

For a *thousand* years before William the Conqueror invaded England and before the Battle of Hastings was fought, Catholic popes had led and strengthened the Christian Church across the world as it weathered persecutions, social and natural catastrophes, schisms, heresies, and all manner of other menaces that threatened to overwhelm it. The papacy had been the indestructible focal point of Christian unity for nearly fifteen hundred years before Martin Luther was even a winkle in his daddy's eye.

While the rest of the world wallowed in the sink-hole of human slavery, the popes consistently stood firm against it. In the depths of the Nazi nightmare, before the United States and other western powers lifted a finger to stop it, the popes placed themselves squarely in the path of Hitler's *Wehrmacht* and did what they could to prevent the slaughter of European Jews. Popes warned the world about the horrors that would follow in the wake of contraception and abortion. The world laughed and then watched as the predictions came true with ghastly precision.

The 264 men who have stood in the shoes of the Fisherman have at least one thing in common: They form the living links in a single chain of Catholic unity, a chain that stretches across Christian history back to Simon Peter himself. It's true that a chain is as strong as its weakest link, and this chain, forged by Christ Himself, has been strained, at times seemingly well beyond the limit, but it has never broken.

In contrast, the Protestant Reformation can boast of nothing similar. While for two thousand years the papacy has stood as a bulwark for the Church against the savage efforts of the Evil One to sift it like wheat, Martin Luther and John Calvin sowed the wind, and today we are reaping a whirlwind of gigantic proportions. Under the guise of adhering to the fine-sounding principle of *sola scriptura* (Latin: Scripture alone), Protestantism has rejected the papacy, and what fruit has that yielded? Doctrinal disunity, blatant contradictions, relativism born of confusion, and fragmentation. By abandoning the rock on which the Church was built, the Reformers could build their new theological structure on only the shifting sands of mere human opinion. But Scripture calls to them, beckoning them home to the Rock of Peter, the one place where they can find, not perfection or sinlessness, but the stability and permanence Christ promised his followers.

"The stone which the builders rejected has become the cornerstone. This is the Lord's doing, and it is marvelous in our eyes" (Psalm 118:22–23).

The rock of Peter, the thing that seems most distasteful to so many about the Catholic Church is, in fact, the answer to their most urgent problems. The papacy is the Lord's doing, not man's, and it ought to be marvelous in their eyes. May God grant that, in time, our separated brethren will see this and come home.

The papacy: rock solid for two thousand years

"*Ubi Petrus, ibi Ecclesia*" runs the ancient Christian axiom: "Where Peter is, there is the Church." This phrase sums up volumes that could be written about the nature and purpose of the papacy. Since the inception of the Church, Christians have understood this truth, whether they lived according to it or not. From Simon Peter forward, the popes have been the fixed center of a pilgrim Church that is passing through the hurricane of this world, buffeted and shaken at times, but always intact. The papacy is the rock on which Christ is building His Church. The rains lash it, the winds pummel it, the floods burst against it, but that Church has not fallen. Nor will it.

There have been many kinds of men who have sat on the Chair of Peter. Many were saints, a few were wicked and scandalous, the great majority have been good and holy men. But all of them have been human and imperfect — *men*, but men protected by the Holy Spirit to carry out a pivotal mission in the life of His Church. Some did extremely well in fulfilling this mission, and others, just a few actually, failed miserably in their personal lives and as leaders, while never managing to breach that shield of grace that prevented them from leading the Church astray.

And that is perhaps the single greatest proof of the divine origin of the papacy. If it were merely a human institution, as its critics and enemies will tell you, it would have collapsed in a heap long ago. You can be sure of that. If the papacy were just a "tradition of men," it would have disintegrated early on, under the sheer weight of human frailty. But it hasn't, and it won't.

It can't.

Christ Himself has been ever faithful to His promise to Simon: "You are rock and upon this rock I will build my Church, and the gates of hell will not prevail against it."

A Parting Thought

Long ago, in his introductory chapter to his magnificent book, *The Spirit of Catholicism,* Karl Adam gave a long quote from Lord Thomas Macaulay (1800-1859), a famous Anglican writer. He expresses better than I could my awe and love for the Church Jesus Christ has built on the Rock of Peter. I thank and praise God with all my heart for inviting me, as He invites everyone, to live in His House:

There is not, and there never was on this earth, a work of human policy so well deserving of examination as the Roman Catholic Church. The history of that Church joins together the two great ages of human civilization. No other institution is left standing which carries the mind back to the times when the smoke of sacrifice rose from the Pantheon, and when camelopards and tigers bounded in the Flavian amphitheatre.

The proudest royal houses are but of yesterday, when compared with the line of the Supreme Pontiffs. That line we trace back in an unbroken series, from the Pope who crowned Napoleon in the nineteenth century to the Pope who crowned Pepin in the eighth; and far beyond the time of Pepin the august dynasty extends, till it is lost in the twilight of fable. The republic of Venice came next in antiquity. But the republic of Venice was modern when compared with the papacy; and the republic of Venice is gone, and the Papacy remains.

The Papacy remains, not in decay, not a mere antique,

but full of life and youthful vigour. The Catholic Church is still sending forth to the farthest ends of the world missionaries as zealous as those who landed in Kent with Augustine, and still confronting hostile kings with the same spirit with which she confronted Attila. . . .

Nor do we see any sign which indicates that the term of her long dominion is approaching. She saw the commencement of all the governments and of all the ecclesiastical establishments that now exist in the world; and we feel no assurance that she is not destined to see the end of them all.

She was great and respected before the Saxon had set foot on Britain, before the Frank had passed the Rhine, when Grecian eloquence still flourished at Antioch, when idols were still worshipped in the temple of Mecca. And she may still exist in undiminished vigour when some traveler from New Zealand shall, in the midst of a vast solitude, take his stand on a broken arch of London Bridge to sketch the ruins of St. Paul's.

All I can add to that is *Deo Gratias*.

About the Author

Patrick Madrid is publisher of the award-winning Envoy magazine, a journal of Catholic apologetics and evangelization (www.envoymagazine.com). A popular speaker and best-selling author, his books include *Surprised by Truth, Any Friend of God's Is a Friend of Mine, Pope Fiction, Surprised by Truth 2,* and the forthcoming *Envoy for Christ.* In addition to his books, he is also the host of the popular EWTN television series "Pope Fiction," the fast-paced new apologetics show that offers biblical and historical answers to many common myths and misconceptions about the papacy. (For program details, please visit www.envoymagazine.com).

He has conducted hundreds of apologetics conferences in English and Spanish across the U.S., as well as throughout Europe, Asia, Latin America, and in the Middle East. He is a veteran of numerous formal public debates with Protestant ministers. Mormon leaders, and other non-Catholic spokesmen. He and his wife are raising their children in the countryside of Central Ohio.

You can contact Patrict Madrid at:
Envoy Magazine
Post Office Box 640
Granville OH 43023
patrickmadrid@hotmail.com

Appendix

A chronological list of the popes

1. St. Peter (32-67)
2. St. Linus (67-76)
3. St. Anacletus (Cletus) 76-88)
4. St. Clement I (88-97)
5. St. Evaristus (97-105)
6. St. Alexander I (105-115)
7. St. Sixtus I (115-125) — also called Xystus I
8. St. Telesphorus (125-136)
9. St. Hyginus (136-140)
10. St. Pius I (140-155)
11. St. Anicetus (155-166)
12. St. Soter (166-175)
13. St. Eleutherius (175-189)
14. St. Victor I (189-199)
15. St. Zephyrinus (199-217)
16. St. Callistus I (217-22)
17. St. Urban I (222-230)
18. St. Pontian (230-235)
19. St. Anterus (235-236)
20. St. Fabian (236-250)
21. St. Cornelius (251-253)
22. St. Lucius I (253-254)
23. St. Stephen I (254-257)
24. St. Sixtus II (257-258)
25. St. Dionysius (260-268)
26. St. Felix I (269-274)
27. St. Eutychian (275-283)
28. St. Caius (283-296) — also called Gaius
29. St. Marcellinus (296-304)
30. St. Marcellus I (308-309)
31. St. Eusebius (309 or 310)
32. St. Miltiades (311-314)
33. St. Sylvester I (314-335)
34. St. Marcus (336)
35. St. Julius I (337-352)
36. Liberius (352-366)
37. Damasus I (366-383)
38. St. Siricius (384-399)
39. St. Anastasius I (399-401)
40. St. Innocent I (401-417)
41. St. Zosimus (417-418)
42. St. Boniface I (418-422)
43. St. Celestine I (422-432)
44. St. Sixtus III (432-440)
45. St. Leo I (the Great) (440-61)
46. St. Hilarius (461-468)
47. St. Simplicius (468-483)
48. St. Felix III (II) (483-492)
49. St. Gelasius I (492-496)
50. Anastasius II (496-498)
51. St. Symmachus (498-514)
52. St. Hormisdas (514-523)
53. St. John I (523-526)

54. St. Felix IV (III) (526-530)
55. Boniface II (530-532)
56. John II (533-535)
57. St. Agapetus I (535-536) —
also called Agapitus I
58. St. Silverius (536-537)
59. Vigilius (537-555)
60. Pelagius I (556-561)
61. John III (561-574)
62. Benedict I (575-579)
63. Pelagius II (579-590)
64. St. Gregory I (the Great)
(590-604)
65. Sabinian (604-606)
66. Boniface III (607)
67. St. Boniface IV (608-615)
68. St. Deusdedit (Adeodatus I)
(615-618)
69. Boniface V (619-625)
70. Honorius I (625-638)
71. Severinus (640)
72. John IV (640-642)
73. Theodore I (642-649)
74. St. Martin I (649-655)
75. St. Eugene I (655-657)
76. St. Vitalian (657-672)
77. Adeodatus (II) (672-676)
78. Donus (676-678)
79. St. Agatho (678-681)
80. St. Leo II (682-683)
81. St. Benedict II (684-685)
82. John V (685-686)
83. Conon (686-687)
84. St. Sergius I (687-701)

85. John VI (701-705)
86. John VII (705-707)
87. Sisinnius (708)
88. Constantine (708-715)
89. St. Gregory II (715-731)
90. St. Gregory III (731-741)
91. St. Zachary (741-752)
Stephen II (752) [Died before
consecration.]
92. Stephen II [III] (752-757)
93. St. Paul I (757-767)
94. Stephen IV (767-772)
95. Adrian I (772-795)
96. St. Leo III (795-816)
97. Stephen V (816-817)
98. St. Paschal I (817-824)
99. Eugene II (824-827)
100. Valentine (827)
101. Gregory IV (827-844)
102. Sergius II (844-847)
103. St. Leo IV (847-855)
104. Benedict III (855-858)
105. St. Nicholas I (the Great)
(858-867)
106. Adrian II (867-872)
107. John VIII (872-882)
108. Marinus I (882-884)
109. St. Adrian III (884-885)
110. Stephen VI (885-891)
111. Formosus (891-896)
112. Boniface VI (896)
113. Stephen VII (896-897)
114. Romanus (897)
115. Theodore II (897)

116. John IX (898-900)
117. Benedict IV (900-903)
118. Leo V (903)
119. Sergius III (904-911)
120. Anastasius III (911-913)
121. Lando (913-914)
122. John X (914-928)
123. Leo VI (928)
124. Stephen VIII (929-931)
125. John XI (931-935)
126. Leo VII (936-939)
127. Stephen IX (939-942)
128. Marinus II (942-946)
129. Agapetus II (946-955)
130. John XII (955-963)
131. Leo VIII (963-964)
132. Benedict V (964)
133. John XIII (965-972)
134. Benedict VI (973-974)
135. Benedict VII (974-983)
136. John XIV (983-984)
137. John XV (985-996)
138. Gregory V (996-999)
139. Sylvester II (999-1003)
140. John XVII (1003)
141. John XVIII (1003-1009)
142. Sergius IV (1009-1012)
143. Benedict VIII (1012-1024)
144. John XIX (1024-1032)
145. Benedict IX (1032-1045)
146. Sylvester III (1045)
147. Benedict IX (1045)
148. Gregory VI (1045-1046)
149. Clement II (1046-1047)

150. Benedict IX (1047-1048).
151. Damasus II (1048)
152. St. Leo IX (1049-1054)
153. Victor II (1055-1057)
154. Stephen X (1057-1058)
155. Nicholas II (1058-1061)
156. Alexander II (1061-1073)
157. St. Gregory VII (1073-1085)
158. Blessed Victor III (1086-1087)
159. Blessed Urban II (1088-1099)
160. Paschal II (1099-1118)
161. Gelasius II (1118-1119)
162. Callistus II (1119-1124)
163. Honorius II (1124-1130)
164. Innocent II (1130-1143)
165. Celestine II (1143-1144)
166. Lucius II (1144-1145)
167. Blessed Eugene III (1145-1153)
168. Anastasius IV (1153-1154)
169. Adrian IV (1154-1159)
170. Alexander III (1159-1181)
171. Lucius III (1181-1185)
172. Urban III (1185-1187)
173. Gregory VIII (1187)
174. Clement III (1187-1191)
175. Celestine III (1191-1198)
176. Innocent III (1198-1216)
177. Honorius III (1216-1227)
178. Gregory IX (1227-1241)
179. Celestine IV (1241)

180. Innocent IV (1243-1254)
181. Alexander IV (1254-1261)
182. Urban IV (1261-1264)
183. Clement IV (1264-1268)
184. Blessed Gregory X (1271-1276)
185. Blessed Innocent V (1276)
186. Adrian V (1276)
187. John XXI (1276-1277)
188. Nicholas III (1277-1280)
189. Martin IV (1281-1285)
190. Honorius IV (1285-1287)
191. Nicholas IV (1288-1292)
192. St. Celestine V (1294)
193. Boniface VIII (1294-1303)
194. Blessed Benedict XI (1303-1304)
195. Clement V (1305-1314)
196. John XXII (1316-1334)
197. Benedict XII (1334-1342)
198. Clement VI (1342-1352)
199. Innocent VI (1352-1362)
200. Blessed Urban V (1362-1370)
201. Gregory XI (1370-1378)
202. Urban VI (1378-1389)
203. Boniface IX (1389-1404)
204. Innocent VII (1406-1406)
205. Gregory XII (1406-1415)
206. Martin V (1417-1431)
207. Eugene IV (1431-1447)
208. Nicholas V (1447-1455)
209. Callistus III (1445-1458)
210. Pius II (1458-1464)

211. Paul II (1464-1471)
212. Sixtus IV (1471-1484)
213. Innocent VIII (1484-1492)
214. Alexander VI (1492-1503)
215. Pius III (1503)
216. Julius II (1503-1513)
217. Leo X (1513-1521)
218. Adrian VI (1522-1523)
219. Clement VII (1523-1534)
220. Paul III (1534-1549)
221. Julius III (1550-1555)
222. Marcellus II (1555)
223. Paul IV (1555-1559)
224. Pius IV (1559-1565)
225. St. Pius V (1566-1572)
226. Gregory XIII (1572-1585)
227. Sixtus V (1585-1590)
228. Urban VII (1590)
229. Gregory XIV (1590-1591)
230. Innocent IX (1591)
231. Clement VIII (1592-1605)
232. Leo XI (1605)
233. Paul V (1605-1621)
234. Gregory XV (1621-1623)
235. Urban VIII (1623-1644)
236. Innocent X (1644-1655)
237. Alexander VII (1655-1667)
238. Clement IX (1667-1669)
239. Clement X (1670-1676)
240. Blessed Innocent XI (1676-1689)
241. Alexander VIII (1689-1691)
242. Innocent XII (1691-1700)

254. Gregory XVI (1831-1846)
255. Ven. Pius IX (1846-1878)
256. Leo XIII (1878-1903)
257. St. Pius X (1903-1914)
258. Benedict XV (1914-1922)
259. Pius XI (1922-1939)
260. Pius XII (1939-1958)
261. John XXIII (1958-1963)
262. Paul VI (1963-1978)
263. John Paul I (1978)
264. John Paul II (1978-)

Recommended Reading

Surprised by Truth 2, Patrick Madrid, (Sophia Institute Press)

Reasons for Hope, Jeffrey Mirus, ed., (Christendom College Press)

The Bones of St. Peter, John Evangelist Walsh (Doubleday & Company)

And On This Rock, Stanley L. Jaki (Trinity Communications)

A History of the Popes, J.N.D. Kelly (Oxford, University Press)

Where Is That in the Bible?, Patrick Madrid, (Our Sunday Visitor)

A Father Who Keeps His Promises, Scott Hahn (Servant)

Surprised by Truth: 11 Converts Give the Biblical and Historical Reasons for Becoming Catholic, Patrick Madrid (Basilica Press)

Rome Sweet Home, Scott and Kimberly Hahn (Ignatius Press)

Making Senses Out of Scripture, Mark Shea (Basilica Press)

Nuts & Bolts, Tim Staples (Basilica Press)

Springtime of Evangelization, Pope John Paul II, introduced by Thomas Williams, L.C. (Basilica Press)

Theology and Sanity, Frank Sheed (Ignatius Press)

Theology for Beginners, Frank Sheed (Servant Press)

By What Authority? An Evangelical Discovers Tradition,
Mark Shea (Our Sunday Visitor)

Upon This Rock, Stephen K. Ray (Ignatius Press)

Any Friend of God's Is a Friend of Mine, Patrick Madrid
(Basilica Press)

Not by Scripture Alone, Robert Sungenis, Patrick Madrid,
et al. (Queenship)

Tradition & Traditions, Yves M.J. Congar (Basilica Press)

Mary and the Fathers of the Church, Luigi Gambero
(Ignatius Press)

Catholic for a Reason, Leon Suprenant, Scott Hahn, et al.
(Emmaus Road)

The Fathers of the Church, Mike Aquilina (Our Sunday
Visitor)

Jesus, Peter & the Keys, David Hess, et al., (Queenship)

Internet Resources

A handy collection of apologetics essays on the papacy is
available on the Internet at ic.net/~erasmus/erasmus4.htm.
While some of the essays there are rather superficial and
therefore less helpful, those by Cardinal John Henry
Newman, David Palm, David Armstrong, and Stephen
Ray are excellent and particularly recommended. (As with
all Internet resources, I recommend you bookmark this site
on your Web browser *and* print out the key essays, just in
case the site is ever closed or for some reason becomes
unavailable.)

Envoy magazine has many helpful articles and links
on Catholic subjects. These are available at no charge at
www.envoymagazine.com.

Select Bibliography

Balthasar, Hans Urs Von, *The Office of Peter and the Structure of the Church* (San Francisco: Ignatius Press, 1986).

Barry, Colman J. O.S.B., *Readings in Church History* (Westminster: Christian Classics, 1985).

Boettner, Loraine, *Roman Catholicism* (Phillipsburg, N.J.: Presbyterian and Reformed, 1962).

Broderick, James, S.J., *Robert Bellarmine: Saint and Scholar* (Westminster: The Newman Press, 1961).

Burke, Cormac, *Authority and Freedom in the Church* (San Francisco, Ignatius Press, 1988).

Burman, Edward, *The Inquisition: Hammer of Heresy* (New York: Dorset Press, 1984).

Carroll, Warren H., *A History of Christendom*, 3 vols. (Front Royal: Christendom Press, 1984-1993).

Catechism of the Catholic Church (Washington: United States Catholic Conference, Inc., 1994).

Congar, Yves M. J., *Tradition and Traditions* (San Diego: Basilica Press, 1998 ed.).

Cross, Donna Woolfolk, *Pope Joan* (New York: Ballantine Books, 1997).

Daniel-Rops, Henri, *The Church of the Apostles and Martyrs* (London: J. M. Dent & Sons, 1960).

Durrell, Lawrence, *Pope Joan* (Woodstock: The Overlook Press, 1984).

Eusebius, *The History of the Church from Christ to Constantine*, G. A. Williamson, editor and translator (New York: Dorset Press, 1965).

Graham, Robert, *Pius XII and the Holocaust*, (New York: The Catholic League, 1988.)

Hebermann, Charles G., et al. eds., *The Catholic Encyclopedia* (New York: Robert Appleton Co., 1902-1912), 15 vols.

Hefele, Charles Joseph D.D., *A History of the Christian Councils From the Original Documents* (Edinburgh: T&T Clark, 1894).

Hudson, Henry T., *Papal Power: Its Origins and Development* (Hertfordshire: Evangelical Press, 1981).

Hughes, Philip, *The Church in Crisis* (Garden City: Image Books, 1964).

——— *A History of the Church*, 3 vols. (London: Sheed and Ward, 1947).

Kelly, J. N. D., *Early Christian Doctrines* (San Francisco: Harper Collins, 1978).

Lubac, Henri de, *Catholicism* (San Francisco: Ignatius Press, 1988).

Mann, Horace K., *The Lives of the Popes*, 20 vols. (London: Kegan, Paul, Trench, Trubner & Co., 1929).

Markus, R. A., *Gregory the Great and His World* (Cambridge: The Cambridge University Press, 1997).

Miller, J. Michael C.S.B., *The Shepherd and the Rock* (Huntington: Our Sunday Visitor Publishing Co., 1994).

Newman, John Henry, *An Essay on the Development of Christian Doctrine* (Notre Dame: University of Notre Dame Press, 1989 ed.).

Nichols, Aidan O.P., *Rome and the Eastern Churches* (Collegeville: The Liturgical Press, 1992).

Panzer, Joel S., *The Popes and Slavery* (Staten Island: Alba House, 1996).

Pastor, Ludwig Freiherr von, *The History of the Popes*, 22 vols. (St. Louis: Herder 1902).

Pernoud, Régine, *The Crusades* (London: Secker & Warburg, 1960).

Powell, James M., *Innocent III* (Washington: Catholic University of America Press, 1994 ed.).

Rahner, Karl, *Foundations of Christian Faith* (New York: Crossroad, 1994).

Ratzinger, Joseph, *Principles of Catholic Theology* (San Francisco: Ignatius Press, 1987).

Ray, Stephen K., *Upon This Rock* (San Francisco: Ignatius Press, 1999).

Roberts, Alexander and Donaldson, James, eds., *The Ante-Nicene Fathers* (Peabody: Hendrickson, 1995).

Robinson, I. S., *The Papacy: Continuity and Innovation* (Cambridge: Cambridge University Press, 1990).

Schaff, Philip, ed., *Nicene and Post Nicene Fathers* (Peabody: Hendrickson, 1994).

Schmaus, Michael, *Dogma* vol. 4, *The Church, Its Origin and Structure* (London, Sheed and Ward, 1972).

Sheed, Frank, *Theology and Sanity* (San Francisco: Ignatius Press, 1993).

Stanford, Peter, *The Legend of Pope Joan: In Search of the Truth* (New York: Holt, 1998).

Tappert, Theodore G., ed., *The Book of Concord: The Confessions of the Evangelical Lutheran Church* (Philadelphia: Fortress Press, 1959 ed.).

Walsh, John Evangelist, *The Bones of St. Peter* (Manila: Sinag-Tala, 1987 ed.).

Walsh, William Thomas, *Characters of the Inquisition* (Rockford: TAN Books, 1987).

Webster, William, *The Church of Rome at the Bar of History* (Edinburgh: The Banner of Truth Trust, 1995).

Westfall, Richard S., *Essays on the Trial of Galileo* (Rome: Vatican Observatory Publications, 1989).

Wiltgen, Ralph M. S.V.D., *The Rhine Flows Into the Tiber: A History of Vatican II* (Rockford: TAN Books, 1985).

Scriptures Cited

Old Testament

New Testament

329

Index

You Can Now
Understand Scripture
as the
First Christians Did.

This exciting new book by renowned Catholic apologist
Mark Shea will deepen your love for the Bible. It
introduces today's Christian
to a way of reading
Scripture that is as old as
the Bible itself. *Making
Senses* gives new
students of the Word
the tools to understand
divine revelation in a
clear, accessible and life-
changing way. Its
fantastic insights will
supercharge your
personal or group
Bible study! - $14.99

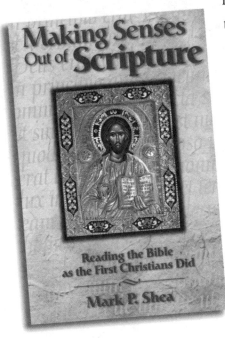

Call Basilica Press toll-free | Catholic Word
800-933-9398 | W5180 Jefferson Street
www.basilicapress.com | Necedah, WI 54646

Do you know someone whose Catholic Faith ended here?

If you're like most Catholics, your answer is "yes", a family member, friend, or co-worker.

Now you can do something about it. You can bring them home to the Church with **Envoy** magazine, an exciting bi-monthly journal of Catholic apologetics and evangelization.

Published by Patrick Madrid, best-selling Catholic author of books like *Surprised by Truth, Surprised by Truth 2, Pope Fiction and Where Is that In the Bible?* **Envoy** magazine will teach you how to explain and defend Catholic truth in a way that works. Each issue gives you cutting-edge information and answers from today's top Catholic apologists, evangelists, and writers. Our articles are consistently fresh, upbeat, useful, and *charitable*.

Envoy magazine will show you how to explain your Catholic Faith intelligently, defend it charitably, and share it *effectively*. It will prepare you to be an ambassador for Christ.

Subscribe today, and the next time you're faced with friends or loved ones who have lost their Catholic Faith (if not their First Communion picture), you can answer their questions and be a light to guide them home.

Bringing Christ to the World

Call 1-800-55-ENVOY - www.envoymagazine.com

Parish and RCIA bulk quantities available.

How to Order

CATHOLIC WORD
Bringing You The Best in Catholic Publishing

Ascension Press, Basilica Press, Lilyfield Press,
St. John Press & Company Publications

W5180 Jefferson St.   Phone: 800-933-9398
Necedah, WI 54646   Fax: 608-565-2025
                       Email: familytrad@aol.com

PO#:_____ Date:_____

Bill To: **Ship To:**

Name:_____   Name: _____
Address:_____   Address: _____
City:_____ State:___ Zip:_____   City:_____State:___ Zip:_____
Phone:_____ Fax:_____
Email: _____

QTY	ISBN	Case	Description	Unit Price	Total
	096-592-2812	20/81	Friendly Defenders Catholic Flash Cards $11.99 NEW!		
	096-592-2804	36	Did Adam & Eve Have Belly Buttons? $12.99		
	096-592-2820	32	The Rapture Trap $11.99 NEW!		
	096-426-1081	40	Surprised By Truth $14.99		
	097-035-8903	44	My Life on the Rock $14.99		
	096-426-1006	28	Pope Fiction $14.99		
	096-426-1065	44	Making Senses Out of Scripture $14.95		
	096-426-1022	72	Nuts and Bolts $11.95		
	193-031-4078	34	Scripture Studies - Galatians $14.95		
	193-031-4000	16	Bible Basics $19.95		
	096-426-109X	84	Any Friend of God's Is A Friend of Mine $9.95		
	096-426-1030	60	Springtime of Evangelization $14.95		
	193-031-4019	36	Lessons from Lives of the Saints $12.95		
	096-714-9215	48	Philadelphia Catholic in King James's Court $12.95		
	096-714-9223	120	Philadelphia Catholic Discussion/Study Guide $3.95		
	093-898-4047	30	Holy Innocents: A Catholic Novel $16.95 NEW!		
	096-701-0209	60	Triumph of God's Kingdom in the Millennium and End Times $14.95		

Subtotal _____
Shipping _____
Total _____

Notes: _____

Call for Bookstore & Parish Discounts

Include $4 for the 1st book and $.50 for each additional book or call for
exact shipping.